*To Tricia, of course, and to Tracey, Nikki and Iain.*
*A man could wish for no better gift than the unconditional love*
*of his family. IM*

*To all those who have helped me in my career, especially Tony Gale,*
*Denver Daniels and my wife Kim. RB*

# CRIMINAL JUSTICE RESEARCH

# Criminal Justice Research
## Inspiration, Influence and Ideation

*Edited by*

IAN K. McKENZIE
*Institute of Criminal Justice Studies, University of Portsmouth*

*and*

RAY BULL
*Department of Psychology, University of Portsmouth*

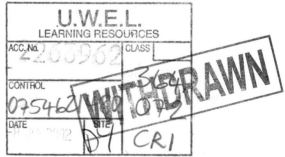

## Ashgate
### DARTMOUTH
Aldershot • Burlington USA • Singapore • Sydney

Published by
Dartmouth Publishing Company
Ashgate Publishing Limited
Gower House
Croft Road
Aldershot
Hampshire GU11 3HR
England

Ashgate Publishing Company
131 Main Street
Burlington, VT 05401-5600 USA

Ashgate website: http://www.ashgate.com

**British Library Cataloguing in Publication Data**
Criminal justice research: inspiration, influence and ideation
   1. Criminal justice, Administration of 2. Criminology
   I. McKenzie, Ian K., 1941– II. Bull, Ray, 1947–
   364

**Library of Congress Control Number:** 2001092172

ISBN 0 7546 2148 0 (HB)
ISBN 0 7546 2153 7 (PB)

Printed and bound in Great Britain by MPG Books Ltd, Bodmin, Cornwall

# Contents

# Contributors

**Harold K. Becker** obtained his Doctor of Criminology degree from the School of Criminology at the University of California at Berkeley, USA. He is a Professor of Criminal Justice at California State University, Long Beach. He has been a Los Angeles police officer, and is currently a researcher, consultant, and evaluator to police and schools on crime prevention programs.

**Donna Lee Becker** has been an elementary and secondary teacher and has co-authored, with Harold Becker, the *Handbook of the World's Police*. Donna has been a writing assistant to Harold, conducting background information gathering, consultancy work, and prepublication editing of all materials.

**Jennifer Brown** is Professor of Psychology and director of the Forensic Psychology masters programme at the University of Surrey, England. She has a special interest in the occupational culture of the police particularly with reference to gender issues and recently with Professor Frances Heidensohn published an international comparison of policewomen's experiences. Formerly head of research at Hampshire Constabulary, England, Professor Brown can claim firsthand knowledge of working within the police culture.

**Ray Bull** is Professor of Psychology in the Department of Psychology at the University of Portsmouth. He is a chartered Forensic Psychologist of the British Psychological Society. For 30 years he has worked with a variety of police forces in several counties. The main focus of his research is the conducting of investigative interviews.

**James Ginger**, a Professor at St Mary's University, San Antonio, Texas, was recently selected by the United States District Court for New Jersey as the independent monitor for the consent decree between U.S. Department of Justice and the New Jersey State Police. He serves as the independent auditor for the consent decree entered into by DOJ and the City of Pittsburgh Police Department. Dr Ginger was the deputy director of the Washington, D.C.-based Police Foundation, and the director of the Southern Police Institute at the University of Louisville, Kentucky.

**Les Johnston** is Professor of Criminology and Research Director at the Institute of Criminal Justice Studies, University of Portsmouth. He has research interests in public, commercial and civil policing, risk and the governance of security. His publications include *The Rebirth of Private Policing*, London: Routledge (1992) and *Policing Britain: Risk, Security and Governance*: Longman (Pearson Education, 2000).

**Ian K. McKenzie**, Principal Lecturer in the Institute of Criminal Justice Studies of the University of Portsmouth, is a former senior police officer of the London Metropolitan Police. Following retirement from the police in 1985, and a period as Chief Psychologist to Fort Worth Police Department, Texas, he 'drifted' into academe. He is author and co-author of a number of books and papers on policing and the interface between psychology and the criminal justice system.

**Robert Reiner** is Professor of Criminology in the Law Department, London School of Economics. He has published a number of books and over one hundred papers on policing and criminal justice topics. He was President of the British Society of Criminology from 1993-6. His current research is a study financed by the Economic and Social Research Council analysing changing media representations of crime and criminal justice since the Second World War.

**Peter J. van Koppen** is a Psychologist, specializing in law and psychology. He is senior researcher at the Netherlands Institute for Criminality and Law Enforcement (NSCR) at Leiden, The Netherlands, and Professor of Law and Psychology at the Department of Law, Antwerp University, Belgium. His areas of interest are decision making in the criminal process, witness statements and identification and evidence.

**Sandra Walklate** is currently Professor of Sociology at Manchester Metropolitan University. She has written extensively on gender, policing and criminal victimisation and has worked both in a professional and voluntary capacity with a range of different victim support organizations. She is currently writing a book on murder for Willan Publishing.

# Foreword

Despite the date inside the front cover, this is really a millennium volume, a book intended to recognise a *fin de siècle*. The book came about because one of us, driving into the University one day in late 1999 and listening to the radio, was fascinated by a discussion programme in which eminent playwrights and authors of literature discussed with much erudition their ideas about the 'top100' plays and books published during the 20th century. As it happened, we had arranged to meet for lunch that day and during the course of that meeting we started to discuss the radio programme. One of us suggested that it would be fascinating to ask a range of criminal justice researchers what they thought were the most important/influential books, documents, papers and so on in the field of criminal justice in the 20th century. At this stage, it was a piece of empirical research we had in mind and what was envisaged was (probably) a tabular list similar to that produced, examined and discussed, for example, by Cohn and Farrington (1994a, 1994b, 1998). That idea did not last for long for we realised (very rapidly) that in order to retain its millennial currency, we would have needed to have started about two or three years earlier. Not a good idea then. However, we are academics and thus are well skilled at seeking to achieve the impossible, often with a minimum of resources, so we kept on gnawing at the bone. Before too long – and still during that single lunch period – we had come up, quite literally on the back of the well known envelope, with the idea for this book. We even had a list of possible authors, which, although subsequently slightly refined, continues to reflect the broad canvas of criminal justice research in the late 20th and early 21st centuries.

As a result of our deliberations, we asked our authors to select no fewer than three pieces of work (and preferably no more than six pieces) published in the 20th century (other than their own) which they believe has had the greatest impact on them both as a researcher and as an individual. Criteria for selection of the works were broad and focussed on published work which had the most substantial influence on policy and/or practice in their field of study or, in some other way, is considered by them to be key to an understanding of CJ issues in the 20th century as they affect the given field of study. Thus the authors were told that items selected for presentation and discussion might be articles, monographs, book chapters, legislation, government documents or any other 'influential' publication. Each was asked to write a description and critique of the selected items (as a sort of literature review) and to discuss the impact of them *on formulating or developing their own research.* In addition we (the editors) encouraged authors to speculate about the direction in which the area in question might be expected to develop in the first 10-15 years of the 21st century.

For our purposes, the definition of criminal justice was (is) a broad one and that is reflected in the combination of criminologists, psychologists, sociologists and experts on social and public administration. It is also reflected in efforts made to ensure that a proportion of the authors exercise their expertise and write about the CJ arena outside the United Kingdom.

Save in the broadest sense, this is not a book which reports on research findings, for all the documents are (and sometimes have been for many years) in the public domain. Rather, we must emphasise, as we did when contacting our contributors, that the principal feature of this text is the opportunity it gives to readers to examine the *intellectual influences* on key figures and the *personal dynamics* of their research initiatives. We were interested in two specific areas. Firstly, to get some insight concerning the influences and underpinnings of each individual's research interest(s); that is, what each contributor finds interesting and why, as well as how it drove (or drives) his or her research efforts. Second, we seek to provide for readers the views of eminent criminal justice researchers about what the key issues are in their preferred area of investigation.

A text such as this could, in theory, be presented in a number of differing ways. However, we have chosen to present the work of our colleagues (and of ourselves) under four headings (parts) which to a greater or lesser extent reflect the location of either the chapter or the research it describes within the criminal justice system.

The four parts are: Part 1: The Criminal Justice Core; Part 2: Police Culture; Part 3: The Police Role; and Part 4: Crime Investigation.

In Part 1: Robert Reiner, in what is probably the most self-revelatory of our chapters, discusses the influences on him *as a criminologist* of a wide range of texts ranging from classical criminological theory to empirical research. Similarly, Sandra Walklate, although drawing slightly more frequently on empirical studies, nevertheless locates her principal work in a dense theoretical frame.

In Part 2, however, the authors (Jennifer Brown, Ian McKenzie and Jim Ginger) are grouped on the basis of the loosely linked theme of an examination of police culture. Each of the authors tells us something about their own experiences 'in the field', not the smallest part of which is a tendency to have been, and perhaps to remain, surprised and disappointed by the anti-intellectualism of the police environment.

In Part 2, Les Johnston and Harold and Donna Becker, examine influences at what might be described as the leading edge of contemporary research. The development on both sides of the Atlantic of alternatives to the 'public police' and, at one and the same time, the consideration of the 'best' way for the 'public police' to undertake their role, has become a growing source of research and debate. The validity of these, and other developments is the core material for the examination of 'futures' in criminal justice and the subsequent development of both private and public policing are of central importance for the development of policing in a democratic society. (In passing it is worth noting that Harold Becker, also a police practitioner, signals some discontent with the relationship between policing and academe.)

Finally, in Part 4, we turn to issues in connection with the investigation of crime. As editors, we are confident that there will always be some people who think that a section such as this should be first not last. However, it does seem to us that, the contributions of Peter van Koppen and Ray Bull, would not exist at all were it not for all the underpinnings of the earlier sections.

As editors we set our authors a daunting task and all have responded magnificently. To invite people to reveal their influences is not unlike a session 'In the Psychiatrist's Chair' and, like the revelations made to that psychiatrist, some of what you will find here is eye-opening and at the same time slightly disturbing. However, as is always the case, it is only you, the reader, who will decide whether or not we have succeeded in our aim of allowing you to examine, the inspirations, influences and thought processes which underpin our authors' research efforts.

Ian McKenzie<br>
Ray Bull<br>
July 2001

## References

Cohn, E.G. and Farrington, D.P. (1994a). Who Are the Most Influential Criminologists in the English Speaking World?, *British Journal of Criminology,* 34: 204-25.

Cohn, E.G. and Farrington, D.P. (1994b). Who Are the Most Cited Scholars in Major American Criminology and Criminal Justice Journals?, *Journal of Criminal Justice,* 22: 517-34.

Cohn, E.G. and Farrington, D.P. (1998). Changes in the Most Cited Scholars in Major International Journals, *British Journal of Criminology,* 38: 156-70.

# PART 1

# THE CRIMINAL JUSTICE CORE

# 1. The First Cut is the Deepest: Criminological Texts and the Return of the Repressed

ROBERT REINER

## Introduction

'Few novels can change your life. This one will.' That was the pledge on the cover of the 1971 novel *The Dice Man* by Luke Rhinehart. Whether or not this was an effective sales pitch only an examination of Panther Books' balance sheets can tell us. However, it is a dubious view of how the influence of books works. It is most implausible that they produce change like tablets of stone newly brought down from Mount Sinai. Books which appear to change us as individuals, and *a fortiori* those that seem to influence social groups as a whole, do so because they effectively resonate with and articulate already ongoing developments which had hitherto been inchoate and unexpressed. 'Fortune favours the mind that is prepared', as Pasteur put it.

The editors of this volume have given us a double mission, to review the texts which have had the greatest influence on our fields as a whole, and to assess their impact on our own research. As argued above, single texts are really the archetypal embodiments of much broader movements of thought, even if they can be taken as their quintessential exemplars. Thus my first mission impossible (MI) is to review the history of twentieth century criminology as represented by its key iconic texts. MI2 is to assess their role in the formulation of my own individual research agenda. There is of course no necessary relation between these two tasks. There is no one-to-one relationship between a discipline as a whole and an individual's intellectual trajectory.

Nonetheless when I reflected upon which criminological texts I would see as the key influences upon my own development I realised that they were close to the norm for criminologists of my generation as shown by a survey conducted by Paul Rock (with my assistance) some years ago (Rock,1994). To my generation of criminologists (those recruited to university posts in the

1960s and 70s) our professional socialisation and development was profoundly marked by what Rock called the 'Big Bang' (ibid.: 134). This was the impact of the foundation in November 1968 of the National Deviancy Conference (NDC), the rallying point for the rapidly emerging 'new' deviance theory and 'new' criminology. To the 'fortunate generation' of academic criminologists recruited in the 1960s and 1970s (Rock, 1988, 1994: 133), which now dominates the profession (at least numerically), the key sacred texts were Howard Becker's *Outsiders* (1963) and Ian Taylor, Paul Walton and Jock Young's *The New Criminology* (1973). These were nominated respectively by 31 per cent and 22 per cent of the 'fortunate generation' as the works that had most influenced them (Rock, 1994: 141). Also frequently cited by this group were David's *Delinquency and Drift* (1964) and Stan Cohen's *Visions of Social Control* (1985). These works were also associated with the 'Big Bang' (although Cohen's book was published considerably later, he had been a central figure in the NDC and its influence, and had edited its first published volume, Cohen, 1971).

Given the prominence of the 'fortunate generation' in the criminological profession, these choices were also predominant in the sample as a whole. However, older and younger generations did cite some different characteristic influences. To the older generation the key figures cited were Cesare Beccaria, Robert Merton, Edwin Sutherland, and – one of their own – Nigel Walker. Younger criminologists frequently nominated Michel Foucault's *Discipline and Punish* (1977), David Garland's *Punishment and Modern Society* (1990) and Carol Smart's (1977). These different generational choices clearly reflect the positions against which the NDC had aimed its 'new' theorisations (classicism and positivism), and some of the more recent theoretical critiques of the 'new' deviance theory/criminology itself (feminism and post-structuralism). Nonetheless it was the choices of the 'fortunate generation' that characterised the sample as a whole (Rock, 1994).

In this Chapter I will consider the development of criminology in the last half of the twentieth century through the prism of five key texts. I shall also indicate how they have influenced me personally. As argued above such texts are usually emblematic of broader currents of thought. Whilst in some cases the quintessential embodiment of a particular criminological development was obvious, in others there were several works of almost equal significance. I have cheated somewhat on the assignment by discussing my five key texts in conjunction with some of the others with which their impact was intertwined. Even more problematically, I have found it impossible to find a choice for the 1990s and the early 21st century. It is always hardest to get any perspective on the period one is living through, and this is especially so at a time of rapid change such as we are experiencing at the turn of the second millennium.

The five texts I will discuss are:

1. Robert Merton's *Social Structure and Anomie* (first published in 1938), the most influential example of 'sociological positivism' in criminology.
2. David Matza's *Delinquency and Drift* (1964), in conjunction with his earlier seminal papers with Gresham Sykes (notably Sykes and Matza 1957). These paved the way for the 'new deviancy' theory of the 1960s, of which Becker's *Outsiders* (Becker, 1963) was the quintessential embodiment.
3. Ian Taylor, Paul Walton and Jock Young's *The New Criminology* (1973), unquestionably the pivotal work of the critical criminologies of the 1960s and 1970s. It has had enormous influence on the subject in many different ways.
4. David Downes and Paul Rock's edited collection *Deviant Interpretations* (Downes and Rock, 1979) pioneered the self-critique of the NDC's influence. I will focus particularly on Stan Cohen's paper in that volume, 'Guilt, Justice and Tolerance: Some Old Concepts for a New Criminology' (only one of the many influential essays by Cohen which I could have chosen, which together chart critically the late twentieth century development of criminology cf. Cohen 1988).
5. The major development since the late 1970s was clearly the proliferation of varieties of self-avowed 'realism', of the Right (heralded by James Q. Wilson's 1975 *Thinking About Crime*), and the Left (notably John Lea and Jock Young's 1984 *What Is To Be Done About Law and Order?*). I will consider both of these, especially Lea and Young.

It is hard to write intellectual history, especially biography or autobiography, without an implied Whig perspective: things can only get better. The most common narrative is the unfolding of present-day understanding, taken as an unquestioned and unqualified truth, out of past fogs of ignorance and confusion. As Cohen puts it, 'intellectual autobiographies always make us sound dumber in the past than we really were in order to give the illusion of continual cerebral progress' (Cohen, 1979:18). Even if today's science sees as far as it does only because it stands on the shoulders of giants, nonetheless, having paid due homage to them, we are usually portrayed as knowing more than those who inspired us. Bracketing out the thorny question of whether this progressive vision is true of the physical sciences, it is certainly not true of the social sciences or the humanities, although of course dedicated followers of fashion, as well as positivist natural scientists *manques,* like to pretend it is.

Criminology, perhaps even more than other areas of social science, is so inherently bound up with essentially contestable issues of ethics and governance that, as reminded us, its would-be knowledge is inseparably implicated with power. But whilst neophilia is a besetting sin of intellectual and academic life, the account of the recent history of criminology that follows is perhaps more guilty of an alternative temptation: nostalgia for a supposed golden age. Recently I have become increasingly concerned about what seems to have been lost since the heyday of the new criminologies – above all a sense of the links between crime, criminal justice and wider social issues and structures. I have to struggle to remind myself that things have also been gained: greater empirical knowledge, some crime prevention techniques that work a little, and more awareness of hitherto neglected dimensions of the injustice of criminal justice, notably gender and race.

Although there has undoubtedly been a narrowing of criminological focus in recent years to the more narrowly pragmatic and policy-oriented (as will be elaborated later), nonetheless there has not been anything like a reversion to the position before what Paul Rock called the 'Big Bang' of the 1960s. Stan Cohen has succinctly summed-up the remit of criminology thus: 'The stuff of criminology consists of only three questions: Why are laws made? Why are they broken? What do we do or what should we do about this?' (Cohen, 1988: 9. See also Lea, 1998: 164). Before the 'Big Bang' most criminology was concentrated almost entirely on the second of these issues, with some limited interest in the third. Although there were precursors who examined the nature and formation definitions of deviance (notably but not only Durkheim), it is only since the 1960s that the first question has clearly been unavoidable in criminology, or that the study of crime control (the third issue) has transcended a narrowly technicist penology. However, since the late 1970s there has certainly been something of a reversion to pre-Big Bang criminology, especially but not only in the USA.

Before embarking on the discussion of my key texts, the narrow parochialism of this chapter must be admitted. It is parochial in a double sense. Firstly it is primarily concerned with criminology in Britain. My first two selections are from the USA, and this testifies to the extent to which there once was greater international cross-fertilisation of criminological ideas. Although some scholars undoubtedly continue to exercise influence throughout the world, this is rare. Ellen Cohn and David Farrington's comparative analyses of journal citations (Cohn and Farrington 1990, 1994, 1998) show that British and American criminologists occupy almost totally different intellectual worlds, at least as indicated by the sources they reference. Only a few criminologists engage in work that is comparative in anything more than a gestural sense (Nelken 1997a). This volume promises to be an exception, with contributors from North America and continental Europe. However, my chapter does focus primarily on British criminology.

This chapter follows most criminology in being parochial in a deeper sense. Cohen's definition of the province of criminology cited above explicitly restricts its ambit to the making and breaking of criminal law. There have of course been many challenges to rooting the ambit of criminology in law, above all in the new deviance theory of the late 1960s, of which Cohen himself was a prominent pioneer. Nonetheless even the 60s debates (in common with such earlier ventures as Sutherland's coinage of the concept of white-collar crime cf. Sutherland, 1949; Nelken, 1997b; Slapper and Tombs, 1999) focused on behaviour which was at the margins of criminalisation. Only a few (notably Stan Cohen in his recent work) have directed criminologists' attention to the relevance for the understanding of wrongdoing of much broader conceptions of human rights violations, especially those organised or connived at by states (Cohen, 1988 chapters.11-14; 1993; 1995; 1997). Perhaps the most vivid indication of this is the virtually complete ignoring of the Holocaust – arguably the greatest crime in history even in a legalistic sense – by criminologists (Morrison 1995:202-3), even though several were either victims of it or the children of victims (including myself). Somehow once offending transcends the small-scale of even the 'organised crime' that occurs on a relatively routine basis it passes off the criminological radar screen. However, whilst it is important to note this double parochialism of most criminology as an agenda for the future, this chapter will concentrate on the key landmarks in the history of the present.

## Robert Merton, Anomie and Social Structure

Merton's paper on anomie, first published in 1938 but today better known in its revised 1957 version (Merton 1957), is both enormously influential in criminology and sociology in general, but also in my own personal development in the subject. It is one of the most frequently cited papers of all time in sociology, throughout the world. As Paul Rock and David Downes say of functionalism in general, the demolition of Merton's theory of anomie in essays and exams has for several generations of students become 'almost an initiation rite of passage' into criminology (Downes and Rock, 1997: 88).

Robert Merton was of course one of the key American social theorists from the 1930s to the early 1960s, and the anomie essay was only a small part of his huge corpus of work. It illustrates David Downes' point that criminology has been a 'rendezvous' subject (cited in Rock 1997:234). Some of the most important contributions have been made not by specialist professional criminologists but by scholars from a variety of disciplines – from Durkheim to Foucault – who have visited the sites of crime and deviance briefly but seminally. During his working life, Merton was probably best known for his meta-theoretical essays on sociology, advocating 'middle-range' theory and offering a critique of the dominant grand theory of the time (particularly in America), functionalism, as embodied above all in the work of his contemporary Talcott Parsons. In addition, he wrote prolifically on many substantive topics, above all on the sociology of science.

To student sociologists of my generation Merton offered a number of attractions. He wrote clearly and vividly, less so than C. Wright Mills, but much more than Talcott Parsons and his other rivals in mainstream sociology. Politically he was what *The New Criminology* dubbed the 'cautious rebel' (Taylor, Walton and Young 1973: 101), so he offered an acceptable critical alternative to the intellectual and political rigidities of Parsonian functionalism. 'Middle range' theory offered a theoretical analysis of concrete subject matters like crime that seemed to steer clear of the rocks of what C. Wright Mills dubbed 'abstracted empiricism' and 'grand theory' (Mills, 1959 chapters 2 and 3).

To me personally reading Merton came at the right time to attract me to sociology in general, and in particular to the study of deviance. As I have written elsewhere (Reiner 1998), I came from an Orthodox Jewish background but by the time I was an undergraduate reading Merton had questioned my childhood faith. However, having lost the clear moral compass of my childhood I was beset by questions about ethics and how one should live. I had no personal experience at all of crime or law enforcement, but had for many years been an avid fan of detective stories, probably as a vicarious way of exploring wrong-doing in a cosy and secure setting. I had been a liberal in my sentiments about punishment from as early in my life as I can remember, and recall being deeply shocked as a young boy by reading about the executions of Derek Bentley and Ruth Ellis. Nonetheless I had implicitly always regarded crime and punishment from what I much later learned to call a 'classical' perspective. I had never thought of criminals other than as wrong-doers deserving punishment, albeit only minimal, proportionate and humanely administered. It was only when I read Merton's essay that a whole new vista appeared to me: the prospect of understanding crime as a phenomenon with social causes, ones which might be removed or at any rate ameliorated by a fairer society. This appealed to so many of the perspectives and values I had espoused in the course of my adolescent distancing from the religion of my parents: faith in reason not revelation; science not superstition; reform not revenge. It was Merton's essay above all that set me on the postgraduate path of reading for an MSc in Sociology at LSE, specialising in deviance as my main interest.

Is Merton's essay merely of historical interest, however, or does anything of value survive the generations of critical demolition since it was first written? As I elaborated in an earlier paper on Merton (Reiner, 1984), it seems to me that his approach in his classic essay on anomie provides a useful basis for a social explanation of rates and patterns of crime and deviance. It has continued to be influential on subsequent theorists, albeit often without acknowledgement. One reason for the common underestimation of Merton's influence is a terminological one. Merton's analysis of crime and deviance centres on the concept of 'anomie'. However, this is closely similar to another of Merton's concepts, 'relative deprivation', which lies at the heart of most socialist or social democratic accounts of crime providing a mediating link between crime, inequality and exclusion (for example Lea and Young, 1984; Box, 1987; Lea, 1992; Young,1997: 487-8, 1999; Taylor, 1997: 274-280, 1999; Downes, 1998; Currie,1998a and b; Reiner, 2000a:81-2). It is strange that Merton himself never related his own concept of relative deprivation to crime, when it is clearly an aspect of his model of anomie.

Merton's essay clearly sets out to provide a framework for understanding patterns of variation in crime and deviance between and within societies. In large part this is intended to explain the problem of American exceptionalism in its high crime levels compared to other industrial democracies. It also offers an analysis of the sources of varying forms of deviance within a society. The theory is so well known that only a brief precis here should suffice (for fuller expositions see Taylor, Walton and Young, 1973 chapter 4; Reiner, 1984: 186-194; Downes and Rock, 1997 chapter 5). Deviance is seen as resulting from pressures induced by 'anomie'– a mismatch between culturally defined aspirations and the legitimate opportunities available in a particular social structure. The strain of anomie results in variations in the extent and pattern of deviance within and between particular societies.

Societies vary in the extent of anomic strain they experience either because of the character of their cultural definitions of success, or because of the degree of disjunction between culturally defined goals and structurally available legitimate means. America is exceptionally anomic and thus crime-prone on both these scores, because its culture is both highly materialistic and meritocratic. Materialistic cultures are particularly susceptible to anomie. Prioritising monetary success is likely to generate anomie because the limits of aspiration are never clearly defined but 'indefinite and relative' (Merton, 1957: 136). Moreover, a materialistic culture stresses the goal of monetary success rather than the legitimate means for their attainment. Winning is everything, so that restraints on how this is to be achieved are secondary and likely to be evaded as competition gets tough – 'nice guys finish last'. The USA is also especially anomie and crime prone because of its meritocratic culture, the mythology of careers open to the talents, with the path from log cabin to the White House, from rags to riches, available to everyone. The structural reality is, however, that opportunities are as differentially distributed in the USA as in the more obviously class and tradition bound European societies. The dissonance between aspirations and legitimate means for their achievement generates, argues Merton, anomie, strains in the regulatory structure, making deviance more likely.

The core of Merton's essay is his consideration of how the overall anomic strain may result in different deviant adaptations. It is this part of his argument that is the most remembered and the most frequently subject to ritualistic slaying in student essays. Merton offers a typology of five possible adaptations depending on whether people accept or reject the cultural goals and/or the legitimate institutionalised means for attaining them (Merton, 1957: 140). The possibilities he outlines are: conformity (accept goals and means); innovation (accept goals, reject means); ritualism (reject goals, accept means); retreatism (reject goals and means); rebellion (reject goals and means, but seek to replace them with a new congruent set). The last four are deviant adaptations, though not necessarily involving crime. Merton offers only sketchy suggestions as to how individuals come to adopt these adaptations. For example, he suggests that ritualism might be a characteristic lower-middle class response, attributable to a combination of limited opportunities and strict socialisation.

As mentioned above, Merton's paper has been subjected to several decades of criticism. These can be divided into questions about the empirical validity of aspects of the analysis; observations about the underdevelopment of parts of the argument (which Merton had conceded in the essay itself, stating that it 'remains but a prelude', ibid.: 160); and attempts at theoretical refutation of its fundamentals. Whilst the first two types of critique imply the need for adjustment and extension of the original arguments, the theoretical attacks purport to call its entire validity into question (Reiner, 1984).

One of the most common criticisms of Merton is that he takes at face value the distribution of crime as indicated by official statistics. Certainly as Merton himself puts it 'it appears from our analysis that the greatest pressures towards deviation are exerted upon the lower strata' (Merton, 1957: 144), because the lack of legitimate opportunities is in absolute terms more significant lower down the social hierarchy. However, Merton stated unambiguously in the very same sentence 'the official crime statistics uniformly showing higher rates in the lower strata are far from complete and reliable'. Far from ignoring suite crime in favour of street crime, Merton discusses at length the phenomenon of crimes of the powerful (ibid.: 141-4). Indeed the analysis of the criminogenic characteristics of American culture per se, with its relentless pressure for material and monetary success, and the emphasis on *relative* not absolute deprivation, seem designed to explain white- collar as well as street crime. Merton clearly indicates that pressures to deviate in response to anomic strain takes many forms and are experienced throughout the social structure. Nonetheless his argument does imply plausibly that legally labelled crime will disproportionately be a phenomenon of lower social strata (although as he rightly says this can never be known conclusively). This is because anomic pressures on lower strata are more likely to take the form of legally defined crime, partly because of the structure of legitimate and illegitimate opportunities, and partly because of the lack of power to influence the law-making and enforcing processes.

The previous point relates to an important area of underdevelopment of the initial paper, explaining the processes underlying different forms of deviant adaptation. This has generated a large body of literature in the sub-cultural tradition, extending Merton's framework to show how and why anomic strain generates different adaptations (for example Cohen 1955; Cloward and Ohlin 1962; Downes 1966). Albert Cohen used the Freudian concept of reaction formation to explain how youths exposed to the success ethos but excluded from legitimate opportunities might engage in violent and destructive behaviour as a way of denying their failure to achieve the goals they had initially incorporated. Cloward and Ohlin introduced the idea of an illegitimate opportunity structure in which people were differentially placed as an explanation of their varying adaptations to anomic strain. Downes related different deviant subcultures to how anomic pressure was experienced by different classes and ethnic groups, mediated by access to housing and other aspects of life chances.

Amongst the more fundamental theoretical criticisms of Merton, the main ones concern: his apparent determinism; the related denial of authenticity to deviant moral choices; the lack of a historical analysis of how and why different cultures and social structures develop; and his faith in the possibilities of social reform to reduce anomic strain. *The New Criminology* argued that in 'classical anomie theory, the typical actor is in a box, in a social position, and he is not to get out until social reformers have opened the opportunity chest... The individual actor – boxed into a fixed social position – is rarely seen to evolve a solution to his problem in his own terms' (Taylor, Walton and Young, 1973: 108).

Although clearly Merton suggests relationships between particular social positions and patterns of deviant response, there is nothing in the model to suggest that this occurs through mechanistic determination. Merton's emphasis is on structure rather than agency, but his analysis is entirely compatible with a dialectical conception of the relationship between structural position and actors' responses. Any postulated relationship between say class and deviance is probabilistic not invariant. Part of the variance can be interpreted as not just attributable to finer aspects of structure (as in Cloward and Ohlin) but to the autonomy of actors ultimately to decide how to define and respond to their situations. All this of course raises the perennial and ultimately insoluble philosophical issues of free-will and determinism, or agency and structure in their sociological guise, but Merton need not be interpreted in a deterministic way. Nor are deviant adaptations necessarily denied moral authenticity. Drug taking, for example, *may* be seen as an example of retreatism, literal 'opiates of the people' to avoid the pain of failure. But in particular instances it may be a form of purposive rebellion, as in the case of hippies or bohemian artists, seeking to supplant the dominant culture of material success.

Laurie Taylor's amusing caricature of anomie theory as portraying society as a rigged fruit machine has become an almost inevitable quote in critiques of Merton. He claims that 'in this analysis nobody appears to ask who put the machine there in the first place and who takes the profits. Criticism of the game is confined to changing the pay-out sequences so that the deprived can get a better deal (increasing educational opportunities, poverty programmes). What at first sight looks like a major critique of society ends up by taking the existing society for granted' (Taylor, 1973: 148). As mentioned earlier, *The New Criminology* similarly castigated Merton for being a 'cautious rebel' (Taylor, Walton and Young, 1973: 101). These criticisms smack of the heady days of the early 1970s before Thatcher and Reagan were even clouds on the horizon. Analytically there is nothing to preclude extending Merton's analysis to a historical examination of why the American Dream has such a materialistic and meritocratic character, and why structural opportunities remain so unequal. Politically, after twenty-five years of neo-liberal economic and social policy 'cautious rebellion' no longer seems such small beer. As I argued nearly twenty years ago, with hindsight 'it seems utopian in the worst sense to dismiss 'increasing educational opportunities' and 'poverty programmes' rather sneeringly as sops to the status quo... Merton's explicitly 'middle-range' theory has been much criticised for its 'caution', but at least it raises what Trotsky might have called 'transitional demands' that point to a realistic strategy of change, rather than utopian postulates of an ideal society' (Reiner 1984: 194).

In sum, Merton's theory of anomie, first advanced in the late 1930s, is hardly surprisingly the criminology of the 'New Deal', redolent of the reformist, Keynesian values and politics the FDR Democrats. However, the era in which it was the virtually unquestioned common-sense of social and criminal justice policy had much to recommend it in terms of growing prosperity, declining inequality, and relatively low crime and disorder, although there was also much hidden corruption, and intolerance of difference (Young 1999). The heart of Merton's analysis, the recognition of a relationship between crime and an acquisitive, unjust society, rightly continues to inspire contemporary social democratic perspectives.

## David Matza: Appreciating Appreciation

David Matza is a key progenitor of the 'Big Bang' in criminology during the 1960s, the epistemological and political break associated in this country above all with the NDC and new deviancy theory. I began studying criminology in the late 1960s, just as all this was getting under way. I well remember being enthralled by the work of Matza, and those such as Becker, Lemert, Polsky, as well as Goffman, Laing and other analysts whose approach was cognate although they did not write on crime (Becker 1963; Lemert 1967; Polsky 1967; Goffman 1963, 1968; Laing 1967).

If Merton introduced me to the idea that crime and deviance could be understood as socially generated, at least in part, the new deviancy theorists led on to yet more exciting prospects. Above all they raised head-on the problematic character of moral categorisations, much more vividly than the arguments of abstract moral philosophy which I was also grappling with personally in the context of dealing with guilt about violating the religious norms I had been brought up with (Reiner 1998: 93-6). In addition the naturalistic, tell-it-like-it-is studies of exotic forms of deviance within the labelling approach had all the voyeuristic fascination of a vicarious walk on the wild side without the dangers of inhaling.

It was hard to find a single representative of the great ferment in 1960s criminology for discussion here. In the end I have settled for Matza rather than Becker, whose 1963 book *Outsiders* is the quintessential text of counter-cultural criminology (it ranks with Merton's essay as one of the most frequently cited texts in criminology). Matza's work appeals to me above all for its stress on the ambiguities and complexities of moral judgement, represented by such key concepts as 'techniques of neutralisation', 'subterranean values', and 'drift'.

Matza published two influential books on deviance in the 1960s, *Delinquency and Drift* and *Becoming Deviant* (Matza 1964, 1969). Although the latter is an important critique of criminological theory, above all of positivist criminology's blotting-out of the links between crime and the state that defines and seeks to regulate crime, it is the former I will concentrate on here. *Delinquency and Drift* itself is largely drawn from some earlier seminal papers Matza co-wrote with Gresham Sykes (Sykes and Matza 1957; Matza and Sykes 1961. Cf. also Matza 1961).

Perhaps the pivotal contribution Matza made is summarised by his own distinction between a 'correctionalist' and an 'appreciative' perspective (made explicit in Matza, 1969 Part 1, but underlying all his work). Whereas positivist criminology (a major target throughout his work) seeks to understand the causes of crime in order to 'correct' them, the 'appreciative' approach recognises that deviants like all other human beings have an inner-life and point of view. Interpreting the deviant's perspective is necessary for understanding deviance, and indeed regulating it if that is the project. I argued earlier that the recognition of deviants' agency is not incompatible with the work of Merton and other sociological positivists, but of course their emphasis is on the effects of structure. Matza grapples with the issues of free-will, responsibility and determinism head-on in his espousal of the ideas of 'soft determinism' (Matza, 1964: 8-9) and 'drift'. 'The fundamental assertion of soft determinism is that human actions are not deprived of freedom because they are causally determined' (Matza, 1964: 9). To understand is not necessarily to forgive. People make their own history, but not under conditions of their own choosing. 'Drift' conveys this constant dialectic between the strains imposed by the situations actors find themselves in and the autonomy they exercise to some degree in their interpretations and reactions.

'Appreciation' does not imply acceptance of deviants' actions. Understanding the deviant's perspective is not incompatible with condemning it, although it may be, depending on the analyst's particular moral and political viewpoint. Perhaps the most consistent theme linking Matza's work is the rejection of the idea of deviants having radically different moral perspectives from the conventional values enshrined in criminal law (a position Matza attributes to subcultural theories). Sykes and Matza (1957) developed the concept of 'techniques of neutralisation' on the basis of interviews with delinquents. These are modes of argument neutralising moral culpability for deviation, but which are found within criminal law itself in its repertoire of excuses and mitigations (although the delinquents have applied them to their own actions in circumstances where the courts did not). Sykes and Matza identified five techniques of neutralisation: denial of responsibility, denial of the victim, denial of injury, condemning the condemners, and the appeal to higher loyalties. These are seen as important aspects of explaining deviance, on the plausible assumption that people do not wish to appear evil to themselves. I certainly have come to recognise them within myself when I act in ways that I would normally condemn.

In their later 1961 paper on delinquency, Sykes and Matza invert the argument. Conventional culture contains 'subterranean' values that are marginalised in everyday life but are licensed for specific occasions: the search for 'kicks' – excitement, risk, thrills, adventure. Delinquents differ not because they enjoy these things but because they do so at conventionally inappropriate times and places. The huge public taste for crime stories testifies to the extent to which conventional people share the delinquents' tastes if not their recklessness. Sykes and Matza extend this point to violence, the use of which is sanctioned indeed glorified in appropriate circumstances (law-enforcement, war, or just standing up for yourself), but condemned in general (although vicariously enjoyed in many forms of entertainment).

Combining these concepts in *Delinquency and Drift*, Matza constructs a powerful case for seeing deviance not as an alien universe but the practices of people whose mental processes and morality are continuous with the conventional. This is of course a partial return to the classical perspective in which crime is seen as rational action (as acknowledged by the Preface to Matza, 1964).

Matza's work was a clear precursor of the labelling perspective and the new deviancy theory of the 1960s. This was above all by calling into question the hitherto taken for granted standpoint of criminal law, and recognising the significance of the criminal justice system itself in creating and shaping the deviance it purports to control. Turning the analytic standpoint on the criminal justice system was undoubtedly one of the great advances of 1960s criminology, making possible such new areas as the study of the police and policing (Reiner, 1997). However, the labelling approach had some clear limitations in its straightforward inversion of the concerns and values of conventional criminology. Its empirical focus was on marginally criminal forms of deviance which could most easily be appreciated rather than condemned (Liazos, 1972). It tended to simply swap an outlaw or underdog identification for earlier criminology's official standpoint. This was most explicit in Becker's essay asking 'Whose side are we on?' (Becker, 1967). Alvin Gouldner's well-known critique of Becker (Gouldner, 1968) argued that the appreciative yet critical stance had to be applied to understanding control no less than deviance. Merely swapping the labels and moral evaluations around was to reproduce the problems of conventional criminology from the other side. Both crime and control were mutually interacting processes shaped by the wider social structure and culture. Gouldner's essay was explicitly a major inspiration for *The New Criminology's* search 'for a fully social theory of deviance' (the book's sub-title), and indeed Gouldner wrote the book's Foreword (Taylor, Walton and Young, 1973:ix-xiv). It is to this I now turn.

### Taylor, Walton and Young's *New Criminology*

*The New Criminology* was undoubtedly the key text of the radical criminology that developed in the late 1960s and 1970s in Britain and North America. It represented a hardening, politically and theoretically, of the 'Big Bang' that had produced the NDC and new deviancy theory. As discussed earlier, Paul Rock's survey of British criminologists in the early 1990s found it to be the second most influential book on his respondents (especially those of the 'fortunate generation'), closely following Becker's *Outsiders* (Rock, 1994: 141).

As the book's sub-title indicates, its agenda is to blaze the trail 'for a fully social theory of deviance'. This is attempted through an 'immanent critique' of existing criminological theories, from eighteenth century classicism to 1960s labelling and conflict theories. Having thus provided the groundwork for their own synthesis in the book's first eight chapters, the authors' concluding ninth chapter then points towards the payoff in two ways. It sets out the 'formal requirements' of 'a fully social theory of deviance' (Taylor, Walton and Young, 1973: 268-78). Finally in the last few pages (ibid.: 278-282) they commit the new criminology to the political project of working towards a crime-free society, the necessary precondition for which is a socialism that accepts 'human diversity'. As the book's concluding sentence puts it: 'The task is to create a society in which the facts of human diversity, whether personal, organic or social, are not subject to the power to criminalize.' (ibid.: 282). The authors themselves amplify this political project in somewhat greater detail in the introductory first chapter they contributed to an edited collection of essays two years later (Taylor, Walton and Young, 1975).

*The New Criminology* is thus really three books in one. It is a critical textbook on criminological theory, on which subsequent generations of budding criminologists have cut their teeth. It is also a sketch of a particular model of how to study crime and deviance: the 'fully social theory' whose formal requirements are set out in Chapter Nine. Finally, it is a political manifesto, asserting that the whole history of criminological theory can be read as establishing the possibility of freedom from crime if a new kind of socialist society is constructed, based on radical equality and tolerance.

As a textbook *The New Criminology* has to a large extent stood the test of time. A plethora of new texts on criminological theory have appeared since 1973, several with their own distinctive virtues. David Downes and Paul Rock's *Understanding Deviance* (first published in 1982, third edition 1997) is the most analytically rigorous and balanced survey of (mainly twentieth century) criminological theory available. Vold's *Theoretical Criminology* (originally published in 1958 and clearly a source for some of *The New Criminology* itself) remains a stimulating and clear student-friendly text in its current incarnation (Vold, Bernard and Snipes 1997). Morrison's *Theoretical Criminology* (1995) is a philosophically and theoretically sophisticated critical reading of the history of criminological theory. Tierney's *Criminology: Theory and Contexts* is a clear, stimulating, rigorous review of post-World War II criminological theories and their social context (Tierney

1996). Jones (1998) is perhaps the most accessible yet comprehensive student introduction.

Yet despite these (and other) rivals, all more up-to-date in their coverage, *The New Criminology* remains an important reference for all students. This is paradoxically for the same reason I never recommend it on its own. It is exceptionally engaging and stimulating as a text precisely because of its polemical stance, its critical reading of past theory as a way of constructing a 'new criminology'. Past theories are interrogated in turn, rejected as limited and partial, but with some kernels salvaged as building blocks of the 'fully social theory'. Thus classical criminology, for example, is said not to suffer from positivism's denial of human autonomy, but its own conception of action is overly rational, and fails to recognise the importance of social structure. Crucially, all theories apart from Marxism, neglect or deny the relationship between capitalism and crime, the significance of structured differences in class power. Classical Marxism on the other hand is overly deterministic, denying any role to human choice and any respect for moral diversity.

The sketch of the *'formal* requirements' of 'a fully social theory' specifies seven elements for it (Taylor, Walton and Young, 1973:270-8). The theory must encompass: (1) The wider origins of the deviant act; (2) Immediate origins of the deviant act; (3) The actual act; (4) Immediate origins of social reaction; (5) Wider origins of social reaction; (6) The outcome of the social reaction on deviants' further reaction; (7) The nature of the deviant process as a whole. This is clearly a synthesis allowing the integration of the valid kernels of past theories that survived the earlier chapters' immanent critique. An analysis of criminogenic aspects social structure and culture such as found say in Merton's model of anomie or in Marxist theories like Bonger's would be examples of element 1. However, they need supplementing by the other elements. How do wider structural pressures translate themselves into the 'immediate origins' of deviance? Much of the repertoire of positive criminology could be relevant here in particular cases, from biological or psychological explanations of individual pathology to 'middle range' sociological theories like Merton's typology of deviant adaptations, subcultural theories, or ecological theories. However, none of the pressures or strains analysed in 1 and 2 (above) fully determine deviance. The actual act must be analysed in part because of the significance of individual's autonomy, but also because of the importance of situational exigencies such as are pointed to by contemporary rational choice perspectives emphasising the role of opportunities in the occurrence of offending. Moreover, as labelling perspectives pointed out, deviance is defined and structured by social reaction. So this too must be analysed in terms of its immediate (4) and wider (5) origins, and their possible outcome in 'secondary' deviance (6). Finally it must always be remembered that these factors are separable only in abstract analysis. Their complex dialectical inter-relationship in the whole living process of deviance and reaction must not be lost sight of (7).

Most research focuses on at most a couple of these elements. Perhaps the most significant exception was the sweeping study of the policing of 'mugging' by Stuart Hall and his colleagues (Hall *et al.* 1978). Although not self-consciously modelled on *The New Criminology*'s 'formal requirements', *Policing the Crisis* certainly comes close to being the multi-layered analysis of the occurrence and reaction to a particular act of deviance that Taylor, Young and Walton called for. Opening out from an analysis of a specific court case in which three black youths in Birmingham were given exemplary sentences for a 'mugging', the book probes the media and police construction of a 'moral panic' around 'mugging' in the early 1970s. It goes on to trace the wider roots of this in a Gramscian account of British culture and political economy, primarily since World War II. Finally the book analyses the social, economic and cultural history and structure of the black community in post-war Britain to probe the pressures that could produce street crime. Although it is probably the most wide-ranging analysis of a particular offence in criminology, as Downes and Rock point out, even *Policing the Crisis* does not really satisfy all seven of the 'formal requirements' in Taylor, Walton and Young's 'fully social theory'. There is little on elements 3, 'the actual act', and 6, 'the outcome of social reaction on deviants' further actions' (Downes and Rock *op cit*: 248).

Most research will inevitably be much more limited. Nonetheless it remains important in my view that researchers are sensitive to the other elements even if they can't tackle them directly. For example, in my book *The Politics of the Police* (first published in 1985; 3rd edn. 2000), I felt it important to combine 'wider' and 'immediate' factors, as well as an emphasis on actual practices. The discussion of police practices (chapter 4 on such matters as the content of police work, crime prevention and detection, and discrimination) and their 'immediate origins' such as police culture (chapter 3), was preceded by a 'wider' and more 'immediate' analysis of their structuring in history (chapters 1 and 2). Chapter 6 was a discussion of legal regulation and accountability, i.e. the 'reaction' to possible police deviance. Nonetheless there is a very little analysis of the structuring of the problems the police are a dialectical reaction to, which a 'fully social theory' of policing would have to encompass.

Whilst *The New Criminology* remains valuable in my view both as a provocative text, and a reminder to 'only connect' in the analysis of deviance and control, its political conclusions were and remain highly problematic. The postulation of a crime-free society based on socialist diversity rapidly came to be seen as utopian in the worst sense – 'left idealism' – by some of the authors themselves in their conversion to 'realism' (which is examined later). There are several obvious and fundamental problems with the dream of the last few pages of *The New Criminology* (278-82). Even if a radically egalitarian socialist society could exist, in which the bulk of current crime – which is related to private property – had disappeared, would there not still be inter-personal conflicts and problems arising out of individual pathologies that would neither be tolerated nor treated non-punitively? Wouldn't Durkheim's arguments about the 'normality' of crime remain valid, i.e. that a society where grosser deviations are fewer might be more sensitive to relatively more minor deviance? However, the biggest problem in the discussion is whether such a socialist society is at all feasible. Clearly in the three decades since its appearance the world has changed in ways that make *The New Criminology*'s project seem ever more unrealisable. Nonetheless it seems to me there is some value in utopian thinking if only as some kind of inspirational myth (cf. Loader, 1998 for a persuasive case urging what he calls 'utopian realism'). Certainly the blinkering out of possibilities beyond the actually existing, as in end of ideology and end of history arguments, involve a self-fulfilling depressing of horizons (Levitas, 1990; Jacoby, 1999). *Pace* Max Weber, an ethics of ultimate ends may sometimes be needed to animate the ethics of responsibility.

### 'There Are More Questions Than Answers': Stan Cohen's 'Guilt, Justice and Tolerance'

*The New Criminology* and *Critical Criminology*, Taylor, Walton and Young's 1975 companion volume of essays, marked the zenith of radical criminology in what Jock Young himself was soon to call its 'left idealist' form. By the late 1970s criticism of this from other radical positions was rife. A seminal contribution to this was made by a 1979 collection of papers edited by David Downes and Paul Rock, with contributions by people who had been closely associated with the NDC (Downes and Rock, 1979). The book is full of important papers criticising aspects of the 'new criminology'. Several papers, notably Paul Rock's, point to the dangers of totalising and of deterministic explanations which lurk in the model of a 'fully social theory of deviance', despite its own protestations to the contrary (Rock, 1979). David Downes, under the captivating title 'Praxis Makes Perfect', mounts a cogent plea for a social democratic, Fabian approach to crime that recognises that socialist societies have proved no better at achieving either 'classlessness' than capitalist ones (Downes, 1979).

It was Stan Cohen's essay 'Guilt, Justice and Tolerance: Some Old Concepts for a New Criminology' that I found especially disturbing and memorable (Cohen, 1979), possibly because it spoke straight to some of the concerns that had first drawn me into studying deviance. Above all it is suffused with complex, subtle and at times agonised probing of the relationship between ethics, justice and crime. It is exceptionally hard to summarise or convey its flavour, perhaps because it is in many ways an internal dialogue, with, in the words of the reggae song, 'more questions than answers'.

The essay begins with a convincing internal critique of new deviancy theory and criminology to develop or make explicit a coherent ethical position on the criteria demarcating what should be regarded as deviant. 'It was less a question of moral nihilism – which is, at least, an established philosophical position – than of selective morality' (**Cohen, 1979:19**). Pot-smokers yes, polluters no. He amusingly deprecated the shifting stances according to different crimes, contexts and audiences. 'If ... deviants were not pathological beings driven by forces beyond their control, then surely as rational, responsible beings they should be punished more severely? Ah no, that's not *quite* what we meant. And when we talked about being on the side of the deviant, did this mean we were actually in favour of what he did? Here our answers were really tortuous... Already apparent in these stances was the vacillation between the image of the deviant as mismanaged victim and the deviant as cultural hero' (Cohen, 1979:18-19). As Cohen notes, these issues were already pointed to by Jock Young in 'Working Class Criminology', which anticipates elements of his later autocritique cf. Young, 1975).

The heart of the essay is a complex consideration of the classical issues of how explanation, especially if it involves 'appreciation' as a methodological stance, can be combined with moral responsibility, guilt, and punishment. This is illustrated by the example of the trials of American officers for their part in the My Lai massacres during the Vietnam War (Cohen, 1979: 28-31). He shows that the Left's arguments against 'scape-goating' relatively junior officers for the sins of the political elite joined with the Right's whitewash of the soldiers to let them off the hook. 'Without some notion of individual responsibility, no credit or blame could be assigned to anybody. Masochistic indictments of the whole culture as 'guilty'... sound virtuous but are politically sterile' (Cohen, 1979: 29).

The confusions were compounded when the deterministic thrust of social structural explanation was combined with the *New Criminology*'s attacks on both determinism and voluntarism in earlier theories (Cohen, 1979: 31-5). There was no attempt at a consistent synthesis. Criminals were depicted in effect as 'rational in the morning, drifting in the afternoon and brutalised in the evening' (Cohen, 1979: 32).

*'Guilt, Justice and Tolerance'* is noteworthy not for its answers but its unsettling questioning of the failure of the new deviancy theories and criminology to confront what are in effect age old problems of moral and political philosophy. These are crucially implicated in criminalisation and control in practice as well as theory. Cohen's own conclusions are worth quoting from. The 'purer' theoretical tasks still remain on the agenda: to reconcile the twists of classical and positivist philosophies with a sociological conception of individual responsibility; to apply an abstract theory of justice to the brute facts of the social order and the possibilities of a different order; to understand what the notions of diversity and tolerance would look like in the good society. But these tasks must be performed with at least one eye open to the day-to-day world of crime and criminal justice politics' (Cohen, 1979: 49-50). However, as Cohen himself anticipated, these more complex issues were being side-stepped yet again by the resurgence in the late 1970s of a more right-wing climate in politics generally and in 'law and order' politics in particular. In criminology this was reflected in the rise of 'realism' across the political spectrum.

### John Lea and Jock Young's *What Is To Be Done About Law and Order?*

*What Is To Be Done About Law and Order?* (Lea and Young, 1984; 2nd edn. 1992) is the flagship of the realist turn by many erstwhile 'new criminologists' during the 1980s, such as Jock Young, John Lea, Richard Kinsey and Roger Matthews. The way had been paved by many articles by Young in particular (perhaps its earliest harbinger was Young, 1975. See also Young, 1979, 1980, Lea and Young, 1982). Ian Taylor had also published a vigorously argued case for a socialist criminal justice policy in 1981. Although it did not overtly label itself 'left realist' it was certainly an attempt to engage in current political debates in a much more concrete and immediate way than *The New Criminology*'s 'left idealism' (Taylor 1981).

'Left realism' was overtly pitched against two main targets: 'left idealism' (as found in the last few pages of *The New Criminology*), and 'administrative criminology' (Young, 1986, 1988, 1994, 1997). The latter is an amalgam of what are really two distinct developments.

The first is the right-wing realism that began to flourish in the USA during the 1970s, quintessentially embodied in James Q. Wilson's *Thinking About Crime* (Wilson, 1975), with its fierce polemic against seeking the 'root causes' of crime. It was already implied by Wilson's subsequent publication of a lengthy tome trying to establish the root causes of crime in 'human nature' (Wilson and Herrnstein, 1985) that his *animus* was really against explanations of crime in terms of social inequality. The revised edition of *Thinking About Crime* makes this explicit (Wilson, 1985: 6, chapter 3).

This should be distinguished from the rational choice/situational crime prevention approach pioneered at the Home Office Research Unit by Ron Clarke and his associates (Mayhew *et al.* 1976; Clarke and Mayhew, 1980; Cornish and Clarke, 1986; Bottoms, 1990; Pease, 1997). Although both are lumped together by Young as 'administrative criminology' because they share a pragmatic emphasis on 'what works', bracketing out issues of aetiology, the politics of the two are different. Situational crime prevention is a key aspect of much broader shifts in criminal justice policy, related to the high volumes of crime in late modern societies. These have been incisively analysed as 'criminologies of everyday life' by David Garland (Garland, 1996, 2000, 2001). Their key characteristic is a concern with actuarial risk reduction rather than moral issues of blame and punishment (Feeley and Simon, 1994). Although clearly part of the broader move towards 'realism' in the last twenty-five years, these policies are not necessarily associated with the political right. They are for example a key feature of New Labour's Crime Reduction Programme (Home Office, 1998; Nuttall, Goldblatt and Lewis, 1998).

'Left realism' proclaims a new departure from previous radical analyses of crime in a number of ways. Most crucially it rejects the playing down of the significance of crime in the everyday sense which was implicit in new deviancy theory and criminology, with their tendencies to constructionism and relativism. Whilst not denying that there are discriminatory dimensions to labelling processes (Lea and Young 1984, Chapter 4), and that legal definitions of crime bear a problematic relationship to different conceptions of social harm or morality, 'left realism' emphasises that 'street crime' is a problem to be taken seriously. This is argued for partly on *a priori* grounds. However, the main arguments are based on empirical evidence from crime surveys. These reveal the particular impact of crime on poorer people, ethnic minorities, women, and the young. In short, crime hits precisely the constituencies with which the left should be concerned with (Lea and Young 1984 Chaps.1 and 2; Kinsey 1984; Kinsey, Lea and Young 1986; Jones, Maclean and Young 1986; Crawford *et al* 1990). Both on the grounds of social justice and pragmatic political considerations, the problem of 'law and order', which is of such concern to these groups, should not be relinquished to conservatives whilst the left awaits some wider socialist transformation (as 'left idealism' implied).

'Left realism' addresses questions of crime causation utilising primarily a form of relative deprivation/anomie model reminiscent of Merton (Lea and Young, 1984 chapter 3 and 6). This is intended to resolve the 'aetiological crisis' supposedly faced by traditional sociological positivism in the face of the rise of crime in the 'affluent society' period of the 1950s and 60s (Young, 1986: 4-6). The analysis of crime is said to revolve around four elements. 'Realism, then, points to a square of crime involving the interaction between police and other agencies of social control, the public, the offender, and the victim' (Young, 1994:103-5). This is an expansion of the analysis of the 'formal requirements' of a 'fully social theory' in *The New Criminology*, spelling out more elaborately the components of crime and social reaction.

'Left realism' is intended above all to develop effective crime control policies that further rather than impugn social justice. It is here that it is at its weakest and most implausible, however. The main arguments seem to revolve around two inter-related elements, greater community involvement and better policing. Effective policing depends upon support from the community, a proposition supported by much empirical evidence showing that the successful clear-up of crime is a function of information provided by the public. This is frustrated increasingly by a drift towards 'militaristic policing' (Lea and Young, 1984; chapter 5). If policing was restricted a 'minimalist' role of reacting to definite breaches of criminal law only, shedding its service and order-maintenance functions (Kinsey, Lea and Young, 1986), and subject to effective democratic accountability (Lea and Young, 1984; chapter 7), then community confidence would be restored. The result would be a virtuous circle as more information led to more crimes being cleared-up and hence even greater public confidence.

It is plausible that if enhanced democratic police accountability – desirable in itself of course – was achieved it could set in train such a benign process. However, it is unlikely that this or any other improvements in police performance could radically boost public protection from crime (Reiner, 2000b chapters 4 and 7). This is because, as left realism itself shows in its analysis of the aetiology of crime, the main determinants of offending are social factors that lie largely outside police control. Improved police accountability and performance are desirable objectives but not panaceas for crime. There remains much truth in the old 'left idealist' position that social justice and inclusion are necessary conditions of crime reduction.

**Conclusion**

Twentieth century criminological theory has traversed a path that is conventionally depicted as moving from positivism (initially primarily individualistic, and subsequently sociological), through the critical questioning of new deviancy theory and radical criminology, to the contemporary 'realist' concern with 'what works?'. Important and stimulating theoretical texts continue to be published in the current era of pragmatism (such as Garland, 1990, 2001; Nelken, 1994; Sparks, 1997; Taylor, 1999; Young, 1999), but undoubtedly the bulk of criminology is now geared to short-run policy concerns (Loader, 1998). Integration is frequently advocated but rarely achieved (Bottoms, 2000). The key texts marking these phases are probably similar to those I have chosen: Merton; Becker; Taylor, Walton and Young; James Q. Wilson, or Lea and Young, according to political preference.

I have offered a slight variant, with Matza rather than Becker as the symbol of the critique of positivism, and Stan Cohen's paper from the 1979 Downes and Rock critique of *The New Criminology* as a bridge to realism. This is intended to underline the importance for criminology of preserving a sense of moral complexity. I quoted earlier Stan Cohen's succinct condensation of the criminological problematic into three questions (Cohen, 1988: 9). The central issues concern why laws are made, why they are broken, and what is or should be done about it? The four C's: the creation, causation and control of crimes. The perennial temptation for criminology is to become the servant of power, focused only on issues of causation and control. The work of Matza, Cohen, Downes, Rock and others reminds us of the questions that are of less interest to the State or the powerful. Where does the content of the norms that define deviance come from, and what is their moral status from different standpoints? How do so-called deviants regard their own conduct? How much moral responsibility do they have for their behaviour in the light of our understanding of the pressures structuring it? How can we understand and evaluate social reactions to deviance? What are the morally negative consequences of efforts to control deviance? Without losing sight of the realist emphasis on the harm that is indeed done by much of what is defined as deviance, the work that has influenced me the most serves as a continuous warning that there are always likely to be negative side-costs of even righteous actions. Dirty Harry rather than Dixon is the quintessential representation of social control. Which is why I have prefaced each edition of my book *The Politics of the Police* with Weber's succinct evocation of what Sartre in *Les Mains Sales* characterised as the dirty hands problem. 'He who lets himself in for politics, that is, for power and force as means, contracts with diabolical powers' (Weber, 1918:123).

## References

Becker, H. (1963). *Outsiders.* New York: Free Press.
Becker, H. (1967). 'Whose Side Are We On?', *Social Problems*, 14:3:239-47.
Bottoms, A. E. (1990). 'Crime Prevention Facing the 1990s', *Policing and Society* 1:1, 3-22.
Bottoms, A. E. (2000). 'The Relationship Between Theory and Research in Criminology' in R, King and E. Wincup (eds), *Doing Research on Crime and Justice.* Oxford: Oxford University Press.
Box, S. (1987). *Recession, Crime and Punishment.* London: Macmillan.
Clarke, R. and Mayhew, P. (eds), (1980). *Designing Out Crime.* London: HMSO.
Cloward, R. and Ohlin, L. (1962). *Delinquency and Opportunity.* New York: Free Press.
Cohen, A. (1955). *Delinquent Boys.* New York: Free Press.
Cohen, S., ed. (1971). *Images of Deviance.* London: Penguin.
Cohen, S. (1979). 'Guilt, Justice and Tolerance: Some Old Concepts for a New Criminology' in D. Downes and P. Rock (eds), *Deviant Interpretations.* Oxford: Martin Robertson.
Cohen, S. (1985). *Visions of Social Control.* Oxford: Blackwell.
Cohen, S. (1988). *Against Criminology.* New Brunswick: Transaction Books.
Cohen, S. (1993). 'Human Rights and Crimes of the State: The Culture of Denial', *Australia and New Zealand Journal of Criminology* 26:1, p.97.
Cohen, S. (1995). 'State Crimes of Previous Regimes: Knowledge, Accountability and the Policing of the Past', *Law and Social Inquiry* 20:1, p.7.
Cohen, S. (1997). 'Crime and Politics: Spot the Difference' in R. Rawlings (ed.), *Law, Society and Economy.* Oxford: Oxford University Press.
Cohn, E. and Farrington, D. (1990). 'Differences Between British and American Criminology: An Analysis of Citations', *British Journal of Criminology* 30:4, 467-82.
Cohn, E. and Farrington,D. (1994). 'Who Are the Most Influential Criminologists in the English-speaking World?', *British Journal of Criminology* 34:2, 204-25.
Cohn, E. and Farrington, D. (1998). 'Changes in the Most-Cited Scholars in Major International Journals Between 1986-90 and 1991-95 ', *British Journal of Criminology* 38:1, 156-170.

Cornish, D. and Clarke, R. (eds), (1986). *The Reasoning Criminal: Rational Choice Perspectives on Offending*. New York: Springer-Verlag.
Crawford, A., Jones, T., Woodhouse, T. and Young, J. (1990). *The Second Islington Crime Survey*. London: Middlesex Polytechnic Centre for Criminology.
Currie, E. (1998a). *Crime and Punishment in America*. New York: Holt.
Currie, E. (1998b). 'Crime and Market Society: Lessons From the United States' in P. Walton and J.Young (eds) *The New Criminology Revisited*. London: Macmillan.
Downes, D. (1966). *The Delinquent Solution*. London: Routledge.
Downes, D. (1979). 'Praxis Makes Perfect: A Critique of Critical Criminology' in D.Downes and P.Rock (eds) *Deviant Interpretations*. Oxford: Martin Robertson.
Downes, D. (1998). ' Toughing It Out: From Labour Opposition to Labour Government' *Policy Studies* 19:1, 191-8.
Downes, D. and Rock, P. eds (1979). *Deviant Interpretations*. Oxford: Martin Robertson.
Downes, D. and Rock, P. (1997). *Understanding Deviance*. 3$^{rd}$ edn. Oxford: Oxford University Press.
Foucault, M. (1977). *Discipline and Punish*. London: Allen Lane.
Garland, D. (1990). *Punishment and Modern Society*. Oxford: Oxford University Press.
Garland, D. (1996). 'The Limits of the Sovereign State: Strategies of Crime Control in Contemporary Society', *British Journal of Criminology* 36:1, 1-27.
Garland, D. (2000). 'The Culture of High Crime Societies: Some Preconditions of Recent 'Law and Order' Policies', *British Journal of Criminology* 40:3 :347-75.
Garland, D. (2001). *The New Culture of Crime Control*. Oxford: Oxford University Press.
Goffman, E. (1963). *Stigma*. Englewood Cliffs: Prentice-Hall.
Goffman, E. (1968). *Asylums*. London: Penguin.
Gouldner, A. (1968). 'The Sociologist As Partisan', *The American Sociologist* May: 103-16.
Hall, S., Critcher, C., Jefferson, T., Clarke, J. and Roberts, B. (1978). *Policing the Crisis*. London: Macmillan.
Home Office (1998). *Crime Reduction Strategy*. News Release 282/98, 21 July. London: Home Office.
Jacoby, R. (1999). *The End of Utopia*. New York: Basic Books.
Jones, S. (1998). *Criminology*. London: Butterworths.
Jones, T., Maclean, B. and Young, J. (1986). *The Islington Crime Survey*. Aldershot: Gower.
Kinsey, R. (1984). *The Merseyside Crime Survey*. Liverpool: Merseyside County Council.
Kinsey, R. Lea, J. and Young, J. (1986). *Losing the Fight Against Crime*. Oxford: Blackwell.
Laing, R. (1967). *The Politics of Experience*. London: Penguin.
Lea, J. (1992). 'The Analysis of Crime' in J.Young and R.Matthews (eds) *Rethinking Criminology: The Realist Debate*. London: Sage.
Lea, J. (1998). 'Criminology and Postmodernity' in P. Walton and J. Young (eds) *The New Criminology Revisited*. London: Macmillan.
Lea, J. and Young, J. (1982). 'The Riots in Britain 1981' in D. Cowell, T. Jones and J. Young (eds) *Policing the Riots*. London: Junction Books.
Lea, J. and Young, J. (1984). *What is to be Done About Law and Order?*. London: Penguin (2nd edn 1992), London: Pluto Press).
Lemert, E. (1967). *Human Deviance: Social Problems and Social Control*. Englewood Cliffs: Prentice-Hall.
Levitas, R. (1990). *The Concept of Utopia*. Deddington: Philip Allen.

Liazos, A. (1972). 'The Poverty of the Sociology of Deviance: Nuts, Sluts and Perverts', *Social Problems* 20:1, 103-20.

Loader, I. (1998). 'Criminology and the Public Sphere: Arguments for Utopian Realism' in P. Walton and J. Young (eds), *The New Criminology Revisited*. London: Macmillan.

Matza, D. (1961). 'Subterranean Traditions of Youth', *Annals of the American Academy of Political and Social Science*, 338.

Matza, D. (1964). *Delinquency and Drift*. New York: Wiley.

Matza, D. (1969). *Becoming Deviant*. Englewood Cliffs: Prentice-Hall.

Mayhew, P., Sturman, A. and Hough, M. (1976). *Crime As Opportunity*. Home Office Research Study 34. London: HMSO.

Merton, R. (1957). 'Social Structure and Anomie' in *Social Theory and Social Structure*. 2nd edn, New York: Free Press. (originally published in *American Sociological Review* 1938).

Mills, C.W. (1959). *The Sociological Imagination*. New York: Free Press.

Morrison, W. (1995). *Theoretical Criminology*. London: Cavendish Publishing.

Nelken, D. (1994). ed. *The Futures of Criminology*. London: Sage.

Nelken, D. (1997a). 'Understanding Criminal Justice Comparatively' in M. Maguire, R. Morgan and R. Reiner (eds), *The Oxford Handbook of Criminology*. 2nd edn, Oxford: Oxford University Press.

Nelken, D. (1997b). 'White-Collar Crime' in M. Maguire, R. Morgan and R. Reiner (eds), *The Oxford Handbook of Criminology*. 2nd edn, Oxford: Oxford University Press.

Nuttall, C., Goldblatt, P. and Lewis, C. eds, (1998). *Reducing Offending*. Home Office Research Study 187. London: Home Office.

Pease, K. (1997). 'Crime Prevention' in M. Maguire, R. Morgan and R. Reiner (eds) *The Oxford Handboook of Criminology*. 2nd edn, Oxford: Oxford University Press.

Polsky, N. (1967). *Hustlers, Beats and Others*. Chicago: Aldine.

Reiner, R. (1984). 'Crime, Law and Deviance: the Durkheim Legacy' in S. Fenton (ed), *Durkheim and Modern Sociology*. Cambridge: Cambridge University Press.

Reiner, R. (1997). 'Policing and the Police' in M. Maguire, R. Morgan and R. Reiner (eds), *The Oxford Handbook of Criminology*. 2nd edn, Oxford: Oxford University Press.

Reiner, R. (1998). 'Copping A Plea' in S.Holdaway and P.Rock (eds), *Thinking About Criminology*. London: UCL Press.

Reiner, R. (2000a). 'Crime and Control in Britain' *Sociology* 34:1, 71-94.

Reiner, R. (2000b). *The Politics of the Police*. 3rd edn, Oxford: Oxford University Press.

Rock, P. (1979). 'The Sociology of Crime, Symbolic Interactionism and Some Problematic Qualities of Radical Criminology' in D. Downes and P. Rock (eds), *Deviant Interpretations*. Oxford: Martin Robertson.

Rock, P. (1988). 'The Present State of British Criminology' *British Journal of Criminology* 28:2, 188-99.

Rock, P. (1994). 'The Social Organization of British Criminology' in M. Maguire, R. Morgan and R. Reiner (eds), *The Oxford Handbook of Criminology*. Oxford: Oxford University Press.

Rock, P. (1997). 'Sociological Theories of Crime' in M. Maguire, R .Morgan and R. Reiner (eds), *The Oxford Handbook of Criminology*. 2nd.edn, Oxford: Oxford University Press.

Slapper, G. and Tombs, S. (1999). *Corporate Crime*. London: Longman.

Smart, C. (1977). *Women, Crime and Criminology*. London: Routledge.

Sparks, R. (1997). 'Recent Social Theory and the Study of Crime and Punishment' in M. Maguire, R. Morgan and R. Reiner (eds), *The Oxford Handbook of Criminology*. Oxford: Oxford University Press.

Sutherland, E. (1949). *White-collar Crime*. New York: Holt, Rinehart and Winston.

Sykes, G. and Matza, D. (1957). 'Techniques of Neutralisation: A Theory of Delinquency', *American Sociological Review* 22:4, 664-70.

Sykes, G. and Matza, D. (1961). 'Juvenile Delinquency and Subterranean Values', *American Sociological Review* 26:4, 712-719.

Taylor, I. (1981). *Law and Order: Arguments for Socialism*. London: Macmillan.

Taylor, I. (1997). 'The Political Economy of Crime' in M. Maguire, R. Morgan and R. Reiner (eds), *The Oxford Handbook of Criminology*. 2nd. edn, Oxford: Oxford University Press.

Taylor, I. (1999). *Crime in Context: A Critical Criminology of Market Societies*. Cambridge: Polity Press.

Taylor, L. (1973). *Deviance and Society*. London: Michael Joseph.

Taylor, I., Walton, P., and Young, J. (1973). *The New Criminology*. London: Routledge.

Taylor, I., Walton, P., and Young, J. (1975) (eds), *Critical Criminology*. London: Routledge.

Tierney, J. (1996). *Criminology: Theory and Context*. Hemel Hempstead: Harvester Wheatsheaf.

Vold, G., Bernard, T., and Snipes, J. (1998). *Theoretical Criminology*. 4th edn, New York: Oxford University Press.

Weber, M. (1918). 'Politics As A Vocation' in H. Gerth and C.W. Mills (eds), *From Max Weber*. London: Routledge, 1948.

Wilson, J.Q. (1975). *Thinking About Crime*. New York: Vintage, (2nd. edn, 1985).

Wilson, J.Q. and Herrnstein, R. (1985). *Crime and Human Nature*. New York: Simon and Schuster.

Young, J. (1975). 'Working-class Criminology' in I. Taylor, P. Walton and J. Young. *Critical Criminology*. London: Routledge.

Young, J. (1979). 'Left Idealism, Reformism and Beyond' in B. Fine, R. Kinsey, J. Lea, S. Picciotto and J. Young (eds), *Capitalism and the Rule of Law*. London: Hutchinson.

Young, J. (1981). 'Thinking Seriously About Crime' in M. Fitzgerald, G. McLennan and J. Pawson (eds), *Crime and Society*. London: Routledge.

Young, J. (1986). 'The Failure of Criminology: The Need for A Radical Realism' in R .Matthews and J. Young (eds), *Confronting Crime*. London: Sage.

Young, J. (1988). 'Radical Criminology in Britain' *British Journal of Criminology* 28:1, 159-83.

Young, J. (1994). 'Incessant Chatter: Recent Paradigms in Criminology' in M.Maguire, R.Morgan and R.Reiner (eds), *The Oxford Handbook of Criminology*. Oxford: Oxford University Press.

Young, J. (1997). 'Left Realist Criminology: Radical in its Analysis, Realist in its Policy' in M. Maguire, R .Morgan and R. Reiner (eds), *The Oxford Handbook of Criminology*. 2nd. edn, Oxford: Oxford University Press.

Young, J. (1999). *The Exclusive Society*. London: Sage.

# 2. Reflections on 'Victims' and 'Victimisation': An Autobiography of Ideas

SANDRA WALKLATE

## Introduction

When asked to consider the three or four key texts that have influenced one's theoretical and/or empirical work in a particular field one is inevitably faced with a number of dilemmas: what to include, and why; what to exclude and why; what was influential when and why; indeed what has influenced you and why? Then, the question arises; how to tell this story? At the risk of being accused of self-indulgence, I have chosen to discuss the texts that have influenced me in the fashion of an autobiography. This, it seems to me, to be the only way to help the reader make sense of what on first consideration might seem to be an odd collections of texts for someone who has spent some considerable time working within the field of victimology. So in some respects the books I have chosen represent the kinds of ideas I think *should* have influenced the development of work on 'victims' and 'victimisation' as much as they represent ideas which have *actually* influenced such developments. My chosen texts are Sparks, Genn and Dodd (1977) *Surveying Victims* (along with the follow-up essay by Genn (1988) on *Multiple Victimisation*); Stanko (1990) *Everyday Violence*, Giddens (1991) *Modernity and Self-Identity*; and Harre (1979) *Social Being*. Each of these texts has been differently influential in both the empirical and conceptual work I have pursued. The potential influence and importance of each needs to be understood both by reference to the nature of victimology and the nature of my own biography in turn. So first we shall turn to a brief overview of the nature of victimology as a vehicle for studying 'victims' and 'victimisation'.

*Victimology, 'Victims' and 'Victimisation'.* The reader will have noted already that I have chosen to put inverted commas around the terms 'victims' and 'victimisation'. This is to indicate what I consider to be their problematic status as terms in either describing or understanding what we have contemporarily come to take for granted in relation to people's experience of crime. These terms are, however, only problematic in my contemporary view of the nature and impact of criminal victimisation. I did not always consider them to be so. Moreover from a point of view, the (sub) discipline of victimology still does not consider these terms as being problematic in any way. So what are the key characteristics of victimology as a (sub)discipline and how does it use these concepts?

In many ways the emergence and development of the (sub) discipline of victimology parallels that of criminology. Early victimological work was concerned to identify different types of victims much in the same way that early criminological work endeavoured to identify different types of criminals. Original concerns such as these reflect the extent to which victimology was as embedded in the ideas of differentiation, determinism and pathology as criminology (Roshier, 1989). Such central concerns notwithstanding, commentators on victimology have identified different strands of victimological thought that can be broadly categorised as positivist, radical and critical (Mawby and Walklate, 1994). It will be of value to say a little about each of these theoretical strands in turn.

Miers (1989) initially assigned the label 'positivist' victimology to a range of victimological work. He identified the key characteristics of this kind of work in the following way:

> The identification of factors which contribute to a non-random pattern of victimisation, a focus on interpersonal crimes of violence, and a concern to identify victims who may have contributed to their own victimisation (Miers, 1989: 3).

In other words this version of victimology is centrally concerned to identify patterns of victimisation; the regularities and precipitative characteristics of victimising events, and thereby to produce victim typologies. This version of victimology privileges traditional conceptions of science and scientific objectivity and, as a consequence, has been very influential in setting the victimological research agenda along a particular path. That path has, for the most part, been characterised (though not exclusively) by the use and development of the criminal victimisation survey (hence the inclusion of the work of Sparks, Genn and Dodd as one of my key texts). Yet despite the beneficial qualities that can be readily identified with positivist victimology largely derived from such survey work, such work does reflect a research agenda that is conceptually and empirically impoverished. Such work shapes the focus and understanding of the 'victim' in very particular ways. This statement requires fuller exploration.

As has already been suggested, positivist victimology is concerned to identify regularities. It reflects a traditional view of science and the scientific knowledge gathering process which is concerned to separate that which is knowable; the observable, the measurable, the objective; from that which is not knowable; belief. Hence the methodological focus on the construction of victim typologies and the search for patterns of victimisation through the use of the criminal victimisation survey. Positivist victimology presumes that such a research process equips us with objective, measurable information that can be used in both the spheres of politics and policy. It is fair to say that the development of the criminal victimisation survey has been clearly influential in placing the question of criminal victimisation on the political and policy agendas. Yet despite the value that can be attached to the empirical findings which positivist victimology has generated, they are nevertheless limited. They are limited in that, for the most part, such work focuses our attention primarily on what has been called 'conventional crime' (Walklate, 1989) illustrated in the definition of positivist victimology offered by Miers (1989). Moreover this version of victimology takes the meaning of the term victim itself to be self-evident. It is evident in the presence of individual suffering or is defined by the legal framework. There is little sense from within this strand of victimological work that on the one hand the state (including the law) contributes to an understanding of victim status or that, on the other hand, it captures a sense of the ways in which individuals may actively resist, campaign against or survive victim status.

The focus of radical victimology is, arguably, somewhat different. Radical victimology, somewhat paralleling (again) a radical criminology, concerns itself with; 'victims of police force, the victims of war, the victims of the correctional system, the victims of state violence, the victims of oppression of any sort.' (Quinney, 1972:315). In other words, for Quinney all of these victims could be rendered visible by calling into question the role of the capitalist state in defining the social construction of both the offender and the victim. Elias (1986) has associated this broader definition of victimology with the whole question of human rights. Indeed, Elias goes so far as to argue that the standards of human rights cannot only provide victimology with its definitional framework but also with 'more objective measures of victimisation' (Elias, 1985: 17). However, during the 1980s there emerged a version of radical victimology that took the victims' agenda in a somewhat different direction from that posited by either Quinney or Elias.

The emergence of radical left realism within criminology/ victimology during the 1980s had an impact in the United Kingdom and elsewhere in its determination to take the victim of crime seriously. Young (1986: 23-4) called for an 'accurate victimology' which started with 'problems as people experience them' and embraced an understanding of the geographically and socially focused distribution of criminal victimisation. Determined to recapture the law and order debate from the Conservative Party to the Labour Party, the policy implications and the research findings emanating from this work need to be put into that broader political context.

Radical left realism was committed to geographically and socially focused surveys. In other words its research agenda endeavoured to incorporate that which was already known about the patterning of victimisation according to age, sex, class and race. As a consequence it has been very successful in offering a much more detailed picture and analysis of who the victims of crime are (being particularly more successful at uncovering incidents of, for example, racial and sexual harassment than national victimisation surveys) and has also included some efforts to explore an understanding of those who are disproportionately victims of 'commercial crime' (Pearce, 1990).

One of the key problems associated with this version of a radical victimology emanates from its use of the term realism. This is an issue to which we shall return. However, in relation to its understanding of 'victims' and 'victimisation' it reflected a clear attempt to situate these concepts within a structural and processual setting even if such an understanding was not fully accomplished or accomplishable. Part of its inability to achieve this lies in its partial understanding of realism and has the resultant effect, according to Smart (1990), of a latent slippage into positivism.

Another version of radicalism that relates to the work of victimology but developed outside of it, is articulated by much of the work conducted under the general heading of feminism. The marginalisation of feminism by victimology has been the subject of comment on more than one occasion. Rock (1986), for example, implies that this has occurred to a certain extent in the choices made by feminists themselves who have regarded the concept of 'victim precipitation', so central to much conventional victimological work, as 'victim blaming' not only in its everyday use but in the way it has been translated in the courts as 'contributory negligence' (Jeffries and Radford, 1984). Some aspects of this uneasy relationship between victimology and feminism are epitomised in their respective use of the terms 'victim' and 'survivor'. The genealogy of the term victim itself connotes the sacrificiant who was frequently female and the word itself, when gendered as in French, is denoted as female. Feminists, recognising the power of such a linguistic heritage, regard the term as emphasising passivity and powerlessness. This contrasts with what they argue is the active resistance to oppression in which most women engage, most of the time, in their everyday life, in order to survive. Hence the feminist preference for the term survivor. But of course, whilst these terms are often presented as oppositional, experientially speaking they frequently are not. It is as possible to think in terms of an active or passive victim as it is to identify an active or passive survivor. Indeed an argument can be mounted which presents these concepts as capturing different elements of the same process (Walklate, 1993) and moreover may be embedded in women's own experiences of their day to day lives (Kirkwood, 1993). However, the challenge posed by feminism to victimology runs much deeper than this conceptual debate.

Feminist work is not in and of itself centrally concerned with criminal victimisation yet many of the areas and issues with which feminists have concerned themselves and campaigned against, are very much about criminal victimisation. Rape, domestic violence, child abuse, are all areas in which feminist informed work has achieved much in documenting both the extent and the impact of such events on women's lives. They are also areas of concern which constitute criminal victimisation. What renders the findings associated with this data different from those of more conventional victimological work is twofold; on the one hand it renders the safe haven of the home a significant arena in which to understand criminal victimisation and on the other hand it poses an underlying mechanism which produces the surface manifestation of this kind of patterning of criminal victimisation; patriarchy. And although there is a danger inherent in feminist work that can leave the impression that women are 'victims' and men are not (Walklate, 2000; Goodey, 1997; Newburn and Stanko, 1994), a consideration of feminism returns us to the question of what do we understand by the terms 'victim' and 'victimisation'. It also returns us to the question of what can meaningfully be understood by the term realism.

Efforts have been made to construct an alternative agenda for victimology incorporating an understanding of both feminism and realism by Mawby and Walklate (1994) through the proposal of a critical victimology. The term critical has been used in a number of different ways to articulate an agenda for victimology (see for example, Miers, 1990, and Fattah, 1991). However, the version of critical victimology proposed by Mawby and

Walklate (1994) endeavoured to address the problematic aspects of both positivist and radical victimology. This was attempted in three ways; by building on the achievements of radical left realism, through an understanding of scientific realism, and in adopting Giddens' (1984) theory of structuration (hence the inclusion of Giddens as a key book in this context). This view of victimology demanded that we move beyond the mere appearance of things towards understanding what generated that appearance. In order to do this it is important to ask the question: what constitutes the real?

In order to understand the nature and impact of social reality, arguably it is necessary to search beneath the 'mere appearances' associated with positivism, and to posit mechanisms by which those appearances are produced. Mawby and Walklate (1994) argued that by leaning on Giddens' theory of structuration, endeavours to research the real need to take account of a number of different processes which contribute to the construction of everyday reality. These are; people's conscious activity, their 'unconscious' activity, the unobserved and unobservable mechanisms that underpin daily life, and the intended and unintended consequences of people's action. In other words this kind of theoretical starting point privileges process over incidence and argues for duality rather than dualism. As such it is reminiscent of some feminist concerns (Harding, 1991) and provides one way of beginning to understand the dynamic relationship between the structural location of women (victimisation) and women's negotiation of that structural location (survival). Thus providing one way of transgressing the imposed dualism of victim or survivor. In the context of victimology this kind of starting point postulates the importance of understanding the processes which go on behind our backs, that contribute to the victims (and the crimes) which we 'see' as well as those we do not 'see', in order to fully understand the 'lived realities' (Genn, 1988) of criminal victimisation. Noticeably, the version of critical victimology proposed by Mawby and Walklate (1994) made no special claims to privilege one form of knowledge over another.

From this brief, and personal, overview of the nature of victimology, it is already possible to trace the influence of some of the authors that I have chosen as my key texts. However, in order to appreciate more fully why these texts were chosen a little needs to be said about my personal involvement with the study of victims of crime.

*A Biographical Diversion*

I began my academic career in January 1975 as a Lecturer in Social Psychology at the (then) Liverpool Polytechnic. I had conducted a post-graduate research degree on 'The University as a Mechanism of Social Control' and was rather passionate about the work of Erving Goffman. My version of social psychology was therefore very much rooted in micro-sociological theory but with ample coverage of the more conventional psychological material. The publication of two books in the late 1970s became the course bibles: Harre and Secord *The Explanation of Social Behaviour* and Harre *Social Being*. This latter text is one we shall be discussing more fully shortly.

My first foray into conducting research into victims of crime was as part of a team which failed to win the contract to conduct the Merseyside Crime Survey during 1982-3. As a part of that process it became known, locally, that someone 'at the poly' was interested in engaging in such research and I was contacted by a then Senior Probation Officer, George Murphy, who was involved with a Liverpool Victim Support Scheme. He wanted someone to get a feel for how the scheme was working and what victims thought of what they were trying to do. All of that was during 1982-4. It was a salutary experience moving from bidding for over £100,000 for a research contract to conducting a piece of work in one's spare time, but it was also a highly rewarding one. That move was certainly a turning point for me both academically and personally.

Over the next 10 years I forged strong links with Victim Support on Merseyside ultimately becoming the deputy chairperson of the Liverpool Crown Court Witness Support Scheme. Over that same time period my views about victims, victimisation and the criminal justice response to such experiences has evolved. At the beginning of the 1980s academic and political interest in the victim of crime was in its early stages. That interest was very much fuelled by a view that the impact of crime, though varied, was not to be taken lightly and my own experience of interviewing victims in Liverpool at that time within three weeks of their victimisation certainly concurred with that position. Academically, the work of Sparks, Genn and Dodd laid the groundwork for the development, application and refinement of the criminal victimisation survey. It was a key source of information for researchers whether in the Home Office or bidding for local victimisation survey contracts. The emergent focus on the crime victim led me to persuade Gordon Smith, then with Unwin Hyman, that there was scope in the market for a text on issues relating to victims and victimology.

On the way to my current thinking about the key concepts which might be relevant towards understanding any social process, including that of criminal victimisation, I have explored feminism, and I have revisited (if I ever left) sociological theory especially as presented in the work of Giddens. During that time I was fortunate enough to secure a major ESC award (with Karen Evans and Penny Fraser) to work on the fear of crime in high crime areas. It was this work that particularly challenged all that had come to be taken for granted about the nature and impact of criminal victimisation. In one of our research areas we found that people, far from being afraid of crime had learned to accommodate its presence to the extent that their sense of well being was not perturbed by its presence. This led me to think much more deeply about 'victims' and 'victimisation' and what these terms might signify and for whom. Of course, this work was not conducted in a vacuum. As a research team we were very responsive to, and reflective of, the 'fear of crime' debate as it was articulated in the early 1990s alongside the continued growth and development of victim support organisations. As an individual my view of those developments was changing.

All the criminal victimisation survey work of the 1980s leant weight to the minimalist argument to at least to take the needs of victims into account; and for others the maximalise argument for victims' rights. Arguably both positions shared a common view of the special status to be accorded to victims of crime. However, as the decade progressed culminating in the first Victims' Charter in 1990, I was less convinced by this 'special status' view as either one which could usefully inform policy or research. Further theoretical reflection about the nature of victimology as a discipline has led me back to some of the literature with which I began my career, as the rest of this chapter will demonstrate. It is within the influence of this literature that I would now argue that 'victims' have the same requirements of the criminal justice system as anyone else: to be treated with respect (Harare, 1979). So how does that story unfold?

## Sparks, Genn and Dodd Surveying Victims (1977)

The research on which this 1977 book is based was primarily concerned to evaluate the efficacy of the criminal victimisation survey as a tool of measurement. Such surveys had, by the time this study was conducted, been conducted in the United States for over ten years. This way of measuring the crime problem had been heralded as the key to solving one of the main criminological dilemmas; that which had been referred to as the 'dark' figure of crime. By asking questions of a sample of the general population about their experiences of crime, whether or not such incidents had been reported to the police, it was hoped that a more accurate picture of the crime problem could be constructed. Indeed the survey conducted for this study, based in three Inner London areas, revealed more than ten times as much crime as was suggested by the police statistics for these areas. However, this study was not about findings such as these. Its main focus of concern was to test the methodology: did criminal victimisation surveys measure what they said they were measuring and what were the main pitfalls associated with them. It was in this latter respect that this study stands as a seminal piece of work. Whilst in many respects some of the methodological issues raised by this study have since been overlooked, its findings are nevertheless still worth reiterating.

The overall conclusion to this study was that it is possible to use the criminal victimisation survey method to gain a more accurate picture of the nature and extent of the crime problem and that this was a worthwhile exercise to engage in. However, the authors suggested that this general conclusion be treated with some caution; there were methodological pitfalls. The methodological pitfalls this study pointed to concerned: the use of the electoral register as a sampling frame; the use of a reverse record check (comparing respondents' responses with police records); the optimum reference period for such surveys (given the problems of respondent recall and telescoping); the question of perception of crime seriousness; and the difficulties of comparison between survey results and police records. The Home Office and others have differentially addressed some of these pitfalls in the subsequent adoption of this method. However, Sparks, Genn and Dodd (1977: 223) conclude that;

> Finally it must be emphasised strongly again that victim surveys can at best produce inferential estimates of the difference between crimes which victims (say that they) reported to the police, and crimes which appear in the police statistics.

Whilst some of the tentative nature of the conclusions to this study have been lost in the intervening period it is nevertheless the case that this was a solid and well argued presentation in overall support of the utilisation of the criminal victimisation survey. It subsequently leant great weight to the adoption of the criminal victimisation survey as a research technique by the

Home Office in the early 1980s. The fact that the findings from such surveys have been used politically both to maximise and minimise the crime problem and people's experience of crime, and at the same time the inherent problems of the methodology have frequently been overlooked, is a result of the work under discussion here. Indeed this text stands as an exemplar of how to present, as transparently as possible, a piece of empirical work. Importantly this is also an interesting piece of work because of some of its findings.

One of their key findings states that:

> In common with other researchers, we found that the distribution of reported victimisation was extremely skewed, and that the number of 'multiple victims' was far greater than would be expected purely by chance. We found no simple theoretical model which would account for this distribution (Sparks, Genn and Dodd, 1977: 219).

Given the attention that has been paid to the phenomenon of 'multiple victimisation' during the 1990s this particular finding is interesting indeed. Not just because of the length of time it has taken policy makers to pay attention to it but also because this constitutes an important link in the development of the understanding of victimisation. It is this issue which Genn revisited in 1988 in discussing some of the interview work which was conducted for the 1977 study. In reflecting on that process she has this to say;

> I found it no longer surprising that a structured questionnaire administered to one household should uncover some thirteen incidents of 'victimisation'. Indeed, it became evident that these incidents could have represented only a small part of the total volume of crimes (as defined in our survey) which had been 'suffered' during the previous twelve-month period. What also became apparent was the fact that the events reported to us in the survey were not regarded as particularly remarkable. *They were just part of life* (Genn, 1988: 93, emphasis added).

This comment, and the essay from which it is taken, not only points to a key limitation of the criminal victimisation survey and its 'event' orientation, it also points to a moment of transgression between positivist victimology and that of a more radical orientation. For example, for those living in violent relationships, or those who are members of ethnic minorities, or for anyone subjected to different forms of harassment, this is just part of life. Those working within the feminist movement had long pointed to the need to recognise the skewed nature of criminal victimisation. However, making sense of such findings within victimology was long, and some would say still is, overdue.

The implications of understanding crime and criminal victimisation as 'just part of life' or what Crawford et al. (1990) were later to call the 'lived reality of crime' is still not fully embraced by academics, politicians or policy makers, yet for many people living in 'high crime areas' or 'high crime situations' this is just what it is. The work of Sparks, Genn and Dodd and the follow-up essay by Genn emanating from that work has been slowly but inexorably influential in shifting the academic and the policy agenda towards an appreciation of this. The criminal victimisation survey has in particular become the standard measuring instrument of much work in the fields of crime, crime prevention and community safety. The exploration of the databases that such surveys have produced has also set the question of multiple victimisation squarely on the policy agenda. Much of this would be far less refined in the absence of the work under discussion here. However, in parallel with such work, other ideas were emerging, largely associated with feminism, which could too claim a concern with criminal victimisation and multiple victimisation. It is to the influence of those ideas that we shall turn next.

## E. A. Stanko: *Everyday Violence* (1990)

The publication of *Everyday Violence* constituted a timely and accessible intervention into the 'fear of crime' debate. That debate had, for the most part of the 1980s, evolved into a dispute concerned with the rationality or otherwise of people's fear of crime. This debate had been fuelled by the different use and interpretation of data generated from the criminal victimisation survey recently completed by the Home Office and those associating themselves with the emergence of radical left realism (see the earlier discussion). Whilst feminist work had long challenged the presumption that the 'fear of crime' was associated with strangers in public places, Stanko's work took that challenge a stage further. She introduced and offered a relatively full exploration of a different way of conceptualising how the findings with respect to the 'fear of crime' might be read. Through the notion of personal safety she introduced a way of thinking about the everyday normality of negotiating danger, what she calls 'climates of unsafety'. Such climates of unsafety are explored in this book for men and for women.

The key message of this book is that people (men *and* women) know how, and under what circumstances, they are more or less safe. They have everyday knowledge that equips them with some insight into the threat posed to them by partners, relatives, work colleagues, or strangers. Everyday knowledge that sensitises people to the likelihood of such known threats coming to fruition. So not only did this book challenge the notion that only public places were unsafe (the presumed safe haven of the home); it also challenged the notion that women's fears were irrational. By implication it also offered us a new way of thinking about the relationship men have to feelings of fear. In so doing this study centres the validity and usefulness of qualitative research tools (somewhat absent from mainstream victimological work) and by implication centres listening to what people say, and taking what they say seriously. To put this in more conventional feminist terms, it more than demonstrated the value of treating people as experts in their own lives.

Of course, this was a book, produced and influenced by ideas and methods, outside of victimology.  The conceptual agenda developed by Stanko in this book has nevertheless gone on to permeate much victim-oriented work. Again it is perhaps commonplace now in crime prevention discourse to talk in terms of personal safety and/or community safety. This was not so much the case at the end of the 1980s. The transgression of the public /private, male/female dichotomies which this text both implicitly and explicitly conjures provides the link to the next text which I think has been very influential in my own and, if not, should be, increasingly influential in the field of victimology.  This is the work of Giddens.

## Giddens: *Modernity and Self-Identity* (1991)

In this book Giddens suggests that there are two key features to the (late) modern world: the globalization of modernity and the radicalisation of modernity. In centring the effects of these features, Giddens draws attention to the complex historical processes that underpin the relationship between any individual, their behaviour, feelings or 'sentiments' and the wider social context in which these are expressed.  In the face of massive and rapid social change, Giddens is particularly interested in theorising the way in which individuals sustain a sense of ontological security. This is defined as 'a sense of continuity and order in events, including those not directly within the perceptual environment of the individual' (ibid.: 243). This notion of ontological security, also referred to as a sense of well being, has permeated much sociological and criminological work and became a central feature of some of the research work conducted within the fear of crime debate during the 1990s. So in some respects the importance and influence of these conceptual ideas is already self-evident. However, it is worth exploring in a little more detail where the value of this kind of conceptual apparatus lies for victimology.

The notion of ontological security encourages us to consider some of the key features of the human condition. For example, whilst we cannot know what the next day will bring we 'colonise the future'; we make plans, we imagine possible course of action, as a way of creating some sense of order (control) where there may, factually, be none. This is part of creating our sense of well being. Such a process presumes that human beings are knowledgeable, self-conscious, reflexive actors who work on and interpret social structures through the everyday practical accomplishment of their lives; sometimes consciously sometimes not. It is when those routine activities become disrupted, that is, when ontological security is threatened, that people become subject to anxiety. This Giddens presumes, following Freud, is part of the natural human condition especially in (late) modern societies. As Giddens (1990: 124) states: 'The risk climate of modernity is thus unsettling for everyone; no one escapes'. So exploring the ways in which people maintain their sense of well being despite much evidence which suggests that this is under constant threat in (late) modern society becomes a key issue, not only for individuals themselves, but also for society. Central to the way in which individuals sustain a sense of ontological security is the way in which individuals construct their own understandings of risk and trust. So from this reading of Giddens three concepts become of central importance: ontological security, risk and trust.

The significance of these ideas, in the context of criminal victimisation, is clear. As the crime prevention industry has moved from *crime* prevention *to victimisation* prevention (Karen, 1990), the change of emphasis for the management and responsibility for the crime problem is clearly signalled (qua. Garland, 1996). Thus not only does the impact of criminal victimisation render problematic an individual's sense of well being, calling into question issues of risk, trust and self-blame, but so do the policy and related institutional political processes call into question exactly the same issues. We are now all exhorted, in different ways, to take responsibility for the crime problem. From this conceptual starting point then 'victims' and 'victimisation', as categories that might invoke difference at a minimum or some kind of special status at a maximum, become difficult to maintain. Such a position is obviously threatening to a (sub) disciplinary area devoted to the study of victims and victimisation. Yet the work of Walklate and Evans (1999) clearly demonstrates the value of challenging the conceptual dualism of these terms when used and applied as if they were non-problematic.

The question of trust, and the social relationships which were both sustained and threatened by trust, became central to understanding some of the mechanisms in play in the research of Walklate and Evans. Nelken (1994) has made a sound argument for the criminological exploration of this concept and feminist work clearly challenges the notion of who are to be considered to be trustworthy men. Yet little of this conceptual thought has penetrated victimology. How might that be achieved? This takes me to the last book that I consider retrospectively to have been influential in my own work and that might offer a conceptual schema from which future victimological work might benefit.

## Harare: *Social Being* (1979)

The powerful influence that this book has had on my own thinking about 'victims' and 'victimisation' has only become apparent latterly. It was never a book that was at the forefront of my mind in the work that I had done until I was asked to write an introductory piece for a book about good practice in working with victims of violence and something on researching victims of crime (Walklate, 2000a; 2000b). As these were in some respects reflective bits of work; one on the research process and the other on good practice, I was led to think a little more deeply about two issues. My own discomfort with the idea of victims having rights by virtue of them being victims and my discomfort with the conceptual debate of victim versus survivor. This reflective process took me back to my social psychological roots and the theoretical work of Rom. Harre.

His book *Social Being*, published in 1979, stood out at that time as an effort to offer a genuinely *social* psychological framework for that discipline. Harre's framework for understanding social life posits six general principles:

- Social life is a cultural achievement;
- Social action is achieved through convention;
- The life of an individual has the structure of a moral career;

- An individual does not have a given and constant personality but has a character that is the property of the social collectives to which they belong;
- There may be social patterns that are above and beyond individual experience; and,
- People are capable of imagining (and acting upon) social structures which are outside of those contemporarily available.

These general principles may not seem so illuminating in the 21st century but they were stark in the late 1970s in the discipline of social psychology dominated at it was then by experimental psychological work and the emergent influence of socio-biology. What is particularly valuable is the way in which Harre develops these principles.

He states:

> I am not disposed to take an optimistic view of human life. The hopes of most young people come to nothing. The disappointment of the middle years of life are followed for those who survive them by the ugliness, pain, and despair of old age. Most human effort it seems to me is ill directed or dissipated in acts of folly. The pervasive tone of life for most people is boredom, but a boredom made more acute by resentment (Harre, 1979: 3).

Having taken this view of the human condition he posits few universal laws. Influenced by the centrality of the practical to be found in the work of Marx and of the expressive found in the work of Veblen, Harre suggests very few universal laws. For example: short-term expressive advantages are preferred to long-term practical gains; social activities will be elaborated under pressure to realise expressive gains; the biological basis of life is a problem not a solution; and perhaps most importantly the deepest human motive is to seek the respect of others. From this last vision of the human condition the other universal conditions follow.

For Harre the maintenance of respect (and by implication the avoidance of contempt) is not just an attitude it is a social relationship. A social relationship that is predicated on human beings as having a sense of agency. That is as being with both autonomy and reflexivity. In other words, human beings are free from either internal or external determinism and are thereby capable of self-knowledge, self- monitoring and self- intervention. As he says; 'The task of the reconstruction of society can be begun by anyone at any time in any face to face encounter' (ibid.: 405). At any moment in time this may be possible, but may not be necessarily easy as an individual's moral career, generated by the opinion of others, may result in 'fateful attributes' that cannot be removed from the individuals to whom they are assigned. But the key mechanism underlying all these processes is respect. So what has all this to do with 'victims' and 'victimisation'?

From the early work of the sub-cultural theorists to the later work of those concerned with trying to make sense of gang violence (Katz, 1988) or black identity (Bourgois, 1994), the idea that some kinds of criminal behaviour are associated with the search for respect is not unusual. As Katz, 2000: 184) says, 'Adolescent violent crime is not more centrally about 'respect' than is adult violence, it is just less sophisticated in hiding its motivation. In contemporary lingo, adolescents may explain an attack by saying the victim "dissed" (disrespected) me.' So if the maintenance of respect is an important motivation for offending behaviour, why not for the victim of such behaviour?

During the 1990s there has emerged an increasingly diverse range of voices all claiming to speak for the victim of crime. A common thread in this emergent concern, whether constructed as the innocent victim of violent crime of the 1960s, the consumer of police services of the 1980s, or the secondary victim of crime of the 1990s, is the increasing consistency with which this victim has been invoked as the symbolic person for whom we should all care. How that care might be constructed has been differently informed dependent upon the kind of crime under discussion and the impact that such crime is presumed to have. So 'domestic' violence requires a differently informed response from murder, for example. Yet arguably the requirement for difference has been exaggerated, at the expense of appreciating the sameness of such experiences. This is not intended to downgrade the impact that traumatic events may have on people's lives but simply to observe that whilst individually oriented practice may be able to take account of the differential impact of different crimes, policy cannot. How to respond then; by ensuring respect.

It should not be forgotten that victims of any kind of crime are people trying to deal with more or less exceptional circumstances in their lives. Some of those circumstances they may feel responsible for, some they may feel are shared with others, some have just happened to them. (*qua* Harre and Secord; 1978). How they deal with such circumstances will be dependent in part upon their own personal resources, the personal resources of those close to them, and the kind of support that they may or may not be offered by the various agencies with whom they have contact. Treating people with respect; that is as individuals with personal resources, is a key mechanism for ensuring that, traumatic circumstances notwithstanding, they are enabled to make use of their resources to make sense of what has happened in their lives. How they might choose to do that is likely to be infinitely variable. Working with an understanding of the search for respect as a key human condition is the clear and central message of the work of Harre.

There are a number of implications that can be derived from the position outlined above. For example, this position challenges any presumed special status to be assigned to the victim of crime. This does not mean to say that such crime does not impact upon people. It does. But it does imply that in terms of practice it is useful to remember; 'victims' are people. In other words, whether male or female, black or white, old or young; the maintenance of respect and the avoidance of contempt is key to making people feel OK; a way of sustaining their sense of well being rather that abusing or undermining it. The connecting threads to the work of Giddens are evident. The challenge posed to the dualistic thinking of victim/survivor, or victim/offender is also evident. The implications for victimology and the associated victim centred organisations are substantial. They both may be a part of the developments that have taken place over the last fifty years. Developments which have arguably taken us too far down the road of the 'culture of fear' (Ferudi, 1997); too far down the road of the therapeutic society. However, remembering that 'victims' are people, is no more or less than a plea to remember that victimhood is not a condition to be recommended. In other words, in the face of increasing diversity and the celebration of difference, there may be still some value in working with, exploring, and learning from, the commonalities inherent in the human condition. The search for respect, arguably is one of these.

**Conclusion**

This chapter has endeavoured to trace the developments within victimology in parallel with assessing the emergence and importance of ideas outside of that discipline for the future development of it. This is first and foremost a personal account. The books I have chosen have differently impacted upon the disciplinary areas with which I have been concerned. It would be my personal wish that some of these ideas had a greater impact than they so far have. However, the impact that this would have in terms of disrupting disciplinary boundaries would be great indeed, especially for those who have forged their links, and the development of their work with such organisations like the World Society of Victimology. Yet it is true to say that a good deal of the most imaginative, and sometimes also the most impactive work, has been generated by those prepared to transgress disciplinary boundaries. This has certainly been the case with criminology. Hopefully, as we enter the 21st century, this will also be the case with victimology. The central importance of moving in this direction lies not just in the health of the discipline alone but lies in the need at the practical level of getting policies in place, which work for people. This is especially important for people who have least resources either personally or financially to help themselves. Frequently all they have and want is the desire to be treated with respect.

## References

Bourgois, P. *In search of respect*. Cambridge: Cambridge University Press.
Crawford, A., Jones, T., Woodhouse, T., Young, J. (1990). *The Second Islington Crime Survey*. Middlesex University: Centre for Criminology.
Elias, R. (1986). *The Politics of Victimisation*. Oxford: Oxford University Press.
Fattah, E.A. (1991). *Understanding Criminal Victimisation*. London: Prentice Hall.
Ferudi, F. (1997). *The Culture of Fear*. London: Cassell.
Garland, D. (1996). The Limits of the Sovereign State. *British Journal of Criminology*. 36(4): 445-71.
Genn, H. (1988). Multiple Victimisation. In M. Maguire and J. Pointing (eds), *Victims of Crime: A New Deal*? Milton Keynes: Open University Press.
Giddens, A. (1984). *The Constitution of Society*. Cambridge: Polity Press.
Giddens, A. (1990). *Modernity and Self-Identity*. Cambridge: Polity Press.
Harding, S. (1991). *Whose Science? Whose Knowledge?* Buckingham: Open University Press.
Goodey, J. (1997). Boys Don't Cry: Masculinities, Fear of Crime and Fearlessness. *British Journal of Criminology*, 37(3), 410-18.
Harre, R. (1979). *Social Being*. Oxford: Basil Blackwell.
Harre, R. and Secord, P. (1978). *The Explanation of Social Behaviour*. Oxford: Basil Blackwell.
Jeffries, S. and Radford, J. (1984). Contributory negligence or being a woman? The car rapist case. In P. Scraton and P. Gordon (eds), *Causes for Concern*. Harmonsworth: Penguin, 154-83.
Karmen, A. (1990). *Introduction to Victimology*. Pacific Grove Ca. Brookes Cole.
Katz, J. (1988). *The Seductions of Crime*. New York: Basic Books.
Katz, J. (2000). The Gang Myth. In S. Karstedt and K-D, Bussman (eds), *Social Dynamics of Crime and Control*. Oxford, Portland Oregon: Hart Publishing.
Kirkwood, C. (1993). *Leaving Abusive Partners*. London: Sage.
Mawby, R. and Walklate, S. (1994). *Critical Victimology*. London: Sage.
Miers, D. (1989). Positivist victimology: a critique. *International Review of Victimology*, 1(1), 3-22.

Miers, D. (1990). Positivist victimology: a critique. Part Two: critical victimology. *International Review of Victimology.* 1(3), 219-30.

Nelken, D. (1994). Whom can you trust? The future of comparative criminology. In D. Nelken (ed), *The Futures of Criminology.* London: Sage.

Newburn, T. and Stanko, E.A. (1994). When men are victims: the failure of victimology. In T. Newburn and E.A. Stanko (eds), *Just Boys Doing Business.* London; Routledge.

Pearce, F. (1990). *The Second Islington Crime Survey: Commercial and Conventional Crime in Islington.* Middlesex University: Centre for Criminology.

Quinney, R. (1972). Who is the victim? *Criminology,* November: 309-29.

Rock, P. (1986). *A View from the Shadows.* Oxford: Clarendon Press.

Roshier, B. (1989). *Controlling Crime.* Milton Keynes: Open University Press.

Smart, C. (1990). Feminist approaches to criminology: or postmodern woman meets atavistic man. In L. Gelsthorpe and A. Morris (eds), *Feminist Perspectives in Criminology.* Buckingham: Open University Press.

Sparks, R., Genn, H., and Dodd, D. (1977). *Surveying Victims.* London: John Wiley.

Stanko, E.A. (1990). *Everyday Violence.* London: Pandora.

Walklate, S. (1989). *Victimology: The Victim and the Criminal Justice Process.* London: Unwin Hyman.

Walklate, S. (1993). Responding to women as consumers of a police service: the UK experience 1980-1990. In J. Vigh and G. Katona (eds), *Social Changes, Crime and Police.* Budapest: Eotvos Lorand University Press.

Walklate, S. (2000). *Gender, Crime and Criminal Justice.* Devon: Willan Publishing.

Walklate, S. (2000a). From the politics to the politicisation of the victim of crime. In H. Kemshall and J. Pritchard (eds), *Good Practice in Working with Victims of Violence.* London: Jessica Kingsley.

Walklate, S. (2000b). Researching Victims. In R. King and E. Wincup (eds), *Doing Research on Crime and Justice.* Oxford: Oxford University Press.

Walklate, S. and Evans, K. (1999). *Zero Tolerance or Community Tolerance? Managing Crime in High Crime Areas.* Aldershot: Ashgate.

Young, J. (1986). The failure of criminology: the need for a radical realism. In R. Matthews and J. Young (eds), *Confronting Crime.* London: Sage.

# PART 2

# POLICE CULTURE

# 3. Beyond Behaviourism: Police Culture Revisited

IAN K. McKENZIE

## Introduction

At the time of passing of the Metropolitan Police Act in the April of 1829, Sir Robert Peel, the Home Secretary, whose political expertise had ensured that the Metropolitan Police force (The Met) would come into being later that year, indicated that he held strongly the view that policing was an artisan occupation and was not an employment for gentlemen. Peel had argued that, with the exception of the first two Commissioners, gentlemen were not to be employed on the grounds that they would have difficulty in associating with 'the men'.The 'men', that is constables, he insisted, would be limited to a wage of three shillings a day and in so doing Peel set the mark on policing as a working class occupation. Peel wrote, 'a three shilling a day man is better than a five shilling a day man. No doubt three shillings a day will not give me all the virtues under heaven, but I do not want them' (McKenzie and Gallagher, 1989).

Peel's insistence that the men of the Met should principally be drawn from the working classes was an astute stance to take. The notion of policing of the people by the people for the people became, and for ever more will be, embedded in ideas about the role of the police, at least in the United Kingdom, as servants of the public, not as an arm of government. However, Peel was roundly mistaken in his view that 'all the virtues under heaven' were not an essential aspect of police recruiting. There are few occupations which expose members to such temptations, opportunities and enticements as occur in the day-to-day activity of law enforcement, order maintenance and crime control.

When I first joined the Metropolitan Police in the late 1950s, thoughts of such temptation were far from my mind. Neither were there thoughts, implicit in Peel's observation, about the proprieties of selection and training of police officers. Nevertheless, by a circuitous route, these matters have

53

become the core of my research interests. Coupled with those two broad topic areas, is a long-standing and abiding commitment to developing and enhancing the relationship between psychology and the criminal justice system, or perhaps more precisely, psychology and policing. In short, my research has been guided by three core areas of academic writing:

- Core behaviorist psychology exemplified by the work of B.F. Skinner, (1959) and knowledge of psychology as it relates to everyday human behaviour and, as a consequence, its application to policing. In particular the work of Elliot Aronson (1984) is key here;
- The literature of policing, exemplified by the work of Robert Reiner (1985) and Herman Goldstein (1977); and,
- More recently the literature of integrity and ethics, principally the work of John Kleinig (1996) and Edwin Delattre (1996). It is on these three areas that the remainder of this chapter will concentrate.

**About behaviorism**

I came to psychology as a student relatively late in my life. Following 15 years or so of police work, I had the good fortune to be granted a scholarship for full-time attendance at university in order to read for a Batchelor's degree in psychology. I came to that experience with a great deal of apprehension of the kind felt by many mature students; at the age of 35 and with 15 years of police service behind me, I was simply concerned about my ability to be able to remember things sufficiently to pass examinations. I suppose it is important at this stage to declare what is an almost inevitable bias, a bias which follows from three years of study in a psychology department with a strongly behaviorist approach to its discipline: I was for a long time a convinced radical behaviorist. Although the radical nature of that position has moderated somewhat over the years, the principles of reinforcement theory continue to permeate my academic thinking.

The writing of B.F. Skinner, and in particular his book, *Science and Human Behavior* (Skinner, 1953) was a huge eyeopener to me. I had come from a background of police work in which the gathering of evidence was (is) of paramount importance. There are, in law, two types of evidence. First, information, real or personal, public or private which tends to establish a fact or facts. Second, circumstantial or presumptive evidence, a form of evidence which is legitimately used, but which is much less powerful than 'real' evidence. On reflection, I am drawn to conclude that as a direct consequence of my policing career, the concentration in behaviourist thinking upon quantified examination of behaviour was, for me, evidence of the first-order, whilst much theorising by other psychologists fell firmly into the second camp. Above all else, it is the Skinnerarian/behaviourist insistence on objectivity which draws me to that conclusion.

Skinner's behaviourism was not drawn from the air without precursors. As with all science, he was, as Issac Newton put it, 'Standing on the shoulders of giants'. Hilgard (1972) points out that the definition of psychology as the study of consciousness, with introspection as the preferred method, was widely accepted in the late 19th and early 20th centuries. Psychologists, principally Catell, (1904), and McDougall (1908) aided and abetted by philosophers like Singer (1911) had become increasingly sceptical about the notion that the path to understanding the nature of human nature was solely that of the examination of consciousness and the application of introspection.

Consequently, behaviourism rejects introspection and the examination of consciousness *as being beyond the remit of psychology as a science.* This stance is taken, not because the behaviourist belief is that the mind does not exist or consciousness is not real (as is sometimes claimed by critics of the behaviourist approach) but because the scientific value of any data produced is limited, principally because of the difficulties associated with their interpretation.

Thus, as Hilgard (1972) puts it,

> The central tenet of behaviorism is, of course, the objectivity of the data to be accepted by science. The facts of observation are to be limited to those of any other science: observable events that can be recorded by an experimenter, often with the aid of precision instruments.

In 1913, J.B. Watson, in what was later to be known as 'the behaviorist manifesto', laid the groundwork for what was to follow. Watson's desire was to eliminate subjectivity and consequent imprecision from the examination of human behaviour. Much of Watson's early behaviourist research concentrated upon the examination and definition of conditioned reflexes (Pavlov, 1927) and led, almost inevitably, to what was sometimes referred as a 'molecular' or 'atomistic' psychology; examining minute behaviours. Indeed, at one stage the notion of behaviourism was sometimes decried as 'muscle twitch' psychology (Watson, 1919), a fate which it survived only as a consequence of Watson's (and others) interests in the 'conditioning' of other aspects of behaviour and in providing behaviourist explanations of such things as verbal behaviour. For example, the 'conditioning of emotional reactions' (note the careful wording of that phrase) demonstrated in the case study of 'little Albert B.' and reported by Watson and Rayner (1920)[1] was a significant movement from the conditioning of eye-lid blinks, or even pulse rate and other visceral responses. The disdain for subjectivity shown by earlier behaviourist psychologists was later 'vigorously exemplified' (Graham, 2000) in the work of B.F. Skinner. Crucially, Catania (1988) has suggested that,

> Of all contemporary psychologists, B. F. Skinner is perhaps the most honored and the most maligned, the most widely recognized and the most misrepresented, the most cited and the most misunderstood.

Skinner's brand of psychology, which he preferred to call 'the experimental examination of behavior', employs a number of basic terms and relationships. At the *operant level,* an organism emits *'entering behavior'*, the source of which (innate, acquired, culturally-determined or species-specific or may emanate from any other cause) is immaterial. This emitted behaviour is capable of modification and control. Such manipulation and control is achieved through the application of the principles of reinforcement. The training or modification process, known as *shaping*, is achieved through the application of appropriate reinforcement when shifts in the behaviour in the required direction occur, or by allowing the *extinguishing* of such behaviour (through non-reinforcement or non-reward) when they are not. Within this paradigm one of the most significant features of learning demonstrated through experimental studies in the laboratory is that of the *partial reinforcement effect.* When reinforcement is provided on an *intermittent schedule* (in other words, when every emission of the behaviour is not necessarily reinforced), the power and frequency of the emitted respond tends to be more powerful and the extinction of the response is more prolonged. Finally, Skinner was able to demonstrate two other important dimensions to human behaviour. The first is that, even though a response may not recently have been reinforced and has apparently extinguished, the behaviour may suddenly reappear though the process known as *spontaneous recovery.* The second is that, where behaviour is randomly emitted and is reinforced by chance rather than by design, it can, nevertheless, increase in frequency. Thus, an organism (say a pigeon) randomly turning in a circle that receives an expected reinforcement in the form of food during the emission of that behaviour, will tend to produce similar circling behaviour, now known as *superstitious behaviour*, in the 'expectation' that further reinforcement will follow.[2]

Catania's (1988) observation, noted above, recognises that most of the notions outlined in the last paragraph are unknown or are ignored by critics; they certainly have remained well beyond the span of knowledge of the majority of lay people. Typically, however, misrepresentation and misunderstanding most commonly attach themselves to Skinner's view of the mind. The type of criticism that Skinner's writing provoked, and continues to provoke, is characterised in the view expressed by Zimmer (1999) that Skinner espoused:

> the notion that Man had no indwelling personality, nor will, intention, self-determinism or personal responsibility, and that modern concepts of freedom and dignity have to fall away so Man could be intelligently controlled to behave as he should.

But Skinner's aversion to explanatory passages using references to inner states, and so on, is not an aversion to inner states or processes *per se*. 'The objection,' wrote Skinner, 'to inner states is not that they do not exist, but that they are not relevant in a functional analysis' (Skinner 1953: 35). Later, Skinner was to write that, 'an adequate science of behavior must consider events taking place within the skin of the organism ... as part of behavior itself'(Skinner 1983: 617). Thus, there is no denial of the existence of events such as thinking, perceiving or other events classified as mental or inner. In this kind of analysis, for example, personality is a judgement made by others on the basis of a perception and interpretation of observed behaviour. In its most radical form, Skinner's argument would be that all behaviour is inevitably controlled through the environmental dynamics of reward, punishment and negative reinforcement, and thus that freedom (from such environmental contingencies) is an impossibility. However, as with other matters 'inside the skin', Skinner would not deny that it is entirely possible for a person to *feel* free, and consequently to *feel* also that he or she has free will, although in truth that freedom is an illusion: one cannot escape from the determining effects of past experience of reward and punishment. The existence of apparently internalised superstitious behaviours, or the spontaneous recovery of behaviours tied to apparently long forgotten associations, are proof enough of that.[3]

The principal difficulty with Skinner's work is not in its application of science, an aspiration for psychology which is still of critical importance, but in his attempts to seek popularisation.  Reading the key scientific papers published by Skinner which were themselves based upon his laboratory studies, is of critical importance in coming to terms with his view of the world.  But Skinner presents a hostage to fortune, when for example, he writes in *Beyond Freedom and Dignity* (1971):

> In what follows, these issues are discussed 'from a scientific point of view,' but this does not mean that the reader will need to know the details of a scientific analysis of behavior. A mere interpretation will suffice...The instances of behavior cited in what follows are not offered as 'proof' of the interpretation. The proof is to be found in the basic analysis. The principles used in interpreting the instances have a plausibility which would be lacking in principles drawn entirely from casual observation (Skinner, 1971: 20-21).

Such a statement, allows critics to say, '[Thus] Skinner's theory is inaccessible to laymen, who must take him on faith, substituting 'plausibility' for logic: if his 'interpretation' sounds plausible, it means that he has valid ('non-casual') reasons for expounding it'(Rand, 1985).

There is no doubt that in the search for scientific verity in psychology, Skinner's approach is beyond reproach.  But in his efforts to try and popularise his views he did himself no service[4].  The opportunity which is presented by writing books for general publication which are themselves based upon the application of true scientific methodology but without adequate explanation of that methodology is foolish.  On the other hand, the rejection of a scientific discourse on the grounds that it is 'inaccessible to laymen' is equally foolish.  The scientific papers published by Albert Einstein expounding the General Theory of Relativity remain, to this day,  largely inaccessible to the lay reader, but that does not diminish the theory to the slightest degree.  It has been left to others, with a less opaque writing style, to attempt to explain these crucial ideas to the lay public.  Skinner would have been wise to have done the same.

Nevertheless, the dynamics of reinforcement theory remain for me a crucial element in understanding the nature of human nature.  Although it is now possible to recognise that Skinner was at best mistaken and at worst disingenuous[5] in some of his observations and pronouncements, the fundamental importance of his work remains unchanged. Many psychologists no longer, as was the case in the behavioural revolution, accept Skinnerian theory as the ultimate psychology.  However, many have no hesitation about accepting its success and even in making use of its methods (Hilgard, 1972). Contemporary thinking amongst psychologists requires that issues such as heredity, hormonal control, subjective states represented by dreams and hallucinations, the nature of memory and the internal processing of information are included in any developing model of man. But behavioural dynamics remain crucial. Perhaps sometimes in the ill-informed debate about cloning, some understanding of the principles of reinforcement might lead people to realise that a cell taken from the DNA of a mass murderer or a war criminal, if cloned into a human being, would probably *not* result in another mass murderer or war criminal! The contingencies cannot ever be the same!

**Enter social psychology**

Despite the foregoing, and regardless of the huge influence that the principles of behaviorist theory had upon me, my understanding of the nature of human nature was hugely enhanced by that discovery of social psychology. In my continuing search for explanations of the sometimes bizarre behaviour I had seen emitted by people, both inside and outside the police force during my career, I started to find myself hugely impressed with this sub-discipline of psychology, in particular the study of the effects that individuals have one on the other, most particularly in small groups. There is much experimental work in this field. Often such experimental work is individually reported in contemporary scientific journals. Occasionally, however, such individual experimentation is gathered together by a gifted author in a single volume. The work of Elliot Aronson, in his book, *The Social Animal* (Aronson, 1972) exemplifies such an approach.

Aronson's book, now in its eighth edition, is, for me at least, quite simply the most accessible (to use a modern publisher's word) and the most useful of a plethora of books on social psychology. His approach, which is straightforward and couched in everyday language, is to allow key aspects of social psychological research, leading up to an understanding of the nature of human nature, to speak for themselves through scientific study. Aronson poses and answers such questions as, Is beauty really in the eye of the beholder? If I want people to believe me, should I speak first or last? What attracts people to each other? What makes people like each other or hate each other? Are there ways to reduce prejudice? Does watching violence on TV make children more aggressive?

Aronson not only demonstrates a wide-ranging understanding of social psychology, but he also manages to convey an enthusiasm for the subject which is almost boundless. The key feature of this work is that the author presents academic findings without using pretentious and academic language. Unfortunately, this remains a feat which other academics far too frequently fail to achieve.

Having come to the study of psychology from the world of practical policing there were a number of key issues in which I was particularly interested. I had often observed during the course of my operational police work that far too many people, often far from unintelligent, could simply be led by the nose into committing a criminal act, their involvement in which they subsequently could not explain. Aronson's chapter dealing with the nature of conformity and compliance (which most recently has been expanded to include contemporary issues such as how people can follow blindly the commands of a cult-leader, even unto suicide) provided an eye-opener to me.

This work is generally well known and only a brief elaboration will be provided here. Although the most cited, and certainly the best known work in this connection is that of Milgram (1963, 1964a, 1964b, 1965, 1974) those studies, which will be described shortly, naturally, build on an extant knowledge base ('on the shoulders of giants'). In 1947 Sherif published research which had demonstrated that, when subjects are asked to make judgements about the extent of movement they saw when a single point of light projected onto a screen in a darkened room, and which remained stationary throughout the experimental study, estimates (which initially were likely to range rather widely) settled down to a narrow range with a consistent central value.[6] When later, the subjects were brought together in small groups, their judgements converged, so that the individual differences became submerged within a small 'envelope' of estimates. Subsequently, Solomon Asch (1958a, 1958b) devised a classic set of experimental studies which revealed beyond question that when faced with a majority of their fellow students agreeing on an incorrect response to a problem posed, an individual subject would tend to conform to the majority view. Aronson suggests that the extent of conformity in the studies is mediated by two important goals in the experimental subject. First, the goal of being correct and second, the goal of staying in the good graces of other people by living up to their expectations. Interestingly, evidence from additional experimental studies shows convincingly that whilst individuals tend to conform in such circumstances, often, the *private* judgements they held continue to be held unchanged. Thus, although findings in experimental studies consistently show that in making judgements about, for example, line length, the number of clicks made by metronome or about the aesthetic value of a piece of modern art, people in groups may have their judgement swayed in the direction of the group norm, at the same time they retain, unimpaired, their own private judgement (Aronson, 1984: 22).

One of the most significant features of these studies is that the results were for Asch, unexpected. The research hypothesis was that subjects would readily be able to resist attempts to manipulate their behaviour:

> Asch himself firmly believed that there would be little, if any, yielding to group pressure (Aronson, 1984:19).

One interpretation of this data is that when reality is unclear, *other people* become a major source of information (Aronson, 1984: 28). There is a strong element of social cohesion which affects the outcome of such studies. When social structure of a group has been manipulated as an experimental variable this has shown that the extent of conformity is strongly attached to whether or not a subject would wish to conform to the views of a given group (Smith, 1995). In one respect, it is possible to argue that the behaviour of individuals in such experiments is based upon the dynamics of reinforcement and punishment discussed above.

According to William James (1890) emotion has both a 'feeling' content and a 'cognitive' content. In a study conducted by Schacter and Singer (1962) subjects were either injected with a synthetic form of adrenalin or with a harmless placebo. All subjects were told that the injection was a vitamin substitute called 'suproxin'.

> some other subjects who received the [Adrenalin] were informed there would be side effects, including palpitations of the heart and hand tremors. These, indeed, are some of the effects of [Adrenalin]. Accordingly, when the subjects experienced the symptoms they had an appropriate explanation. In effect, when the symptoms appeared they would say to themselves, 'my heart is pounding and my hands are shaking because of this injection I received and for no other reason.' But other subjects were not forewarned about the symptoms (Aronson, 1984: 29).

During the experimental phase a confederate of the experimenter, appearing to be in a euphoric state of mind or alternatively to be angry, joined the injected subject. When subjects had been given the placebo or had been warned about the physiological effects of the injection, they were not greatly influenced by the behaviour of the others.  Where, however, subjects were experiencing a strong physiological response, the origins of which were not clear, they interpreted and reported their own feelings as either anger or euphoria.

Once again, a clear indication of the extent to which, regardless of strength of personality, the behaviour of each of us may be manipulated by external (environmental) variables.  Nowhere is the evidence of this stronger than in the classic studies undertaken by Stanley Milgram (1963, 1964a, 1964b, 1965, 1974) at Yale University.  Using a 'shock generator', Milgram was able to demonstrate around 65 per cent of the subjects employed would administer an electric shock of up to 450v, to another person who had failed to produce the correct response in a simple 'memory' task.

Aronson describes the experiment as follows:

> subjects volunteer for an experiment advertised as a study of learning and memory.... When the volunteer appears at the lab for his appointment he is paired with another participant, a somewhat stern experimenter in a technician's coat, explains that they will be testing the effects of punishment on learning ... the subject and his partner draw slips to determine roles; the subject draws the role of teacher.  He is led to a 'shock generator' which has an instrument panel with a row of 30 toggle switches, calibrated from a low level of 15v and extending through levels of moderate and severe shock to a high of 450 volts (Aronson, 1984: 38).

The teacher is instructed by the 'technician' that each time  the learner fails to produce a correct word-pair, he must administer an electric shock and that on each repeated failure he should increase the voltage to the next level (an increase of fifteen volts).

Although at various stages there are sounds of complaint from the learner as an electric shock is delivered, on each occasion the technician responds with 'prods' designed to ensure that the teacher continues.  The extent to which a subject would respond in an obedient manner to the dictates of the technician was measured by the maximum amount of shock that the subject would administer before refusing to continue.

No subject stopped prior to 300 volts. Milgram found that 65 per cent of the subjects continued to obey throughout the study, continuing all the way to the end of the shock series.  This was so despite the fact that groups of people, including and psychiatrists and psychologists, as well as lay people, suggested that no more than 1 per cent of any group would go to the end of the shock generator.

There is a danger of over interpreting this result. It does not follow from the study that 65 per cent of people will simply do what they are told. It does not even follow that (if ethical approval for such a study could be obtained) a similar proportion of subjects would in the early 21st century, respond in the same way. Rather these studies indicate a general malleability in human behaviour, particularly when subjected to controlling contingencies by an authority figure (although some people remain able to resist). The technician was, after all, apparently a scientist in a prestigious university. 'In our society... such people are held commonly to be responsible, benevolent people, of high integrity' (Aronson, 1984: 41). Whilst it is tempting to accept the accuracy of Milgram's (1974) suggestion that obedience to authority is a necessary requirement for communal life and has probably been built into our species by evolution, there is little evidence to support this assertion.

Nevertheless, Aronson's conclusion to this section is, for me, one of the most significant observations in my continuing studies of the 'nature of human nature'. Aronson writes:

> We harbour a myth of our personal invulnerability ... but we have seen how the forces of the actual situation override those values and self-conceptions (Aronson, 1984: 43).

It is this, above all, which has led me in my research, particularly that examining the nature of police interviewing and interrogation, but also in my efforts to try to understand the behaviour of both the police and their clients in less coercive circumstances.

Aronson distinguishes three kinds of response to social influence: *compliance, identification*, and *internalisation*.

*Compliance*, he argues, is the term best used to describe the mode of behaviour which is motivated by a desire to gain reward or avoid punishment.

*Identification* is a response to social influence brought about by an individual's desire to be like the influencer. But, identification is different from compliance in that the individual comes to believe in the opinions and values he or she adopts.

> Thus, if an individual finds a person or group attractive or appealing in some way, he will be inclined to accept influence from that person or group and adopt similar values and attitudes (Aronson, 1984: 32).

*Internalisation* is the process through which a value or belief becomes permanent and deeply rooted.

Rewards and punishments (the delivery of which may be redefined in one sense at least as the application of *power*) are important means through which people learn behaviours, attitudes and values. They are the initial determinants of compliance, although identification and internalisation require additional dynamics. For identification, the crucial component is attractiveness. In internalisation, the important component is credibility.

There is a remarkably good fit between the dynamics identified by Aronson and the thinking which underpins Gudjonsson's (1999) views about the processes which lead people to make false confessions. Similarly, material drawn from the studies noted above formed the underpinning of the observational research undertaken by Irving (1980) for the Royal Commission on Criminal Procedure (RCCP, 1881). Indeed, in both cases, they serve(d) as the psychological dynamics which, at that time, dictated the structure, process and practice of interviewing suspects in British policing.

I knew nothing of this theorising at the time when I was commencing my research into aspects of non verbal communication in police interrogation (McKenzie, 1981). However, I also began to realise that there was a huge gap in police training as it was then delivered. There had been a substantial concentration upon law and police procedure as the core issues in the preparation of recruits and probationers. The training had never really included aspects of social psychology, a fact which increasingly dumbfounded me as I delved more into the field. This led to the development, for the Metropolitan Police recruit and probationer training programme, of policing skills training (Burns Howell, McKenzie and Kember, 1980): a programme embedded in the law and police procedure aspects of recruits training but adding to it, social skills, social psychology, and racism awareness. There is insufficient space here to dwell on its detail, however, an independent evaluation by Bull and Horncastle (1988, 1989, 1994) was later to confirm that the training initiative had been successful in most of its elements. Unfortunately, much of it was abandoned during the late 1990s in favour of more pragmatic law enforcement dynamics in recruit and probationer training.

As with social psychology in police training, police interviewing of suspects, usually referred to at that time as interrogation, was the subject of practically no training at all. However, one of the effects of the report by the Royal Commission on Criminal Procedure was the later publication and (somewhat delayed) implementation of the Police and Criminal Evidence Act 1984. After the implementation of that legislation, which included strict controls aimed at reducing the most coercive aspects of the police handling of prisoners and of the interviewing of them, I was able with Barry Irving (Irving and McKenzie, 1988) to undertake empirical observational research which sought to identify the changes in interviewing practice brought about through that legislation. In the UK, much of the continuing work in that field has now passed to other people (see Bull, this volume). However, in the USA, much remains to be done (see McKenzie, 2001).

**Policing and police studies**

Until the mid 1980s, at least in the UK, there was no single, separate discipline which treated the police as suitable for academic study in their own right. Although it is true to say that policing and police issues were sometimes dealt with in criminology courses, stand-alone policing courses were a rarity. This was not the case in the USA, perhaps not surprisingly in view of the Law Enforcement Assistance Act 1965 (LEAA) and the Law Enforcement Education Programme (LEEP) which accompanied it. Both went along way in financing police education in the 1970s.[7] Even in the 1980s, it has been estimated that there were in the USA, close to 300 Criminal Justice colleges offering specific education to police officers.[8] In England and Wales, at the start of the 1980s there was no organised police education whatsoever, although that did not deter a handful of people from seeking academic qualifications.

In the early 1980s, I had the good fortune to be selected by the Police Staff College at Bramshill to serve, for a short period, as a visiting lecturer at the John Jay College of Criminal Justice in New York City. I was asked to teach a comparative course examining policing in the U K *vis-à-vis* that of the USA. At that time there was no single text which laid side-by-side these two policing environments. On my return to the UK, in early 1982, I decided to do it for myself. It was a long task.[9] When the book was later completed and published (McKenzie and Gallagher, 1989) it was a simple fact that it could not have been completed without the insights provided by two specific volumes: Robert Reiner's (1985) text *The Politics of the Police,* and Herman Goldstein's (1977) *Policing a Free Society.*

Reiner's book, now in its third edition (Reiner, 2000), is considered by me and many of my colleagues, to be the defining source of the content of a police studies course. The chapter headings of the first edition tell it all: The Birth of the Blues – The Establishment of Professional Policing in Britain

1829 to 1856; The Rise and Fall of Police Legitimacy 1856 to 1981; Cop Culture; Demystified the Police: The Media Presentation of Policing; Police Powers and Accountability; Conclusion, From Scarman to Newman – a Watershed in Policing?

The core of the book is concerned with Reiner's argument that while policing is a political activity, the politicisation is not overt or partisan. The argument is based upon substantial research not the least of which is material drawn from Reiner's earlier work, *The Blue Coated Worker* (Reiner, 1978). The key element of the argument is that Reiner seeks to demonstrate, successfully in my view, that police efforts to ensure and maintain their acceptance by the public are threatened on the one hand by conservative policies which polarise conflict, and on the other by a refusal or failure, or at least until very recently, of many on the left to accept the legitimacy of police activity.

Although I found the political arguments both acceptable and persuasive, my principle delight was in the chapter on 'cop culture'. As Reiner (1985: 85) puts it:

> An understanding of how police officers see the social world and their role in it - 'cop culture' - is crucial to an analysis of what they do, and their broad political function.

Reiner provides a typology (occasionally drawn from other sources, but never before martialled in this way) of both the police and their clients, which had (and still has) me nodding my head in approval. The 'Clients' are identified as:

- *Good class villains,* professional criminals the pursuit of whom is seen as being challenging and rewarding;
- *Police property,* low status, powerless groups, seen as being problematic or distasteful;
- *Rubbish,* people who waste police time by making calls which are unworthy of attention or which result from matters which are the individual's own fault;
- *Challengers,* these are individuals whose work allows them access to the closed world of policing, these include lawyers, doctors and, to some extent, social workers. Efforts are made to minimise their intrusion;

- *Disarmers*, people who can weaken or neutralise police work because they are perceived as being socially vulnerable. When police are dealing with such people they might expect that even standard police responses would be the subject of special criticism;
- *Do-gooders*, principled, anti-police activists; and,
- *Politicians*, remote unrealistic ivory tower idealists.

Threatened by groups such as these, the police tend, according to this analysis, to bond and stand by each other. This in its turn leads to the creation of a culture of policing, which has the following core characteristics; conservatism, a tendency to macho behaviour, embedded racial prejudice, and an insistence upon the need for pragmatism, summarised by the recognition of the need for initiative in the application of everyday police activity. Reiner points out that there is a highly practical central tenet to police activity, and consequently to police culture, which suggests that, 'You can't play it by the book'.

One of the key questions that has always been asked is how such a non-standard view of the world can be maintained, particularly in the face of evidence that such values and attitudes can easily be counterproductive. One need look no further than the dynamics of small group behaviour which I have discussed above in my examination of Elliott Aronson's book, *The Social Animal*. The early searches which were undertaken to identify and define a police personality (often based upon the idea of authoritarianism) were doomed to failure. The research showed, and it should come as no surprise, that as a general rule it is not authoritarian people that join the police service (Skolnick, 1969; Cochrane and Butler, 1980; Butler, 1982) but that extant negative attitudes, which may not differ significantly from the normal population, are 'accentuated with [police] work experience' (Reiner, 1985: 102). It is police service that leads them to authoritarian values and attitudes. If this is so, and it does appear to be the case, then it is achieved through the application of internalised rewards and punishments and through an unconscious and unintentional application of the dynamics of conformity and compliance. That is through what is colloquially known as the 'canteen culture'.

There is sometimes a view expressed that the existence of a particular (in the sense of special) police culture is 'a bad thing'. I remain uncertain about whether this is correct. It does seem to me that in a world in which police officers are expected to deal with the most vicious, violent and vindictive elements in society, any strategy (intentional or otherwise) which can provide support for them is of value.

The second book in this section, Goldstein's (1977) *Policing a Free Society*, has in some ways a similar theme. The principal focus of this book is an examination of the anomaly which exists as a result of the need to provide coercive constraining forces in a society which is built upon notions of freedom. Goldstein's concerns are not in conducting an examination of the dynamics of police culture but rather in creating a structure which seeks to explain how such an apparent anomaly can be managed. Amongst other things, Goldstein argues strongly for a limitation in the discretion which can be exercised by police officers in the course of their duty. James Q. Wilson (1968) has pointed out that one of the peculiarities of policing is that discretion increases as one moves *down* the hierarchy. Goldstein's view is that the application of such discretion on the streets is often invisible, and consequently inequitable, for it amounts to selective enforcement through the systematic ignoring of some types of offence or by the over enthusiastic application of the law in respect of others. Therefore, Goldstein argues, the structure and limits of police discretion need to be more clearly defined.

> If discretion is to be exercised in an equitable manner, it must be structured; discretionary areas must be defined; policies must be developed and articulated; the official responsible for setting policies must be designated; opportunities must be afforded for citizens to react to policies before they are promulgated; systems of accountability must be established; forms of control must be instituted; and ample provision must be made to enable persons affected by discretionary decisions to review the basis on which they were made (Goldstein, 1977: 110).

There is, not surprisingly, a recognition that such conditions will not be achieved with ease and that the police will naturally be resistant to such notions. It does seem, in part at least, that some of these matters have been addressed in England and Wales through the provisions of the Police and Criminal Evidence Act 1984 and other more recent legislation. Although, by and large, there remains much to be done.

## Integrity

Goldstein (1977) also contains a chapter on police corruption. The book, of course, contains much of considerable value. However, Goldstein makes a fundamental error in classifying the issue of integrity as solely a matter relating to corruption. Police integrity is far more than that. These points are well made in both the books I take as my key texts here: John Kleinig's (1997) *The Ethics of Policing*, supplemented by the cogent examination of police integrity and ethics by Edwin Delattre's (1996) *Character and Cops,* my final choices.

For a number of years now the police service has sought to enhance the extent of their professionalism and for some this has become a search for inclusion in the club of 'the professions'. I do not at this moment wish to enter into a debate about the nature of professionalism or about the desire of some that the police service should become a profession. I do believe, however, that even though the police service aspires to becoming a learned profession, the achievement of that aim is unlikely.

However, aspiring to *professionalism* is another matter. But, such an aspiration carries with it some particular concerns, one of which is at the core of the integrity debate. It is very clear that the key feature that overarches both the aspiration to learned profession status and the desire to become a profession, is that there exists in the professional environment, a code of ethics. Despite a number of attempts so to do, the British police service has manifestly failed to provide a widely accepted code of ethics for its workforce, and even today the topic can only be described as a large black hole. John Kleinig (1997) has suggested that the Primary Objects of the Metropolitan Police, formulated by the Met's first commissioners Rowan and Mayne, are a 'Codes of Ethics'. I for one have never seen those words in that way, and neither, I suspect, have many others.

Nevertheless, the underpinning – the foundation – of integrity must be the existence of specific instructions – called codes or guidelines – which are aimed at providing support in ethical decision-making to those who are at the coal face; codes or guidelines which affect not the performance of duties (although they may do that as well) but which are principally aimed at affecting the values of the service. This is a shift from what has been called 'rule driven' policing to 'value driven' policing.[10] But such a shift comes at a cost.

First, of course, such a shift can only be achieved by the police service if it can agree, hopefully on a national basis, to the development of a code of ethics which is acceptable to all. Second, it requires a recognition that there are substantial problems with the implementation of such notions. As the New York police department learned in their efforts to implement such a programme, value driven guidelines remain a top-down delivery.  As Kleinig (1996) puts it,

> Even within professedly value-driven departments, the existing hierarchical structure and political accountability of management make it unlikely that, even if they should be granted it, line officers will be permitted to exercise significant professional discretion within ethical guidelines  (1996: 39).

It is therefore the very hierarchical structure of policing – which might readily be coupled with the militaristic nature of the organisation – that makes implementation of such a code problematic.[11]

Thus, even when such a code (or its associated philosophy) is in place, it cannot be assumed that its existence will have the desired effect.  Much of the literature of police corruption deals with what I have always called 'Heavy End' corruption; direct involvement in serious criminal activity, the taking of bribes to do or not to do things, the application of 'protection' and so on.  Theories of police corruption – why cops become corrupt – are both controversial and numerous.  They range from the absence of police standards, through police professionalism and morality, into inadequate public support and inadequate rates of pay (see Rowe, 1987 for a complete outline of these).

As Rowe points out, these are simple descriptions of things which are complex and that, furthermore, corruption is not the sole prerogative of police organisations. The dynamics of personal and social weakness lie in us all and the debate which seeks to apportion 'blame' for corruption on one or the other is perennial. Indeed in the context of human weakness, Steffan (1979) has suggested that even the notion of original sin is not without dispute. He told a gathering of theologians:

> You blame it on Adam, he blamed it on Eve and she blamed the serpent. But I am here to tell you that the origin of original sin was the apple, the reward for being evil.

This idea that it is temptation, and surrender to it,  that lies at the root of police corruption is only part of the equation.  As Simpson (1997) has pointed out, deviance in officers may also be viewed as a response to their special situation, a situation which consists of normal social ambition (which includes sex, power and status as well as financial reward) coupled with extraordinary opportunity.

We must not forget, however, that despite my reference to heavy-end corruption, most illicit police activity is behaviour carried out by those that the Knapp Commission (1973) called 'the grass eaters'; police officers involved in minor infractions and the acceptance of pay offs that come almost as an adjunct to police work.

Finally, I turn to the role of trustworthiness and its place in integrity. Trustworthiness is the trait of deserving trust or confidence. Again, I suggest that there are two levels to this dynamic. The extent to which the public can (and do) trust the police and, second, the extent to which the police service trusts itself.

In the context of the first dimension, surveys have repeatedly shown that at the general level, the police fare quite well in the level of their acceptance by the public and that on the dimension of trustworthiness, lawyers and journalists are often seen as more lacking However, when one looks at certain minority groups and their attitudes to the trustworthiness of the police, then one finds a different story. In particular, the young and members of some minority ethnic groups seem to have a strong distrust of the police. I do not intend to rehearse the reasons for this. They are well known.

Trustworthiness is strongly associated, may even be identical with, the extent to which the police have the confidence of the public and, as Berry, Izatt, Mawby, Walley and Wright (1998: 210) have pointed out, this is a substantial part of the *image* of the police; an image that can be managed. But those authors also point out that 'the confidence of the internal customers of an organisation must be maintained'. I take this to refer to the employees of an organisation, in this context both civilians and those that have taken the oath of allegiance. And it is worth noting that many police officers, particularly in the contect of the investigation of complaints, suggest that, 'they (the Bosses) can always get you' (Kleinig, 1996: 292).[12]

Police officers often bemoan the fact that they get little respect from the public. Respect is not a response one can demand, it is one that must be earned. As Delattre (1996: 43) puts it,

> Able leaders understand that nobody can really serve as an example by *trying* to do so. When we see an attempt to set an example, we suspect it is phony and not deeply rooted. People become real exemplars, trusted and looked up to, by being what they appear to be.

To that extent, although there are many others, there is one key area in which the image of the police service must be adjusted; that is through the development of a truly independent complaints and discipline system. The attempt to set an example, to   investigate rigorously allegations of impropriety, is suspected by many people to be phony.

As an observer of police behaviour now for close to 40 years, I regret to say that there is a discernable and common pattern to many, if not all, allegations of misconduct made against police regardless of whether the allegation is one of unfairness or of misuse of deadly force or somewhere in between. At first denied, there is later (usually after some incisive enquiry) an acceptance of the allegation but only as an aberration. That is followed by an effort to explain/justify behaviour as that emanating from 'one rotten apple in the barrel'.

This practice in which allegations of misconduct pass through the sequential process of denial, enquiry, and grudging acceptance (but only as an individual's aberration) may be seen in all types of allegation made against the police, made by all kinds of people, in all police areas. It is quite easy to see why it might be that people do not – will not – accept the rotten apple explanation. To them it seems as if the barrel itself is made of rotten wood.


**Conclusion**

It is relatively easy to argue that a failure of integrity in a police officer is the sole responsibility of the officer him or herself. That would be a stance taken, for example, by a person of a humanistic persuasion. From a behavioristic point of view however, it is not difficult to see that the search would be for the dynamics of reinforcement and punishment which lie behind the emission of such behaviour. The Milgram studies in particular, suggest that even the most severe of deviant behaviours can be manipulated though the intervention of an 'authority figure'[13] and can be supported by only minor environmental changes (increases of only 15 volts on the shock generator are seductively small and therefore easier to justify to oneself). Thus, it may be argued, where the small breaches of integrity go unchecked, the possibility (some might argue probability) is that the behaviour will shift (be shaped) through the reinforcement achieved through a positive outcome. For the cognitive behaviorist, the reinforcement dynamic might be further extended through the notion that additional or alternative contingencies are provided through the reinforcement achieved as a consequence of not getting caught. It is, in my view, not likely that a person ends up in receipt of huge illicit payments, unless there is a process (sometimes called the 'slippery slope') which leads to it.

If, in addition to this analysis, the corrupt or unacceptable behaviour is seen in the context of small group dynamics, it takes on a slightly different hue.

When in the mid 1970s, the corrupt activities of the Metropolitan Police Obscene Publications Squad came to light (Reiner, 1997: 6), it was soon revealed that, although a significant number of officers had received large sums of money to ignore the activities of pornographers in the West End of London, some officers had not used the cash for personal benefit. Some of them when given their 'brown envelope' on a Friday afternoon had immediately put it in a desk drawer, where it *remained untouched* until found by the investigators. True, they did not report the deviance, but neither (apparently) did they see themselves as 'corrupted' like their colleagues. In the context of the small group, and of Reiner's cop culture, it is easy to see how such a thing could happen. The recent publication of the report on Police Integrity by Her Majesty's Inspector of Constabulary (HMIC, 1999) must become the driving force behind research into corruption, integrity and in particular the behavioural associations and operants, as well as the cultural dynamics which drive and sustain it. It is to this area that future research should be directed.

# Notes

1. Watson and Rayner (1920) presented 'little Albert' '... suddenly and for the first time, successively with a white rat, a rabbit, a dog a monkey, with masks with and without hair, cotton wool, burning newspapers, etc. ... *At no time did this infant ever show any fear in any situation*' (emphasis in original). In a second session, ('at eight months twenty-six days of age') the experimenters provoked a fear reaction in the infant. First, Rosalie Rayner, 'caused the child to turn its head and fixate her moving hand'. Then J.B. Watson, three times, struck 'a sharp blow' with a hammer on a suspended metal bar ('four feet in length and three-fourths of an inch in diameter'). 'The child started violently, his breathing was checked on the arms raised in a characteristic manner. On the second stimulation the same thing occurred, and in addition the lips began to pucker and tremble. On the third stimulation the child broke into a sudden crying fit'. In what appears to be some concern about the ethics of their activity ('At first there was considerable hesitation upon our part in making the attempt to set up fear reactions experimentally. A certain responsibility attaches to such a procedure.') the experimenters delayed for close to three months before continuing. When Albert was eleven months and three days of age, their concerns set aside, Watson and Rayner set about a programme in which the presentation of the rat was accompanied by hammer blows to the

metal bar. Quite soon the conditioning resulted in fear responses occurring as soon as the rat was presented, but also resulted in a degree of generalisation in which similar fear responses were produced through the presentation of the rabbit, the dog, a fur coat, a Santa Claus mask, and cotton wool.

2.  Similar behaviours may be seen in, for example, sportsmen and women, who before attempting a high-jump or defending a wicket or taking a free kick, will perform some kind of 'ritual' behaviour; kicking the ground three times, polishing the ball on clothing, touching a cap or other head gear or any one of a wide range of alternative behaviours. They are sustained, according to reinforcement theory, by the occasional 'reward' achieved when the act which follows them is successful and they are more powerfully supported because the effect of *occasional* success is one of 'partial reinforcement' albeit on an unstructured (but nevertheless ratio-based) schedule.

3.  When pondering this relationship I often find myself speculating on the similarity between the inherent determinism of the Skinnerian paradigm and that of Freudian theory.

4.  J.B. Watson had been a contributor to the popular press (Wozniak, 1994).

5.  Another word that might be used here is 'naive'. When I was an undergraduate, the third year classes on behaviorist theory which I attended were led by Prof. Leslie Reid, a former student of B.F. Skinner. Professor Skinner frequently came to England, and would stay with Professor Reid. Reid told us that he had been with Skinner in a pub and that they had sat for some time watching a man playing a one-armed-bandit gaming machine. After a while he turned and said, 'The only thing that machine would do for me would be to strengthen my right arm'. The belief that profound knowledge of reinforcement theory (or any theory about the human condition) makes one immune from its effects is, surely, naive in the extreme.

6.  The apparent movement seen by the subjects in this experimental study are not real. The so called autokinetic effect, results from the brain's inability to deal with a *complete* lack of movement. The perceived movements are erratic, in both direction and extent.

7.  Palmiotto (1997) suggests that, following the award of nearly $19 million by the US Department of Justice's Office of Law Enforcement Administration (OLEO), 'seventeen states began police science courses and college degree programs [and] twenty states initiated and expanded police standards and training programs' (p:25).

8.  Whether this is in fact an accurate figure is debatable. Many of the colleges claiming to provide 'education' seem in hindsight to have been providing 'training', and there is a clear distinction between the two. Training is a process through which information on procedures and on the rules which guide those procedures is provided. Education, by contrast, is the provision of contextualising knowledge which seeks to provide the student with a broad understanding of the 'whys' (and the theories of why) as well as the 'hows'. Put in another way, although the division is far from perfect, training is about skills, and education is about broad knowledge and understanding.

9. My excuse is that I was working contemporaneously on my PhD.

10. Rule driven policing exists where adherence to pre-formulated rules is the nadir of police supervision (although some might see it as the zenith), where '... increasingly bulky Patrol Guides have become impossibly detailed ...' where, '... they frequently fail to address the subtle operational needs of officers' and where '.... following the endless directives is most often a function of supervision ...' By contrast, the value approach encourages decision-making that looks '... not merely to behavioural guidelines but to the values implicit in the confronting situation and the values to be realised by the decisions to be undertaken.' (Kleinig, 1996: 38).

11. In their instructions to the Metropolitan Police (1829) Colonel Charles Rowan and Sir Richard Mayne noted that '... something must necessarily be left to the intelligence and discretion of individuals; and according to the degree in which they show themselves possessed to these qualities and to their zeal, activity and judgement, on all occasions, will be their claims to future promotion and reward.' In a later edition of the Metropolitan Police Instruction Book the text indicates that in the exercise of initiative and discretion, when an officer has acted correctly the Commissioner will support him. Faced with what still remains, a draconian discipline code and with what is still a strong tendency towards 'negative and fault-finding supervision' (PSI, 1981) - at least in the context of police complaints investigation - officers treat such a notion with derision.

12. See note 11.

13. The reinforcement dynamic is here one of *negative* reinforcement. Negative reinforcement (which is not the same as punishment) produces behaviour, sometimes known as 'escape' or 'avoidance' behaviour, which is emitted in an effort to nullify an aversive stimulus. Thus the behaviour of 'key pressing' in the Milgram studies may be seen as a response to the 'orders' of the technician. Similarly, the negative reinforcer for the corrupt police officer is the expectation that a failure to accept the 'brown envelope' will be greeted with ridicule by colleagues.

# References

Asch, S. (1958a). Studies of Independence and Conformity: A Minority of One Against a Unanimous Majority. *Psychological Monographs* 70: Whole No. 416.
Asch, S. (1958b). Effects of Group Pressure on Modification and Distortion of Judgements. In Maccoby E. E., Newcombe T. M. and Hartley E. L. (eds), *Readings in Social Psychology*. New York: Holt Reinhart and Winston.
Argyle, M. (1975). *Bodily Communication*. London: Methuen.
Aronson, E. (1984). *The Social Animal* (4th edn). New York, W.H. Freeman.
Aronson, E. (1999). *The Social Animal* (8th edn). New York, W.H. Freeman.
Berry, G., Izatt. J., Mawby, R., Walley, L, and Wright, A (1998). *Practical Police Management*. (2nd edn). London: Police Review Publishing Co.

Bull, R.C.H. and Horncastle, P. (1988). Evaluating Training: The London Metropolitan Police's Recruit Training in Human Awareness / Policing Skills. In P. Southgate (eds), *New Directions in Police Training*. London: HMSO.

Bull, R.C.H. and Horncastle, P. (1989). An Evaluation of Human Awareness Training. In R. Morgan and D. Smith (eds), *Coming to Terms with Policing*. London: Tavistock.

Bull, R.C.H. and Horncastle, P. (1994). Evaluation of Police Recruit Training Involving Psychology. *Psychology, Crime and Law*, 1, 157-163.

Burns-Howell, A.J., McKenzie, I.K. and Kember, R. (1980). *Human Awareness Training for Recruits and Probationers*. London: Metropolitan Police.

Butler, A.J. (1982). An Examination of the Influence of Training and Work Experience on the Attitudes and Perceptions of Police Officers. Unpublished Manuscript. Bramshill, Hants: Police Staff College.

Catania, A.C. and Harnad , S. (1988). *The Selection of Behaviour: the Operant Behaviorism of B.F. Skinner, Comments and Consequences*. Cambridge: Cambridge University Press.

Catell, J.M. (1904). The Conceptions and Methods of Psychology. *Popular Science Monthly, 46*,176- 86.

Cochrane, R. and Butler, A.J. (1980). The Values of Police Officers, Recruits and Civilians in England. *The Journal of Police Science and Administration, 8.*

Delattre, E.J. (1996). *Character and Cops.* Washington DC: The AEI Press.

Goldstein, H. (1977). *Policing a Free Society.* Cambridge, Mass: Ballinger

Graham, G. (2000). Behaviorism. *Stanford Encyclopaedia of Philosophy. http:// plato.stanford.edu/entries/behaviorism/*

Gudjonsson, G. (1992). *The Psychology of Interrogations, Confessions and Testimony.* Chichester: Wiley.

Hilgard, E. (1972). Behaviorism. In H. Eysenck, W Arnold and R. Meili (eds), *Encyclopedia of Psychology: A-K.* London: Fontana.

HMIC (1999). *Police Integrity: Securing and Maintaining Public Confidence.* London: Home Office

Irving, B. (1980). *Police Interrogation. A Case Study of Current Practice*, Royal Commission on Criminal Procedure, Research Study No. 2. London; HMSO.

Irving, B. and McKenzie, I.K. (1988). *Regulating Custodial Interviews.* London: Police Foundation.

James, W. (1890). *Principles of Psychology.* New York: Smith.

Kleinig, J. (1996). *The Ethics of Policing.* Cambridge: Cambridge University Press.

Knapp Commission (1973). *Report on Police Corruption.* New York: Brasillier.

McDougal, W. (1908). *Introduction to Social Psychology.* New York: G.P. Putnam's Sons.

McKenzie, I.K. (1981). Non-verbal Communication in Interrogation. Unpublished Masters Dissertation: University of Exeter.

McKenzie, I.K. (2001). Investigative Interviewing and Interrogation. In J. Gubrium and J. Holstein (eds),. *The Handbook of Interviewing.* Thousand Oaks, CA: Sage.

McKenzie, I.K. and Gallagher, G.P. (1998). *Behind the Uniform: The Police of Britain and America.* Hemel Hempstead: Harvester Wheatsheaf.

Milgram, S. (1963). Behavioral Study of Obedience. *Journal of Abnormal and Social Psychology. 67*, 371-378.

Milgram, S. (1964a). Group Pressure and Action Against a Person. *Journal of Abnormal and Social Psychology* 69:137-143.

Milgram, S. (1964b). Issues in the Study of Obedience: A Reply to Baumrind. *American Psychologist*, 19: 848-852.

Milgram, S. (1965). Some Conditions of Obedience and Disobedience to Authority. *Human Relations* 18: 848-852.

Milgram, S. (1974). *Obedience to Authority: An Experimental View*. New York: Harper and Row.

Palmiotto, M.J. (1997). *Policing: Concepts, Strategies and Current Issues in American Police Forces*. Durham, NC: Carolina Academic Press.

Pavlov, I. (1927). *Conditioned Reflexes*. New York: Oxford University Press.

Rand, A. (1985). *Philosophy, Who Needs It?* (Chapter 13) New York: New American Library.

RCCP. (1981). *Royal Commission on Criminal Procedure: Report*. HMSO. London.

Reiner, R. (1978). *The Blue Coated Worker*. Cambridge: Cambridge University Press.

Reiner, R. (1985). *The Politics of the Police*. Hemel Hempstead: Harvester Wheatsheaf.

Reiner, R. (2000). *The Politics of the Police (3rd Edn)*. Oxford: Oxford University Press.

Rowe, D. (1987) Introduction to the new edition. In R.H Ward, and R. McCormack (eds),. *Managing Police Corruption: International Perspectives*. Chicago, Ill: OICJ.

Schachter, S. and Singer, J. (1962). Cognitive, Social and Physiological Determinants of Emotional State. Psychological Review,. 69: 379-399.

Singer, E.A. (1927). Mind as an Observable Object. *Journal of Philosophical and Psychological Science Methodology,* 8: 180-186.

Simpson, A. E. (1977). *The Literature of Police Corruption*. New York, NY: McGraw Hill.

Skinner, B.F. (1953). *Science and Human Behavior.* New York: The Free Press.

Skinner, B.F. (1971). *Beyond Freedom and Dignity.* New York: Bantam Books.

Skinner, B.F. (1985). News From Nowhere, 1984. *The Behaviour Analyst*, 8: 5-14

Skinner, B.F. (1983). Behaviorism at Fifty. *Behavioral and Brain Science, 7*: 615-621.

Skolnick, J. (1969). *The Politics of Protest*. New York: Bantam Books.

Smith, P.B. (1995). Social influence processes. In M. Argyle and A. Coleman (eds), *Social Psychology*. Harlow: Longman.

Steffan, L. (1979). Quoted in Souryal, S.S., Etiology of Police Corruption: An Inside View. *Police Chief*, December, 80-83.

Watson, J.B. and Rayner, R. (1920). Conditioned Emotional Reactions. *The Journal of Experimental Psychology*. 3, 1-14.

Watson, J.B. (1919). *Psychology From the Standpoint of A Behaviorist*. London: Routledge.

Wozniak, R.H. (1994). *Reflex, Habit and Implicit Response: The Early Elaboration of Theoretical and Methodological Behaviorism 1915 - 1928*. London: Routledge.

Zimmer,G.(1999).B.F Skinner, Behavioral Psychologist: *http://www.sntp.net/behaviorism/ skinner.htm*

# 4. Researching Equality: The Case of Women Police

JENNIFER BROWN

## Introduction

Gender as a focus of research within criminal justice research is a rather late contender as an analytic device to examine policing. Not an issue to attract significant funding , nor considered a mainstream interest, nonetheless there has been in recent years a burgeoning of studies examining the roles and experiences of women police officers. In part this growth in research activity has been stimulated by an increased self confidence in women officers to challenge sexist behaviour and take their cases to industrial tribunal. The research output has been part of a iterative cycle which has contributed to raising awareness in police women themselves, and contributing to a greater understanding of the lot of women officers. Gender issues has proved a fruitful topic for the increasing numbers of officers undertaking degree level study and required to do research dissertations. The Police Service has gone through something of a revolution of thinking about its women officers and has taken great strides in developing equal opportunities policies and procedures. This is a very different picture from when I started researching equal opportunities within policing a decade ago. The Equal Opportunities Commission (EOC) had just published its report into the Metropolitan Police Service (EOC, 1990). This indicated that women were the subject of (illegal) quotas in some departments, were restricted in terms of their career development and were often deployed along traditional, or stereotypical, gender lines. The police service in Britain had been rather dilatory in its response to the Sex Discrimination Act (SDA) 1975 and very little had been done to prepare for integration. Little research was available either from the UK or elsewhere on the contemporary position of women police officers.

There were three distinct points of reference that stimulated my research interest. The first was an admiration for the early twentieth century women pioneers who advanced the right to vote and to enter areas of work that had, hitherto, been exclusively male domains. My curiosity was wetted in terms of what made these particular women different? Why had they not just accepted the world as they found it? What were the circumstances of their lives and personalities that motivated them to challenge and change the status quo? The second was an experience I had when being given an introduction by a woman sergeant to the police force where I had recently arrived to take over the research department. As we walked around a police station amidst nude calenders and sexual innuendo, in response to my question, 'Do you mind?' she answered, 'Mind what?'. I was struck by her acceptance and her apparent discounting of the ambient sexism that surrounded her. The third was an intriguing result of the first major study I conducted whilst working for the police (Brown and Campbell, 1990). This was an examination of stress amongst police officers. When reviewing gender difference one startling finding emerged. It was that a significant source of stress for women police officers was the prejudice and discrimination they experienced from their male colleagues. I was fired by a sense of injustice that some 70 or so years since Edith Smith had become the first policewoman there was still a disabling environment that arose from an informal occupational culture which remained antagonistic to women's presence in policing. My research activity followed a rather classic pattern given my training as a psychologist: description, explanation and finally some attempt at prediction. Along the way five specific texts provided inspiration, concepts and methodological tools that helped fashion my ideas:

- *The British Policewoman* by Joan Lock (1979);
- *Breaking and Entering* by Susan Martin (1980);
- *Policewomen and Equality* by Sandra Jones (1986);
- *Women in Control* by Frances Heidensohn (1992) and,
- *From Social Worker to Crime Fighter* by Dorothy Schulz (1995).

I have been fortunate in having met all the authors. They share an enthusiasm for their subject and a generosity in facilitating and extending my own researches. They do indeed represent that 'companionship' afforded by kindred spirits which is characterised by Frances Heidensohn in her own reflective essay on sources for her researches into women and the criminal justice system (Heidensohn, 1998).

**Descriptions and incidence rates**

In 1990 I undertook an empirical investigation to examine the experiences of women police officers. The status of equal opportunities within the British Police Service had been jolted into action by the race discrimination case of Detective Constable Singh and his claim against the Nottinghamshire Constabulary and by Alison Halford's sex discrimination case that she had been passed over for promotion on the grounds of her gender (Gregory and Lees, 1999). Women then represented about 12 per cent of the police establishment and Assistant Chief Constable Halford was the sole chief officer outside the London Metropolitan Police. Despite the SDA, which the three police staff associations had fought unsuccessfully to exclude policing from its provisions, and a Home Office circular (87/1989), there had been a little development of equal opportunities policies (Walklate, 1966). My efforts to initiate the research were met with horror in some quarters and were it not for the fortuitous timing of Vee Nield's general secretaryship of the Police Federation and the intervention of my chief constable, John Hoddinott, the research would never have got underway. When looking for a starting point to develop the conceptual basis of the research, I found Sandra Jones' book *Policewomen and Equality* published in 1986. This proved a further piece of good fortune as Sandra was later to write a technical reference to the Home Office verifying the soundness of my research design for that originating study.

Sandra begins her book with the following:

> When I first suggested, to a senior policeman, the possibility of a research study of the present role of policewomen, the idea was greeted with amused scepticism.

Supported through funding from the Equal Opportunities Commission, Sandra undertook the first empirical investigation in Britain of the contemporary position of policewomen some ten years after the passing of the SDA. Using a combination of qualitative interviews and a questionnaire survey she documented a detailed analysis of the promotion and deployment of women officers and offered an engaging account of the discourses employed by men that sought to keep women in their place. Some five or six years later in my own study, I was able to use Sandra's data as a baseline against which to compare women's experiences and to use them to develop a theme touched on, but not extensively covered in her book; the sexual harassment experienced by women in police. The discourse that Sandra presented in chapter seven of her book under the heading 'ritual arguments and constraints' showed me the importance of retaining a qualitative dimension to research in this area as well as outlining justifications used by men for limiting women's incursions into mainstream policing: namely their emotional instability and physical inferiority. These were the themes and an analytical approach I was to develop later. As mentioned above, Sandra provided me with some invaluable help at a stage of the project when I despaired that it would go ahead. Having designed the study there was considerable resistance from within the police service for it to proceed. This was borne of concern as to what the study might find at the time the service was defending itself in the Halford industrial tribunal. Sandra reviewed the research design and warmly endorsed the study. This provided me with the confidence that the research was indeed technically robust and likely to be able to withstand hostile criticism of its results.

The other significant inspiration for this first study was Joan Lock's book published in 1979, *The British Policewoman*. Joan had been a serving police officer herself and was motivated to research her own and contemporaries' histories because none existed. Not academically trained, Joan described her 'magpie method' of collecting information from the Public Record Office, Imperial War Museum, Fawcett Collection, the London Museum and the Metropolitan Police Library. She also managed to locate some of the original women police pioneers from whom she acquired memories and pictures that illustrated the book. Given no structure to the evolution and development of policewomen's roles and responsibilities in policing Joan developed a collating and indexing system. In this way she identified not only the major players such as Margaret Damer Dawson, Mary Allen, Nina Boyle, Mrs Stanley, Dorothy Peto but many of the lesser well known early pioneers. She also provide a chronology of major events and achievements. This was charted in the book: creation of the Women Police Volunteers and Women Police Service; the work of Sir John Baird's Committee on the Employment of Women on Police Duties. Nancy Astor, Britain's first woman Member of Parliament sat on this committee. The arguments rehearsed by the Committee as to whether to continue to employ women officers ranged from their physical fitness (evidence from one witness, Dr Letitia Fairfield indicated that there was

> no problem whatsoever in women doing eight hours at a stretch but ... ladies who had been well fed and not pushed into factories at fourteen would

undoubtedly have better reserves of endurance and last better in the long run (Lock, 1979: 118).)

to the issue of an integrated or separated women's police.

Joan's work helped me in two particular ways. Firstly it provided some answers to my question about what characterised these early pioneers to challenge the *status quo* in the way that they did, and to fight for women's presence in policing. Joan's analysis suggested that in part it was their middle and upper class confidence and independent means, their sense of adventure in breaking taboos by their involvement in the suffrage campaigns, and perhaps most intriguingly, their lack of imagination. Joan argues that not thinking ahead or anticipating the barriers or minding the comments and taunts, that inevitably accompany challenges to the system, were actually helpful in forging their way through the minefields of prejudice and resistance. Secondly, and this was no more than some subtle hints, were issues about the sexuality of some of these early women pioneers. The question this posed for me was could there be here, a possible explanation for the pioneer police women's styles and forcefulness. Did their unconventional relationships provide a train of thinking that if they defied pressure to marry and swapped the influence of fathers for husbands, could they also defy custom and attain fulfilment through occupations that had previously been solely masculine domains? The stories of these early pioneers also presented a graphic account of the differences in style illustrated by the contrast between the masculinised Mary Allen striding around in boots, breeches and Sam Browne belt and Mrs Stanley who clearly used her femininity as a charm offensive. So here we have early examples of the dichotomies that characterised later analyses and anticipated conceptual work being conducted the other side of the Atlantic by Susan Martin. Joan's book showed that the early policewomen faced much the same prejudices that Sandra Jones documented for her 1986 contemporary snapshot. From Joan I got treated to tea and biscuits as well as her wealth of knowledge and memorabilia as we talked about the early days of women in policing. I discovered through Joan, an unusual source for depicting attitudes towards women police officers, that of cartoons. I began my own collection of these when visiting the National Police Library at Bramshill. This collection proved a rich source of primary evidence that I returned to when working with Frances Heidensohn during a later study. I followed Joan's footsteps to the sources of primary documents that she had located. I am not sure much had been disturbed at the time I was searching through this material from the time of Joan's discoveries some twenty years previously.

That first study, funded through the Home Office Police Award Scheme, was undertaken in collaboration with Sergeant Rhona Anderson and Dr. Elizabeth Campbell and provided a descriptive account of the incidence of sexual harassment and sex discrimination of women officers (Anderson, Brown and Campbell, 1993). We found an endemic scale of sexual harassment with over 90 per cent of women indicating they worked in an ambient sexualised environment. As with Sandra Jones' (1986) study, women were deployed differently from men and were less satisfied with their career progression. Despite the passage of the SDA and the implementation of the recommendations of Home Office Circular 87 of 1989, many women officers were reluctant to use their force's grievance procedures to make formal complaints or take their cases to Industrial Tribunals. Through parallel research activity, which attempted to tease out more detailed aspects of police women's deployment patterns (Brown, Maidment and Bull, 1992; Coffey, Brown, and Savage, 1992) I discovered the work of Susan Martin.

Martin can lay claim to producing the first scholarly study of women in US policing, defining a typology of women officers that formed the foundation of much later research. *Breaking and Entering* was Susan Martin's ground breaking study of women police published in 1979. She was working on a doctorate in Sociology intending to look at women in non-traditional occupations. She was also teaching a course entitled 'Theories of Deviance and Crime' to police officers. One of her police officer students explained that the Washington DC police department was experimenting by putting women on patrol and Susan described the light bulb going on in her head and she had found her PhD topic. In pursuing her research, some of the impediments that dogged my own attempts were clearly evident in her research experience. The 'experiment' had been running for a year and initially Susan wanted to conduct follow-up interviews with officers but names were not released so this avenue of research was unavailable. Instead she joined the police reserve in order to conduct a participant observation study. Her role included a training assignment to one of the police districts. Interestingly she wore a uniform, including a Sam Browne belt and handcuffs, working patrol with both men and women officers for about nine months. She kept copious field notes and requested interviews with officers. Throughout the data collection she had a key informant who was a detective and working on her own masters thesis.

This work produced the *police*women /police*women* dichotomy as a way to conceptualise female officers' coping adaptations. Thus the *police*woman is tough, assertive, independent, loyal to the organisation, ambitious and eager for promotion. The police*woman* is service oriented, passive and likely to gravitate towards non-patrol assignments and avoids promotion. The mechanism of stereotyping which forges these adaptations are identified as de-feminisation and de-professionalisation.. This makes rather more explicit Joan Lock's analytical insights. In *Breaking and Entering* Martin works through the consequences of these processes and charts how women's presence disrupts the prevalent norms and solidarity of policemen. She identified the following paradox (p. 108):

> men fear that women will fail to uphold the [male] norms of policing, thus making their work more difficult and less rewarding. Yet they also fear that if women do fulfil the norms, the meaning of masculinity and femininity becomes blurred. If women can perform the role of policemen (a word that blends occupational and sex roles) the defining social characteristics of an officer and a man are no longer exclusively his; women threaten the men's sense of their own masculine identity.

Interestingly Sandra Jones reversed Martin's classification leading her to contemplate *police*men and police*men* (p. 172). She speculated that the more service orientated policeman would experience similar marginalisation to that experienced by policewomen, but reflected 'one wonders whether the impact of holding a minority belief among male peers in a male dominated organisation has quite the same consequences for a man as it has for women officers.' This provided me with a golden nugget to think about and subsequently explore issues of identity and the impact of occupational socialisation on officers holding a minority status (as either female, from and ethnic minority or having an alternative sexual orientation). More immediately Susan Martin's typology, linked as it was to coping adaptations, lead me to look more closely at the stress reactions experienced by policewomen brought on by the attitudes of their male colleagues (Brown and Campbell, 1994; Brown, Campbell and Fife-Schaw, 1996; Brown, 2000) and their ways of coping. Here, with my research collaborators, we were able to explore the adverse impacts on women officers of some of the mechanisms identified and documented by Martin. My research into occupational stress showed that women officers do suffer adversely from aspects of the police occupational culture that support men: solidarity, camaraderie, after hours socialising and drinking, exchanges of war stories of violence and sexual conquests. These serve to reinforce men's images of themselves and map onto their stereotype of what it was to be a police officer. Being 'other' by virtue of gender meant not fitting so readily the prevailing cultural norm. Women cope and adapt but at a personal cost. Martin in *Breaking and Entering* (p. 186) had suggested that women

> adopt a number of coping strategies to maximise their effectiveness, including a strong emphasis on professionalism, assertiveness, occupational achievement, and loyalty to the department.

We found that women officers were likely to minimise the negative impact of sexual harassment on their psychological well-being and instead re-locate some of that distress onto frustrated career ambitions as this was a more acceptable and recognised source of irritation laid at the 'bosses' which they could share with their male colleagues.

**Explanatory framework**

As I and colleagues were beginning to publish research findings on policewomen, Frances Heidensohn produced the results of her US/UK comparative study *Women in Control* in 1992. Frances had been amongst the first in a line of distinguished feminist criminologists who insisted that women's experiences of the criminal justice system could not be subsumed under the rubric of male models and theories. Putting women in the frame has been a hallmark of her work (Heidensohn, 1998). Much of her earlier work had been in the area of women offenders. When researching material for a book on women and crime (Heidensohn, 1985) she found very little on the topic of gender and policing. Her acute observational skills homed in on the fact that literature on Anglo-American models of policing largely ignored the distinctive entry of women into both systems. This together with ideas about social control that emerged from her work on women and crime, lead her to formulate an ambitious cross cultural comparison of different professions in the US, UK, and Israel. The scaled down project that emerged drew on several strands of social theory: the sociology of social control and of policing, occupational sociology and social deviance (Heidensohn, 1998).

Interestingly, Frances acknowledges the work of both Sandra Jones and Susan Martin as important precursor studies. This is emphasized in the following quotation from *Women in Control* (p. 86):

It is important to remember that [*police*women and police*women*] represent the two ends of a continuum and that many women will demonstrate some characteristics of both these role adaptations. Often they struggle to achieve a balance between the defeminised and de-professionalized role (Jones, 86: 172). This advice is often forgotten and Martin's typology is rendered merely, for example, as female officers tended to adopt two principles of coping.

Heidensohn sees Martins's contribution as identifying:

two sets of variables as crucial: one represented by organizational factors such as power, opportunity, and the numbers of women employed, and second by, culturally established sex role norms.

These two variable sets were to be picked up by Frances and me later, when we collaborated on an international comparison of women in policing and represented two axes of a model we were jointly to develop. The third axis of this model was based on the concepts Frances developed from her empirical investigation into the experience of women officers in the USA and UK. When embarking on this comparative project there were few conceptual tools available. In *Women in Control* she lays out the conceptual basis which provided me, and many other researchers, with the basic framework within which to construct and compare women officers' experiences. These concepts (a sense of mission, pioneers, partners, transformational scenes, professionalism, soft cops, female cop culture and top cops) are written in Frances' inimical style that resonate with meaning. Transformational scenes derives from that part of a pantomime when the heroine is transformed from her shy, impoverished persona into a beautiful and well-dressed princess. This refers to experiences by police women when they demonstrate their capabilities as good officers and offset the impediment of gender. These may be dramatic such as an exciting arrest or rather more mundane such as demonstration of basic street policing skills.

One of the other concepts Frances identified was the idea of professionalism. Whereas Sandra Jones documents beliefs men have concerning female officers' lack of professionalism (p. 88-91), Frances discusses (p. 144-46) women officers' view that professionalism was their way of demonstrating their skills (as indeed had Susan Martin earlier). This was done by going by the book, doing things properly, treating the public, including offenders, well and working extremely hard.

The conceptual tools articulated by Frances inspired me to extend the range of my own research inquiries and apply to policing experiences of women within Europe (Brown, 1997) and between Australia, the US and the UK (Brown, 1998). These have proved to be powerful and sustainable conceptualisations that are readily applicable cross culturally and have greatly assisted the project of explicating the developmental phases of women's entry, progression and integration within policing (Brown, Hazenberg and Ormiston, 1999).

When reviewing *Women in Control* in 1993 I wrote:

> It was necessary to rely on grounded concepts derived from the research study itself. Herein lies a difficulty with the analytical framework for the empirical data. It is not entirely clear which concepts derive from the experience of women themselves and those that were imposed on the existing tool kit.

Then, I was concerned about the specificity of the derived concepts and their ability to stand up to wider comparisons. Since using the Heidensohn model I have revised my view and consider her theoretical work to be amongst the most important and robust in this area of research. It provided me with the basis for two developments. Firstly it enabled me to identify a series of temporal stages: entry, restriction, integration, take-off, reform and tip-over that seemed to reflect the distinct phases through which jurisdictions responded to the demands of equality for women in policing. These stages were applied to police jurisdictions in Europe and I found evidence to support this analytical frame (Brown, 1998). Working with colleagues, the second advance was applying a further cross cultural frame and describing policing jurisdictions as European, Colonial and Anglo American (Brown, Hazenberg and Ormiston, 1999). We found the tools offered by Frances were applicable to this extended range of jurisdictions. So now I had the next iteration of a theoretical model. I could look at processes of discrimination across cultures occurring at various stages of women's integration into policing. We found strong recurring patterns within the jurisdictions we studied.

## Integrating research strands

In trying to move the research on, I felt that Frances' conceptual tools (which looked at process) could be developed further: the structural properties of police organisations and the temporal context charting the developmental sequence as women moved towards integration into policing. These strands of research came together and resulted in the collaboration between Frances

Heidensohn and me, published in 2000, called *Gender and Policing*. The concepts developed by Frances in *Women in Control* were demonstrably applicable to other police jurisdictions and provided us with one axis of our elaborated model. The second axis was the properties of numbers, or more precisely, the ratio of women to men in police organisations. Sandra Jones had made reference to the theoretical work of Moss Kanter but it was not until I read Susan Martin's (1989) paper on work supported by the American Police Foundation, that showed how the structural properties and occupational culture of the work organisation maintain barriers to the integration of women in policing, that I began thinking how these ideas might be checked out.

Kanter's (1977) argument is that the relative proportions of men and women in the workplace impacts the relationships between them and the distribution of power and promotion. Kanter (1977: 966) proposes that a skew of 80 per cent : 20 per cent in the workplace results in those in the smaller group being seen as 'tokens' and those in the larger group as 'dominants'; a 60 per cent : 40 per cent ratio constitutes a tilted group where individuals are split as majority : minority members ; between 40 per cent and 60 per cent, the group becomes balanced. Highly visible tokens (such as women) will attract a disproportionate share of attention and are susceptible to an exaggeration of difference because the small numbers exacerbate the application of social stereotyping. The generalisations that follow from the application of stereotyping are made to fit the particular individual. These processes lead to job performance-pressures (in terms of lack of privacy within the organisation) in which competence is taken as a measure of the general ability of the whole of the person's social category rather than as a measure of the individual's achievement. As a consequence, tokens may cope by working harder and over-achieving or attempting to limit their visibility and avoid risks or controversy. This fits well with the *police*woman police*woman* typology. Thus tokens become 'mistake-avoidance sensitive'; have an exaggerated fear of failure at important tasks or key events, and; worry about retaliation by envious dominant group members. Dominants in organisations, on the other hand, continually assert or reclaim the group solidarity and exaggerate those occupational symbols and values that differentiate them from the tokens. Kanter shows how men in the majority dramatise their feats of drinking and sexual prowess through exaggerated displays of aggression and potency.

Our third axis was time. A temporal dimension to psychological research is rare (Chase, 1998). I have always been drawn to accounts of pioneering women and felt that the longevity of antipathy towards women officers required some historical research. I have been inspired here by

Dorothy Schulz and Joan Lock who have written police women histories reflecting experiences on both sides of the Atlantic. Dorothy, formerly a captain in the New York Transit Police, herself a pioneer policewoman, having met Felicia Shpritzer the first woman sergeant of the NYPD, was encouraged by her to join the International Association of Women Police (IAWP). The 1980s conferences were marked by the new generation of women officers trying to take over from the old guard of earlier pioneers. It was a merging of an interest in history and the career developments of different generations of women officers that got Dorothy started on a Doctorate. At that time there was virtually nothing available by way of scholarly research and she had to revert to primary sources. This involved searching the archives of New York City Library where there were special collections containing reports of many police departments. A little used branch of the New York Public Library housed early international Association of Policewomen newsletters. The Public Library had been a project of Lady Nancy Astor and it was her personal collection of documents that were unearthed by Dorothy. Encouragement from the doctoral supervisory panel lead to a broadening of scope to identify the role played by the Women's Temperance Movement and other organisations associated with moral hygiene (prostitution and immorality). These groups were instrumental in arguing the case for the appointment of policewomen. This emphasis on the moral imperative underpinning women's recruitment into the police as the guardian of sexual morality in part explains the contemporary discomfort that policemen exhibit in the presence of policewomen. Hunt (1990) asserts that the consequence of a feminisation of policing is dire for men as this reduces their latitude for laddish behaviour and increases their risk of exposure to punishment. *From Social Worker to Crime Fighter* (Schulz, 1995), documents the move of women officers from welfare concerns to their involvement within mainstream policing. This tension was also evident in British police women's move from the separate policewomen's department to integration charted by Joan Lock. Thus numbers and time provided further dimensions for a more contextualised analysis within which to examine the processes implicated in harassing and discriminatory behaviour by policemen, and the management of these by policewomen. The opportunity to participate in the First Australasian Conference of Policewomen and the first joint conference of the European Network of Police Women and International Association of Women Police provided the opportunity for Frances Heidensohn and myself to conduct a truly international survey to work through some of these theoretical ideas. Our methodology adopted both a qualitative and quantitative dimension (that had proved so effective in Sandra Jones' earlier work). We also borrowed and adapted techniques developed by Dorothy Schulz and Joan Lock in tackling archival research. The typologising of police women by Martin gave us insights into how to develop this as an analytic device.

From our quantitative research findings we were able to show the universality of discriminatory behaviours that characterise policing jurisdictions. We were also able to demonstrate there was not a strict application of the Kanter gender ratio model. Rather than bureaurocratising out discriminatory treatment as ratios become balanced, we found a U-shaped statistical relationship suggesting there to be different discriminatory dynamics at work when women are in either the majority or minority. A synthesis of Sandra Jones' rituals and arguments and Susan Martin's de-feminisation/de-professionalisation thesis enabled us to explore the sustainability of gender disabling devices. Through a 'discourse analysis' of cartoon and other contemporary material, we were able to show the paradox inherent in the idea of *police woman*. Women were represented not only as a force of superior morality but also as potential seductresses. Moreover, the cartoonists in particular deployed the device of showing (less glamorous) women officers to be condemnatory of their more glamorous counterparts: no solidarity of the sisterhood possible here. Our empirical data did indeed demonstrate, as Sandra Jones had predicted, that women do oscillate between the extremes of Susan Martin's typology and, moreover, that there were differences over time and variants, especially amongst more senior women officers.

In *Gender and Policing* rather than typing women and seeing how these types worked in different jurisdictions, we offered a different taxonomy that tried to reflect policing styles within jurisdictions and saw how women managed within these. Thus we defined 'cops' as those who hail from the tradition of Anglo-American policing (a tradition we gave the shorthand 'colonial' because this represents a policing model that had originated with (usually) British colonial power and had since evolved into a national police organisation following independence), 'gendarmes' which derived from the military models of continental European policing; and finally 'transitionals' by which we meant those jurisdictions in Eastern Europe nearly emerged from totalitarian governments. We then presented evidence, based on these types of policing jurisdictions, of the levels of sexual harassment experienced by women police officers and jurisdictions' attitudes towards women's victimization.

## Next steps

My present researches are taking me into more psychological territory. I wanted to germinate the seeds of ideas I had gleaned from Joan Lock, discussed earlier. I want to explore the ways in which female officers maintained elements of their personal identity (i.e. as a woman) in the hostile environment of the police occupational culture and how they adopt a police identity through the process of socialisation. The token dynamics explicated by Martin (Martin and Jurik, 1998) gave me a starting point to explore the maintenance of dual or triple identities of officers as women, who belong to a minority ethnic group, and/or who have an alternative sexual orientation. Some preliminary work has been published on this (Wootten and Brown, 2000). Through qualitative interviewing it was possible to reveal the processes whereby individuals suppress aspects of their personal identity and accentuate their stereotypical attributes of what it is to be a police officer. As they become more confident in the police role, their other identities are in tension and compete for expression. Eventually the officer feels that their personal and police identities are incompatible and they may leave the service or they are able to reconcile the competition and achieve a manageable integration. The gay women officers had quite different coping adaptation. They were either 'out' in an 'in your face' way; partially 'out', for example, to immediate colleagues; or remained 'in the closet'. The fears of exposure that had characterised the early women pioneer officers remain fears today – for some. The next set of studies sought to look at the perception of officers towards colleagues with multiple identities. By starting with the notion of a normative stereotype of the straight, white, male I am currently looking at the perceptions related to difference and predict that the greater distance from the norm the more difficult it will be for the officer to integrate successfully into the police. Research I have supervised at masters level has demonstrated that this prediction does hold up empirically (Thomas, 1999, Rapley, 2000).

I also seek to take a leaf from Sandra Jones' work and chart not just problems but offer some solutions to developing the next generation of equal opportunities policies for policing. In Sandra's work she had proposed (p. 175-181) that forces needed to publish a definitive statement of equal opportunities policy supported by a specific set of operational guidelines; raise the awareness of police managers to implement and enforce the policies; make organisational provisions such as part-time working flexible shifts; and provide training in conflict resolution and assertiveness. By and large much of this has been achieved. All forces within the UK have explicit equal opportunities policies and established grievance procedures. Much progress has been made on flexible working and career opportunities have opened-up to women officers. Recent research by Holdaway and Parker (1997) shows that the aspirational gap between men and women officers is closing but conversion into activating promotion has not. Holdaway and Parker (1998) found there still to be attitudinal biases amongst policemen that preserve gender differences in terms of beliefs about women, career commitment, and physical suitability for policing. They found women officers more likely to feel unsupported or positively blocked by male supervisors especially when attempting ranks above sergeant. Their suggested reason for this was male senior officers' concerns about the minority status of women and their consequent ability to manage male subordinates. However, they also make the important point that not all limits on aspirations or achievement are due to the exertion of male control but are a function of the part women themselves play. The new work in which I am involved is as a consultant to a steering group setting a 'gender agenda' through which women officers are empowered to fulfill their potential in the full spectrum of policing duties, serving at every rank whilst maintaining a work-life balance. The aims of such an agenda are to: achieve a gender balance across the rank structure and specialism consistent with the proportion of women in the economically active population; have women represented in influential policy forums; develop a work/home balance to produce appropriate resources (equipment training opportunities) so as to enable women officers to do their jobs effectively.

## Conclusion

There were parallel developments in researching the position of women both sides of the Atlantic. In Joan Lock and Dorothy Schulz we have former police officers turning their minds to writing their own and their contemporaries histories. Their books were 'first', in that little existed before. They pioneered methods in archival research and located sources which have been invaluable to scholars who followed. Not only did they identify the major landmarks in the progression of women in policing they also provided accounts from the early women pioneers whose stories would otherwise have been lost. Sandra Jones and Susan Martin share a deep personal commitment to this area of research and respectively produced the first empirical studies of contemporary policewomen's experiences either side of the Atlantic. Susan's typology has stimulated much research activity whilst Sandra's data provided key benchmarking results. Both found it difficult to remain within this area of research and it was for others to capitalise on the baselines of data and analysis they established and the theoretical underpinnings that they originated. Frances Heidensohn has perhaps had the most enduring research interest and the evolution of her thinking converged with mine when producing *Gender and Policing*. We argue in our book (Brown and Heidensohn, 2000) that the psychological and sociological layers of the research provided both an individually centered analysis examining impacts of the occupational culture and an account of the structural constraints within which women manage their police careers. Our interests have diverged somewhat since, as Frances has turned her attention to the dynamics of policewomen's networks and I pursue the more individualistic analysis of competing identities.

In assessing the contributions made by their respective work Joan Lock hoped that hers brought the subject of policewomen to notice particularly to academic and feminist writers especially as there appeared at the time of her writings to be an anti police bias in the subjects they tackled. Joan also felt her research efforts proved a valuable link for researchers to connect with prostitution, women's employment, child welfare, and the development of the position of women. Her subsequent articles drew attention to issues relevant to the development of equal opportunities at a time during which little or no energy was expended on such matters. Her cogent commentaries which appeared in *Police Review* anticipated, and possibly helped to precipitate, much that was to change in the deployment of women officers. She drew attention to the difficulties of being a working police mother, (*Police Review*, 30 January 1987) becoming a dog handler, (*Police Review*, 24 April 1987) and her question How Long Must She Wait (*Police Review*, 11 September 1987) prompted a response from Alison Halford (1987) that was cited in the subsequent discipline inquiry as an example of Halford's breach of the Discipline Code (Halford, 1993).

Dorothy Schulz hoped her work has made more people take seriously the early roles of women in policing; that it has made a contribution to police history, women's history and the history of work and professions by paying attention to a group that had previously received none. She is optimistic that women in policing today are stimulated to learn more about their roots and when breaking with the past do not neglect their own histories. She feels it is time to move from introspective analysis of sexual harassment and sex discrimination to accounts of the experiences of women who are succeeding. Her own research attention is being directed at more senior women officers.

She thinks that by claiming women's distinctness (often presented as a reforming presence in policing) this could lead once again to separation between men and women's policing roles. Susan Martin hopes to broaden the theoretical understanding of the stresses and problems of women officers entering policing, and beyond that to an examination of 'tokens' generally. Some of the policy recommendation of the Police Foundation work were taken seriously and some of the issues related to difference were dealt with more sensitively. Also she hopes that research has shown the importance of affirmative action policy in increasing the number of women officers. Sandra Jones' work laid out many of the practical recommendations that were to be implemented by the police service subsequently. Her study provided important benchmarking data and her questionnaire survey was a template for much research that was to follow. Frances Heidensohn's avowed aim is to put women in the frame of criminal justice research. She has certainly achieved this with *Women in Control*. The other significant aspiration for her work is to stimulate debate. If the policing typology offered in *Gender and Policing* is the subject of commentary, further analysis and refutation then Frances would be more that satisfied.

In assessing my own contribution then, the Anderson, Brown and Campbell (1993) study was the first national empirical account documenting the incidence of sexual harassment within British policing. It coincided with a report from Her Majesty's Inspectorate of Constabulary (1993) and provoked a good deal of interest. It elicited a response from the police service accepting the need to engage more actively with the issue of equal opportunities in policing. Much work has since been done in generating more effective policies and commitment has been greater in implementing them. The first woman chief constable, Pauline Clare was appointed Chief Constable of Lancashire in 1995. Since then, both the Dorset and the Wiltshire Constabularies have appointed women chiefs. The equality debate has been further stimulated in the UK by the Macpherson Inquiry (1999) into the police management of the murder of black teenager Stephen Lawrence. This provokes questions about the next generation of equal opportunities policies: should gender, race and sexual orientation merge to create a diversity programme because problems and solutions are common or should there be a single issue approach because underlying causes and intervention have distinctive elements. I hope the research direction I am currently taking may contribute to this debate.

# References

Anderson, R., Brown, J., and Campbell, E.A. (1993). *Aspects of Sex Discrimination in Police Forces in England and Wales*. London: Home Office Police Research Group.

Brown, J.M. (1997). European Policewomen: a Comparative Research Perspective. *International Journal of the Sociology of Law*, 25, 1-19.

Brown, J.M. (1998). Comparing Charges: Experience of Women Police Officers Serving in Australia, British Isles and United States of America. *International Journal of Police Science and Management*. 1, 227-240.

Brown, J.M. (2000). Occupational Culture as a Factor in the Stress of Police Officers. In Leishman, F., Loveday, B., and Savage, S. (eds), *Core Issues in Policing* 2nd Ed. London: Longman.

Brown, J.M. and Campbell, E.A. (1990). Sources of Occupational Stress in the Police. *Work and Stress*, 4, 305-318.

Brown, J.M. and Campbell, E.A. 1994). *Stress and Policing*. Chichester: Wiley.

Brown, J.M., Campbell, E.A., and Fife-Schaw, C. (1995). Adverse Impacts Experienced by Police Officers Following Exposure to Sex Discrimination and Sexual Harassment. *Stress Medicine*, 11, 221-228.

Brown, J.M., Hazenberg, A., and Ormiston, C. (1998). Policewomen; an International Comparison. In Mawby, R. (ed), *Comparative Policy: Issues for the Twenty-first Century*. London: UCL.

Brown J.M., and Heidensohn, F. (2000). *Gender and Policing*. London: Macmillan.

Brown, J.M., Maidment, A., and Bull, R. (1992). Appropriate Skill Matching or Gender Bias in Deployment of Male and Female Police Officers. *Policing and Society*, 2, 1-15.

Coffey, S., Brown, J.M., and Savage, S. (1992). Policewomen's Career Aspirations; Some Reflections on the Role and Capabilities of Women in Policing in Britain. *Police Studies*, 15, 1, 13-19.

Chase, J. (1995). Historical Analysis in Psychological Research in Breakwell, G., Hammond, S., and Fife-Schaw, C. (eds), *Research Methods in Psychology*. London: Sage.

Equal Opportunities Commission (1990). *Managing to Make Progress*. London: Receiver for the Metropolitan Police.

Gregory, J., and Lees, S. (1999). *Policing and Sexual Assault*. London: Routledge.

Halford, A. (1987). Until the 12th of Never. *Police Review* 9th October 2019.

Halford, A. (1993). *No Way up the Greasy Pole*. London: Constable.

Heidensohn, F. (1985). *Women and Crime*. London: Macmillan.

Heidensohn, F. (1992). *Women in Control? The Role of Women in Law Enforcement*. Oxford: Clarendon.

Heidensohn, F (1998). Translations and Refutations; an Analysis of Changing Perspectives in Criminology. In Holdaway, S., and Rock, P. (eds), *Thinking about Criminology*. London: UCL Press.

Her Majesty's Inspectorate of Constabulary (1993). *Equal Opportunities in the Police Service*. London: Home Office.

Holdaway, S., and Parker, S. (1997). *Equal Opportunities in South Yorkshire Police*. University of Sheffield.

Holdaway, S. and Parker, S. (1998). Policing Women Policing: Uniform Patrol, Promotion and Representation in CID. British Journal of Criminology, 38, 40-60.

Holdaway, S., and Parker, S. (1997). *Equal Opportunities in South Yorkshire Police.* University of Sheffield.

Holdaway, S. and Parker, S. (1998). Policing Women Policing: Uniform Patrol, Promotion and Representation in CID. *British Journal of Criminology*, 38, 40-60.

Home Office (1989). *Circular 87/89 : Equal Opportunities: Policies in the Police Service in England and Wales.* London: Home Office.

Hunt, J. (1990). The Logic of Sexism among Police. *Women and Criminal Justice*, 2, 3-30.

Jones, S. (1986). *Policewomen and Equality; Formal Policy and Informal Practice.* London: Macmillan.

Kanter, R.M. (1977). Some Effects of Proportions on Group Life: Skewed Sex Ratios and Responses to Token Women. *American Journal of Sociology*, 82, 965-90.

Lock, J. (1979). *The British Policewoman: Her Story.* London: Hale.

Martin, S.E. (1980). *Breaking and Entering.* Berkeley: University of California Press.

Martin, S.E. (1989). Women in Policing; the 80s and Beyond. In Kenney, D. (ed), *Police and Policing; Contemporary Issues.* New York: Praeger.

Martin, S.E. and Jurik, N. (1996). *Doing Justice Doing Gender: Women in Law and Criminal Justice Occupations.* Thousands Oaks, CA: Sage.

Macpherson Sir W. (1999). *The Stephen Lawrence Enquiry.* Cm 4262-1. London: HMSO.

Rapley, M. (2000). *The Perceptions of Minorities in the Workplace: an Exploratory Study.* Masters Dissertation University of Surrey.

Schulz, D. (1995). *From Social Worker to Crime Fighter.* Westport, CT: Praeger.

Thomas, A. (2000). *Gender and Race as Aspects of Organizational Acceptance.* Masters Dissertation University of Surrey.

Walklate, S. (1995). Equal Opportunities and the Future of Policing. In Leishman, F., Loveday, B., and Savage, S. (eds), *Core Issues in Policing.* London: Longman.

Wootten, I. and Brown, J.M. (2000). Balancing Occupational and Personal Identities; the Experience of Lesbian and Gay Officers. *BPS Lesbian and Gay Psychology Section Newsletter*, 4, 6-13

# 5. Under Observation: Leadership in American Policing

JAMES GINGER

## Introduction

On April 17, 1997, the US Department of Justice implemented an historic consent decree with the City of Pittsburgh, Pennsylvania, marking the first time in American history that the federal branch of American government became a significant partner in the management and supervisory functions of a local police agency. The consent decree, a legal maneuver in lieu of civil litigation, gives the Department of Justice the ability to stipulate – with the 'consent' of the City of Pittsburgh – dramatic changes in Pittsburgh Bureau of Police practices of policy development, training, supervision, discipline, internal investigations, and personnel practices.[1] In effect the decree has become one of the most significant pieces of police 'literature' in the 20th century, laying out, as it were, a clear, articulate and demanding statement concerning acceptable methods of police supervision, management and operations in the US in the 21st century. In effect, the decree is purportedly designed to bring 'the rule of law' back into the lexicon of American policing.

Local control over the police function has been a foundational tenet of American policing since its development, a strong fear of centralized control over the policing function far outweighing cost savings and economies of scale in operations. The American fear of centralized police has even been credited with the delay of the advent of a state police function in many states in the US. Nevertheless, the Department of Justice followed the ground breaking action in Pittsburgh with a similar decree in Steubenville, Ohio in 1998, and the New Jersey State Police in 1999. Based on articles in American newspapers, the Department of Justice is currently considering or actively

---

1.     United States of America v. The City of Pittsburgh, Pittsburgh Bureau of Police and Department of Public Safety, Federal District Court for the Western District of Pennsylvania, Civil Number 97-0354,1997.

pursuing similar consent decrees in New York, New York; Los Angeles, California; Chicago, Illinois; Buffalo, New York; Indianapolis, Indiana; Scottsdale, Arizona; Riverside, California; Columbus, Ohio, and a host of other local police agencies.  The consent decree in New Jersey purportedly has the same goals as the Pittsburgh and the Steubenville decrees: to bring the rule of law back into the process of American policing.

How did a country with a well-recognized paranoia concerning centralized police come to such a series of events?  The answer to that question may best come from an anecdotal review of a career in American policing, combined with a careful review of the literature regarding policing in America over the past 35 years.  Such a process finds a career – subjected to the influences and constraints of the phenomena identified in the literature – which has flowed through multiple changes as it struggled to have an effect on the institution of policing.

I began my career in American policing in 1969.  Classified as a survivor of the police selection process (a mathematically rigorous one, if not methodologically so – twenty of us made it through a testing process that began with more than 2,000 hopefuls) I was assigned to a more senior officer for field training.  My career started with a version of the same speech that virtually every American police recruit received in the late 1960s: 'Son, forget what you learned in the Academy.  I'm going to show you how it's really done'. That admonition, and the one that followed, 'Keep your mouth shut and your ears open!' set the tone for what passed for field training in the late 1960s.  What followed was a mentorship that lasted for nine months, and, in truth, despite its lack of structure, documentation, assessment or systemic development, served as an excellent indoctrination for what passed as 'good policing' at the time.

Witticisms, legends, admonitions, stereotypes, warnings, and demands were interwoven with some spectacular demonstrations of effective police work. The mentorship included some exceptional learning mechanisms. Perhaps the most effective of these was a 20 minute lesson delivered on a late summer's evening.  As we pulled our police cruiser to the curb, in the shadow of a tree, that prevented the streetlight from illuminating the interior of our car – it was the late 1960s, after all, and urban unrest included, in our city as well as many others, attempts to 'off the pig' which included sniping – my mentor shut off the engine – there was no need to roll down the windows, since police cruisers were not air conditioned against the August heat – and advised me to 'listen, and tell me what you hear'. Within 20 minutes, we had attuned my ears to 'know' what was going on in a neighbourhood simply by listening.

Marital discord, front-porch discourse, back-porch deals, intercourse – all fell under the purview of the police (enhanced by the necessity to leave windows and doors open for ventilation against the August heat). A new meaning of 'reasonable expectation of privacy' became readily apparent.

These processes continued for nine months, remarkably, impressing upon the 'new guy' all of the institutional, oral history of the department, and, unknowingly, placing me in the box that Jerome Skolnick had warned all of us about only two years earlier. As a college student who had just changed his degree plan from English to Criminal Justice, I had not yet 'met' Mr Skolnick, but his work had clearly captured what would be my work for the next several years. At the same time that I was being socialized into my new career, Kenneth Culp Davis (1969) was answering Skolnick's work, which identified may problems in American policing, but offered few solutions, with his own. Davis' work provided the solutions that Skolnick overlooked. These two pieces of literature defined my career in policing for the next 15 years. They also go a long way toward answering the question first posed in this chapter: 'How did a country with a well-recognized paranoia concerning centralized police come to the point that the federal government could be directly involved in controlling municipal police practice?'

In 1967, Jerome Skolnick penned a truly seminal piece, *Justice Without Trial: Law Enforcement in a Democratic Society*. Skolnick's treatment of the police in that text was excoriated by the police, ignored by those responsible for ensuring police accountability, and, by those willing to think objectively, recognized as an honest and meaningful treatment between the dichotomy established in the phrase 'law and order'. Skolnick identified serious, pervasive, and constitutionally grave problems in American policing based on his careful analysis of the policing process in a large American city. Two years after Skolnick was carefully identifying serious problems with the process of providing policing services in America, Kenneth Culp Davis, an attorney, provided a nearly perfect counter-point to the problems identified by Skolnick. In two texts, Discretionary *Justice: A Preliminary Inquiry* (1969) and *Police Discretion* (1975), Davis literally sketched out the *solution* to many of the problems identified by Skolnick. His work as well was promptly ignored by American law enforcement leadership.

By 1977, having fully digested the problems identified by Skolnick and the solutions suggested by Davis – the intervening eight years saw me steep myself in the literature on criminal justice, with degrees in sociology and criminal justice, and a masters in criminal justice – I had virtually given up hope of having a meaningful impact on the field from the inside. The socialization process was too strong to be controlled, I reasoned, by simple policy or training at the academy. My first admonition ('Forget everything you learned at the Academy!') was still being used to 'really train' new recruits. My tenure as a policy writer for my agency allowed me to develop policy, but it was being truly taught and implemented by mentors who, at best took a dim view of attempts to regularize and structure police discretion, and who, at worst, actively worked to teach new recruits 'real' policy: the policy of the street. Real change it seemed, could only come from getting to the 'new recruits' before they became recruits. Building a cadre of those who understood the issues identified by Skolnick and at least partially resolved by Davis seemed the only way to effect change. My career shifted from that of an 'insider' to that of an 'outsider', teaching at the college level, and hardening potential police recruits against the types of mentorships that encouraged – and in cases even demanded – unbridled exercise of discretion. For the most part, in America policing *was* the unbridled exercise of discretion in the attempt to achieve 'law and order'. This style of policing continued virtually unabated, through the 1980s.

Nearly 15 years after Skolnick warned us of the eventual outcomes, William Geller (Geller and Scott, 1992) sketched a detailed picture of the *results* 'in the field' of ignoring Skolnick and Davis. In *Deadly Force: What we Know* Geller depicts the results of basically unbridled discretion in American policing. A series of supporting pieces by others fleshes out Geller's picture of the extent to which we had allowed police discretion to all but suborn the Constitution in the name of effective law enforcement. Allegations of implementation of a policing system which ensured effectiveness by selectively denying basic constitutional protections, over the course of 25 years, appears to be the direct progenitor of the move to redirect the policing practice of selected American cities by the Civil Rights Division of the US Department of Justice.

Soon, it was clear that 'change' would not come from inoculating large numbers of potential recruits against the indoctrination they would receive from their field mentors. The problems of unbridled discretion began to become difficult to manage in the late 1980s in America. Most police departments had been coerced into staffing internal affairs divisions, charged with investigating citizens' complaints of improper police treatment. Some departments had even gone so far as to implement civilian review boards to review police behavior. In the late 1980s, American civil law changed, allowing citizens to sue police agencies for improper training, poor tactics, lax supervision, ineffective policy, and ineffectual leadership – and to claim monetary compensation for the damages these failures caused. To be sure, many of the resulting civil suits were spurious, and many were dismissed as such by American courts. But some of the civil suits were well grounded, resulting in shocking verdicts against police officers, supervisors, and city, county and sate governments.

The works of Skolnick, Davis, Geller, and others, allow us to understand better the impact of a serious dichotomy in American policing: the rule of law v. law and order. No one argues that the police should not be empowered to use discretion in the day-to-day practice of their jobs. In fact, as Davis argues, it is essential. But unbridled discretion, in the face of a job that is dangerous and constantly focused on effectiveness, *can* lead to abuse. The following paragraphs assess the impact on the field of policing of its refusal to take notice from Skolnick and its willingness to ignore Davis, and provides some insight into the reliance on civil litigation and consent decrees to effect change.

**Justice Without Trial: The Tip of the Iceberg**

Virtually at the same time I was being prepared to take to the streets as a rookie police officer, Jerome Skolnick (1967) was infuriating police executives with his excoriating expose of policing in America. In setting the scene for his 1967 text, Skolnick (1967: 3-4) notes that:

> In reading about the American police, especially through the period of the 1930s, one feels that constitutional issues of legality have been almost too remote to be of immediate concern. Not that American police conformed to the rule of law. Rather, they seem so far out of line that a writer summarizing a major American study of police practices entitled his book *Our Lawless Police* [and] found practices so appalling and sadistic as to pose no intellectual issue for civilized men.

Skolnick's willingness to bring the battle unabashedly to the practitioners of policing in the 1960s may have sealed his work's fate. It did little to inure him to police officers and leaders. But quickly, things got worse!

Skolnick methodically develops the idea that the basic dichotomy between the rule of law and 'law and order'– expecting the police to deliver policing services within the pale of the rule of law presents serious opportunities for police officers to abuse their discretion in the enforcement of the law.  Skolnick (1967: 42) notes that the interaction between this dichotomy and the police officer's 'working personality':

> yields a dangerous impetus to avoid the encumbrances of the court system by simply engaging in 'street corner justice'.

In developing his hypothesis, Skolnick places at center court, the concept of the 'symbolic assailant' (the typical 'shorthand to identify certain kinds of people... who use gesture, language, and attire that the policeman has come to recognize as a prelude to violence' (Skolnick, 1967: 45)).  Skolnick continues, eerily sketching, in 1967, the precursor to complaints of an entire race of people in America in the 1990s when he quotes from Thomas Adams' (1963) litany of indicators of 'cause' to select an individual for field interrogation:

- Persons who do not 'belong' where they are observed;
- Automobiles which do not 'look right';
- Persons who attempt to avoid or evade the officer;
- Persons who are visibly 'rattled' when near the policeman; and,
- Exaggerated unconcern over contact with the officer (Adams, 1963: 28).

In short, 'cause' existed if the officer 'felt' the symbolic assailant did not belong, looked wrong, or was either too comfortable or too uncomfortable in the presence of the police.  As Skolnick notes, the 'symbolic assailant' is whatever the police officer thinks he is: 'a young man may suggest the threat of violence to the policeman by his manner of walking or 'strutting', the insolence of his demeanor, being registered by the policeman as a possible preamble to later attack.  Signs vary from 'area to area.' (Skolnick, 1967: 46) and, he could easily have added, from police officer to police officer.

Perhaps more importantly, Skolnick notes that the 'danger' of which the symbolic assailant is the perceptual harbinger need not have been experienced personally; it is a matter of socialization.  The police officer, Skolnick notes, 'identifies with his fellow cop who has been beaten, perhaps fatally, by a gang of young thugs' (Skolnick, 1967: 48).  And, lest we assume that the police officer's perceptions are based on whim or fancy, Skolnick spends valuable space quoting James Baldwin, in *Nobody Knows My Name,* preserving for those who study the police perhaps one of the most powerful commentaries on policing America's ghettos:

The only way to police in a ghetto is to be oppressive. None of the Police Commissioner's men, even with the best will in the world, have any way of understanding the lives led by the people they swagger about in twos and threes controlling. Their very presence is an insult, and it would be, even if they spent their entire day feeding gumdrops to children. They represent the force of the white world, and that world's criminal profit and ease, to keep the black man corralled up here, in his place. The badge, the gun in the holster, and the swinging club make vivid what will happen should his rebellion become overt (Baldwin, 1962: 65-67).

Using this chilling starting point, Skolnick identifies four catalysts to the 'police culture': social isolation, police solidarity, danger, and social isolation and authority. His conclusion: by organization and social interaction, police are conservative, authoritarian, conventional, and highly dependent upon each other and 'the system' for support and protection from danger. It is the,

> combination of danger and authority found in the task of the policeman [which] unavoidably combine to frustrate procedural regularity... Danger typically yields self-defensive conduct, conduct that must strain to be impulsive because danger arouses fear and anxiety so easily. Authority under such conditions becomes a resource to reduce perceived threats rather than a series of reflective judgments arrived at calmly (Skolnick, 1967: 67).

By the time Skolnick's work had penetrated to the level of the 'well-read street cop', his intellectual argument ran stone against the 'reality' of policing. As a member of the cadre Skolnick referenced, having been duly socialized into its beliefs and attitudes, I could see the 'reality' of policing. Policing was a dangerous job. We *were* the 'thin blue line'. Our 'authority' was the only thing that stood between civilization and anarchy. 'Procedural regularity' simply got in the way. The 'thinking policeman' however, had ready evidence to support Skolnick's arguments: at times, police officers *did* abuse their power, and at times, the abuse was significant. The question became one of determining how to stop the isolated abuse without ruining the entire system of policing. Many of us thought that 'good policy' might be an answer, but Skolnick had cast doubt on that as well.

Noting the primeval nature of the danger-authority structure of policing along with the rule of law versus the 'law and order' dichotomy inherent in the job, Skolnick suggests that policy and procedure, aimed at controlling the discretion necessary in a danger-authority based environment, 'take on a "frilly" character, or at least tend to be reduced to a secondary position in the face of circumstances seen as threatening' (Skolnick, 1967: 67). He continues, later, relating a non-discrimination policy issued by the chief of police in the American police agency he studied as the basis for *Justice Without Trial.*

> The policy read:
> As a matter of policy, the following words and any other similar derogatory words shall not be used by members and employees in the course of their official duties or at any time as to bring the ... Department in to disrepute. These words are ...
>
> The most common display of a lack of courtesy or objectivity is the use by an officer of unsuitable or offensive language or mannerisms. There is a particular need to refrain from language that has a derogatory connotation with reference to race, color, religion, or nationality. Such usage by the police causes deep resentments and antagonism against them.

Skolnick, with amazing prescience, predicts that policy and procedure cannot (or perhaps more clearly will not) change what danger and authority have wrought. Noting that police officers, like all of us, will engage in any activities rationally reasonable to 'put the best light on his competence and dependability when his record is examined by superiors. Thus, the perceived necessity of measures of departmental [performance] results in the development of techniques ... To enlarge the magnitude of the criteria for measuring their performance' (Skolnick, 1967: 118).

The problem, as Skolnick notes, lies not among the officers or even the chiefs of police who lead the officers. Instead, 'the problem stems from the well-motivated attempts of [these people] to develop measurable standards of efficiency. Unfortunately, meeting these standards tends to become an end in itself, a transformation found in many organizations' (Skolnick, 1967: 118). That police officers will produce that which they see in their best interests to produce is a truism that doubtlessly affects the operation of every police agency in America – indeed in the world. As long as the focus is on 'results', the danger-authority nexus will militate for a law *versus* order dichotomy: forging a system in which creative police officers work, despite the 'system', policies, procedures, rules, regulations and statutes, to ensure that the appropriate 'results' are attained. Or, as Skolnick predicts, 'Thus, the standard of efficiency employed in police departments may not only undermine due process of law, but also the basic standard of justice – that those equally culpable shall be given equal punishment' (Skolnick, 1967: 118).

The 'craftsman's administrative bias' is offered by Skolnick as the explanation of the process which allows the police officer to draw a distinction between the criminal *statutory law* and criminal *process* as defined by the Constitution. The *process* is that which stands in the way of enforcement of the *law*, and, as such, is worth less than the *law*. Finding creative ways around the *process* is justifiable, after all, as that is the way one remains efficient! As Skolnick suggests, 'when [the policeman] sees a black girl and a white serviceman enter a hotel together, he assumes an act of prostitution is in the offing. To him, these are not constitutionally protected citizens, but predictable actors whose misbehaviour he usually judges correctly'(Skolnick, 1967: 202). The Constitution takes on the role of obstacle, not the *raison d'etre*, and the police officer's creative guises to enforce the *statutory law* are seen as appropriate responses to the obstacles thrown in his way by the Constitution.

Skolnick summarizes his findings succinctly, noting that:

> Five features of the policeman's occupational environment weaken the conception of the rule of law as a primary objective of police conduct. One is the social psychology of police work ... the relation between occupational environment, working personality and the rule of law. Second, is the policeman's stake in maintaining his position of authority, especially his interest in bolstering accepted patterns of enforcement. Third is police socialization, especially as it influences the policeman's administrative bias. A related factor is the pressure put upon individual policemen to 'produce'–to be efficient rather than legal when the two norms are in conflict. Finally, there is the policeman's opportunity to behave inconsistently with the rule of law as a result of the low visibility of much of his conduct (Skolnick, 1967: 231).

Enigmatically, Skolnick tells us what we have yet to come to fully realize: that we have worshiped at the feet of the wrong paradigm! A policing function based on professionalism, efficiency, and production will create just that which the Pittsburgh-Department of Justice consent decree was designed to address: efficiency absent an allegiance to the rule of law.

'Such a conception of professionalism', argues Skolnick, 'not only fails to bridge the gap between the maintenance of order and the rule of law. In addition, it comes to serve as an ideology undermining the capacity of police to be accountable to the rule of law. The idea of organization based on principles of administrative efficiency is often misunderstood by officials who are themselves responsible for administering such organizations. In practice, standardized rules and procedures are frequently molded to facilitate the tasks of acting officials... [yet] the policeman is a decidedly 'non-mechanical' official (Skolnick, 1967: 236).

Despite Skolnick's lucid warnings, in the years immediately following his work in *Justice Without Trial*, the activity called *policing* in America became known as law enforcement as agencies began to officially de-emphasize their order maintenance roles and to focus instead on the one practice that Skolnick argued would lead to the demise of the rule of Constitutional law: enforcement of the statutory law. Decades of bureaucratic policing led to the development of 'justice without trial', discretionary police actions designed to reduce the 'obstacles' of Constitutional protections and to meet out a craftsman's justice on the street corner, absent the peculiar demands and constraints of prosecutors, judges, juries and Constitutions--all in the name of bureaucratized efficiency.

Just as presciently, Skolnick suggests that:

> If the police are ever to develop a conception of *legal* as opposed to *managerial* professionalism, they will do so only if the surrounding community demands compliance with the rule of law by rewarding police for such compliance, instead of looking to the police as an institution solely responsible for controlling criminality. In practice, however, the reverse has been true. The police function in a milieu tending to support, normatively and substantively, the idea of administrative efficiency that has become the hallmark of police professionalism. Legality, as expressed by both the criminal courts community with which the police have direct contact, and the political community responsible for the working conditions and prerogatives of police, is a weak ideal' (Skolnick, 1967: 239-240).

Bureaucratic professionalism, Skolnick argues, is exactly the wrong structure for policing, noting that Warren Bennis, in 1965, had soundly criticized bureaucratic structures because:

- Bureaucracy does not adequately allow for personal growth and development of mature personalities;
- It develops conformity and 'group-think;'
- It does not take into account the 'informal' organization and ... emergent and unanticipated problems;
- Its systems of control and authority are hopelessly outdated;
- It has no adequate juridical process;
- It does not possess adequate means for resolving differences and conflict between ranks, and most particularly, between functional groups; and,

- Communication (and innovative ideas) are thwarted or distorted due to hierarchical division. (Bennis, 1965: 32)

The predictions of Skolnick's analysis have come to pass in many American police agencies, judging from front page news. Over the years. Rodney King, Abner Louima, and Amadou Dialou, have become icons for perceptions among the community of a policing-institution run amok. Complaints of racial profiling and race-based decision making on the part of the police appear to be part of the impetus for the US Department of Justice Civil Rights Division's attention to specific police agencies, demanding properly supported searches and detentions, limited use of force, and an effective system to control for race-based decision making by police.

Worse, it is not as if Skolnick were the only one who warned us about the inherent dichotomy between policing and the rule of law. Egon Bittner admonished us about police officers' tendencies to take 'four foot leaps over three foot ditches' in 1970, and noted that the dichotomy would lead to the 'widespread use of arrests without intent to prosecute' (Bittner, 1970: 42). Van Maanen warned us about the police officers' intolerance for the 'asshole' as a threat to order in 1978 (Van Maanen, 1978: 221-238). These conceptual admonitions soon gave rise to quantitative studies that provided some insight into the impact on policing of the dichotomy between the rule of law and 'law and order'. (See for example, Geller and Karales, 1981; Geller and Karales, 1981, Fyfe, 1981; Sparger and Geocapassi,1992; Geller and Scott, 1992). These quantitative studies soon gave way to front-page headlines about 'four-foot leaps' and other police actions against 'assholes'.

By the time the reality of Skolnick's predictions, and those of his peers, had hit the front pages of America's newspapers, a cadre of us were working on solutions. Personally, having seen the failure by then of two alternative strategies – first, working from within to write policy to regularize discretion and training those policies at the academy level, and second, inoculating pre-recruits at the college level to the dangers of the abuse of police discretion – it was clear that resolution of the issues identified by Skolnick would not come from 'the bottom' of police organizations. It would need to come, we reasoned, from 'the top': the executive and managerial levels.

Ironically, however, within two years of Skolnick's *Justice Without Trial*, Kenneth Culp Davis published a text specifically focused on providing an alternative perspective of the managerial professionalism model critiqued by Skolnick in 1967. Davis' *Discretionary Justice* (1969) clearly, succinctly and persuasively offered the policing profession a new paradigm, designed to ameliorate or eliminate the rule of law versus 'law and order' dichotomy noted by Skolnick.

## Police Discretion: Administrative Rulemaking as A Mechanism for Navigating the Ice Field of Bureaucratic Policing

In 1969, with the publication of *Discretionary Justice,* and in 1975, with the publication of *Police Discretion,* Kenneth Culp Davis called for a radical shift in paradigm – away from bureaucratic decision making executed through a patrol officer's ability to arbitrarily select which laws would and would not be enforced on his beat, toward a process of administrative rulemaking which would, if implemented, bring back into policing's lexicon the concept of rule of law. Had Davis' argument caught on in the 1970s and 1980s, many of the front-page headlines from America's news media could have been avoided, and the police could have been an effective mechanism for local intervention to diagnose, assess and prevent criminal activity and disorder. As with Skolnick's work before him, however, Davis was virtually ignored by the professionals running America's police agencies. The rule of law continued to be held hostage by bureaucratic decision making and control and the myth of full enforcement of the criminal law.

Davis' tenets were quite remarkable – simple, expansive and yet elegant: the major problem with policing (as Skolnick correctly identified) was the unbridled discretion that allowed equally situated persons to be treated disparately. The myth of full enforcement of the law, in reality, was tacitly suborned by the reality of selective enforcement, and it was this process of allowing individual police officers to determine which laws would and would not be enforced on their individual beats which gave rise to the ability to ignore the rule of law. That many police administrators in America, to this day, deny that selective enforcement exists, that they still swear allegiance to the myth of full enforcement of the law, testifies to the failure of Davis' argument. Its failure, however, does nothing to reduce the *power* of the argument. While both of Davis' texts offer important insight into a potential process which would bring the rule of law back into the lexicon of American policing, the following paragraphs will focus on *Discretionary Justice,* as it appears to offer exceptional insight into many of the issues Department of Justice consent decrees are designed to address.

As an example, the Pittsburgh consent decree requires police management to carefully scrutinize 'discretionary arrests'[2] such as disorderly conduct and obstruction of justice. Davis notes that 'most arrests for disorderly conduct involve an abuse of power by the arresting officer, as most of the officers we have interviewed readily acknowledge' (Davis, 1969: 15). The abuse of power comes from the process which Skolnick would have referred to as justice without trial: an arrest for a misdemeanor, transport to jail, booking into the justice system, with the associated searches and yielding of property, posting of bond, and appearing for trial only to find the officer's failure to appear to deliver testimony results in a dismissal without judicial review. Under the bureaucratic model of policing, this is administrative efficiency; nowhere is the rule of law to be seen.

Davis' suggestion for bringing the rule of law back into the process of policing is administrative rulemaking, a process which, as he describes in *Police Discretion,* predates his discussion for police operations by nearly 30 years. The federal Administrative Procedures Act of 1946 sets the basic tenets for administrative rulemaking, and Davis recommends the following practice:

> The agency makes its studies [of the proposed actions and rules], perhaps consults some affected parties informally, and prepares proposed rules. The ... rules are published, along with invitations for written comments ... The agency simply receives whatever written materials interested parties care to submit, has its staff sift and summarize ... and makes revisions ... as it sees fit. Then it publishes the final rules, along with the 'concise general statement of their basis and purpose'. Anyone may apply to the agency for changes in the rules at any time (Davis, 1969: 106).

Davis notes that the 'procedure is highly efficient [and] democratic.

> Bureaucrats of American policing seized on the rules, but not the process, keeping the rules to themselves and those whom they wanted to control - patrolmen - but keeping those most affected by the rules - the public - in the dark. The concept of rule of law continued to be held hostage by the process of managerial professionalism.

---

2.      United States v. City of Pittsburgh, p. 8, 12-B.

Davis' concept is remarkably simple: if unbridled, police discretion opens numerous avenues for abuse – creative policing methods used to overcome the obstacles offered up by the Constitution. The answer, then, must lie in appropriately confining, structuring and checking discretion in policing, in a way that causes police officers to be cognizant of the power of discretion, and the need for allegiance to the rule of law. Davis' mechanisms for accomplishing this, too, are remarkably simple. As he notes: unnecessary discretionary power should be cut back, and necessary discretionary power should be properly confined, structured and checked (Davis, 1969: 55-67). Two simple steps would suffice: eliminate all discretion that is not essential; confine, structure and check all discretion that is essential. Structuring discretion consists of practices that provide plans, policy statements, open rules, open findings, and open precedents. Checking discretion includes both administrative and judicial review of discretionary actions. Confining discretion consists of the process of administrative rule making, with open standards, open processes, open comment on intent, and open discussion of decisions with those affected by the decisions (Davis, 1969: 55-67).

*Confining Discretion*

The purpose of confining discretion, Davis suggests, is to keep discretionary power within designated boundaries. He argues that confining discretion can be accomplished by 'narrowing the gap between what an administrator and his staff understand about the law they administer, and what outsiders to the agency have opportunity to understand. The goal in any good system should be to narrow that gap as much as feasible'(Davis, 1969: 60). The best means of accomplishing this, Davis suggests, is to use a process which only recently has made its way into effective police training – but has yet to make its way *through the police to the community:* the process of using scenarios to flesh out policy questions and place understandable boundaries around what an officer can and cannot do under specific circumstances. Davis suggests '(1) a hypothetical set of facts, (2) a statement of the problem raised by the facts, (3) an indication of the agency's answer to the problem, and where appropriate, (4) a statement of the agency's reasons for its position'. (Davis, 1969: 61). Davis argues that an 'agency which uses three tools for making law--adjudication, rules in the form of generalizations , and rules in the form of hypotheticals [scenarios] – is much better equipped to serve the public interest than an agency which limits itself to the first two of the three tools' (Davis, 1969: 61).

A careful reader notes immediately that *openness* is a critical component of Davis' argument. It is *the* element that makes unbridled police discretion difficult to exercise. With Davis' concept of 'openness', not only would the police decide *how and when* its officers should take enforcement action, they have given notice to the public of the intended process, and have provided an 'appeals' process for those who feel that discretionary enforcement has been unfairly applied. Contrast this with a note in *Police Discretion* which recounts a 1974 exchange at a conference with a police captain from San Antonio,

> an individual far ahead of most of his colleagues, [who] was advocating police rules, and he carried his audience [of Texas police administrators] with him in expressing embarrassment when rules that he drafted leaked out to the press while they were still tentative. To my question of why he had not systematically planned to give the rules to the press, he expressed astonishment – and he still had his audience with him: 'We don't want the press to publish our thinking until we've made up our minds. We'll publish our rules when we get them finished, but not before then' (Davis, 1975: 101).

Ten years later, when I completed publication of the San Antonio Police Department's (SAPD) first set of general orders, we 'published' them by placing copies in every branch library in the city – but only after we had them completed. There was no allowance for 'notice and comment, 'and there still is none in most police agencies. The bureaucrats have seized upon the control aspects of rule-making, and now, in most police agencies, 'general manuals' guide even the most mundane activities of patrol officers – and other officers as well – but most of those manuals are kept secret, often requiring Freedom of Information Act requests to obtain even parts of them. Notice and comment, hypotheticals and scenarios, and public input are virtually non-existent. Again, public release of information is a cornerstone of the consent decrees developed by the US Department of Justice, requiring local agencies to release to those they police data regarding their methods of policing.[3]

---

3.  United States of America v. State of New Jersey, Division of State Police *of the Department of Law and Public Safety*, in the Federal District Court for New Jersey, Civil Number 99-5970(MLC), p. 4.

*Structuring Discretion*

Returning to Davis, his argument regarding structuring discretion is similarly simple: structuring discretion requires the administrator to 'regularize it, organize it, produce order in it, so that ... decisions affecting individual practices will achieve a higher quality of justice' (Davis, 1969: 97). The purpose of structuring discretion is to control the manner of the exercise of discretionary power within boundaries. Davis suggests that this can be accomplished through 'seven instruments' that are 'most useful in the structuring of discretionary power: open plans, open policy statements, open rules, open findings, open reasons, open precedents, and fair informal procedures' (Davis, 1969: 98). Davis identifies openness as the 'natural enemy of arbitrariness, and a natural ally in the fight against injustice' (*ibid.*).

Perhaps the best example of structured discretion at work, in direct juxtaposition to unbridled discretion in policing, is the Tampa Police Department in the late 1980s and early 1990s. Facing a rising crime rate and its handmaiden, increasing drug use, the TPD formed a series of high-impact anti-crime squads known as 'QUAD-Squads'. These squads were so-named, officially, because they operated within a chosen quadrant of the city, focusing on a 'zero-tolerance' policy of enforcement of any and all statutes and ordinances. Those who knew the culture of policing could not overlook the reference to the 'street name' for Quaaludes: Quads. Nevertheless, these 'QUAD-Squads deployed across the city, often leaving more than just arrests in their wake. Frequently, the communities receiving this largess of increased police attention and intolerance revolted, throwing rocks, bottles, epithets, and in some cases even burning police vehicles.

After a series of community confrontations, and a management study by the Police Foundation, directed by this author, the public safety director for the city changed markedly the method in which the TPD was managed. In an open session with community residents, the department introduced the findings of the Police Foundation management study, and created *citizen based task forces* to assess and implement Foundation recommendations on training, supervision, policy (including use of force policies), discipline, and other processes of the department. The QUAD-squad methodology was modified, including a community planning component that identified for the police community concerns: drug hot spots, crime hot spots, specific offenders, etc. Following this openness, in the face of what had been a highly closed and discretionary system, implementation of QUAD-squad sweeps were followed by community parades, celebrating the 'taking back' of 'our streets', with open praise for the police attention that had been focused on issues and problems identified by the community. Other elements of openness in Tampa resulted in a citizens' task force rewriting key components of the department's deadly force policy, as well as providing input into proposed policies in other areas.

Davis' 'openness' argument – although not specifically tested by the City of Tampa – is buttressed by the results in that city: it proved to be the natural enemy of arbitrariness and a natural ally in the fight against injustice. Davis provides a set of excellent processes by which a police can implement 'rule of law' policing that values equally the constitutional and statutory law.

*Open plans* serve to put 'on notice' the community affected by a planned enforcement action, notifying them that perceived issues are to be addressed, and inviting comment on the proposed action, generating inclusiveness and 'ownership'.

*Open policy statements* 'close the gap between what the agency and its staff know about the agency's law and policy and what an outsider can know *(ibid.* p. 104). Generally consisting of an announcement of a plan of action in a given area, the process of openness structures discretion by placing those affected by the plan on notice concerning what is and is not acceptable behavior on the part of the officers implementing the plan. Open policy includes a series of reasoned opinions, supporting the proposed policies.

*Open precedents* generate the one thing perhaps most needed in a policing function equally committed to the rule of law and law enforcement: consistency. Consistency, Davis argues, 'is clearly desirable for two main reasons: Equality is a major ingredient of justice, and striving for consistency reduces arbitrariness' *(ibid.* p. 107). Consistency in treatment at the hands of the police, and that *all citizens* are treated fairly *vis-à-vis* the rule of law is an overarching goal that, by the interpretation of a careful read, can be seen as one of the goals of the Department of Justice's consent decrees.

*Fair informal procedures* generate understanding of policy, rule and expectations, and, according to Davis, are 'valuable weapons in the fight against arbitrary exercise of discretion' *(ibid.* p. 111). He adds, 'in coming decades, I think justice will gain if less attention is given to the overworked subjects of judicial review and formal hearings, and if more time and energy are devoted to cutting paths into the wilderness of non-hearing procedures'.

In my experience, after having reviewed, in detail, internal affairs files for more than a dozen American police agencies, the vast majority of citizens' complaints against police officers would be addressed through Davis' 'openness' philosophy. Rudeness, attitude, and other 'conduct' issues related to the way police officers treat individuals under their care and protection account for the majority of citizens' complaints. Another large block of complaints are found to be 'exonerated', which in police parlance means that the officer behaved according to policy (but just as importantly, that the behavior, which was within police policy, generated strong discontent among a member of the department's constituency).

A discussion of the 'average' citizen's complaint and how Davis' philosophy of openness would affect the policing process may be in order. The paragraphs below should be instructive of the potential for openness to affect police-citizen interaction and to reinvigorate the concept of rule of law in American policing.

Robert Andersen, a resident of the inner city of a major metropolitan area in the US, sits on his front porch on a particularly warm summer evening in August, drinking a few beers, and trying to 'beat the heat' by 'dissin'' with some of his friends – playing one-up in the insult department. Things got a little loud. Mr Andersen and his friends are African-American. Two police officers – who undoubtedly are statistically white, since nearly 75 per cent of the department's patrol officers are – accost Mr Andersen on his front porch, noting the beer and the apparent tender age of several of Mr Andersen's friends, whom, the officers allege, appear to be under-age.

Mr Andersen – and his friends – take umbrage at the intervention into a seemingly innocuous Friday evening indulgence. Words are exchanged; a small crowd gathers, and Mr Andersen goes to jail for 'disorderly conduct'. The entire incident takes less than 10 minutes. In the mind's eye of the community – four of Mr Andersen's friends and five or six members of the crowd, Mr Andersen was just rousted by the cops for being black.

Monday morning, immediately before work – he works as a computer programmer for an inner-city youth services agency – Mr Andersen files a complaint with the police department's internal affairs unit, alleging racial intolerance.

*Under the Typical Police Bureaucratic Management System*: A formal investigation is conducted into the incident. The investigation is completed in six months, four months after Mr Andersen, who can ill-afford to miss too much work, pleads guilty to disorderly conduct and pays a small fine. Based on his guilty plea, and a careful review of the officers' actions (and the reasons for those actions) Internal Affairs (IA) Department 'exonerates' the two officers – finding that they behaved within policy, and noting that Mr Andersen plead guilty to disorderly conduct. Although the department has articulated an 'arrest as a last resort'[4] policy, the arrest is technically legal, and the officers insist it had to be done to avoid 'a situation'. The IA investigator misses the fact that neither officer appeared at the scheduled trial of Mr Andersen for the disorderly conduct charges. As best as Mr Andersen can tell, 'exonerated' means that racial intolerance is OK by the PD.

*Under an Open Processes Police Management System*: The police department, in response to budgetary constraints and community concerns has articulated an 'arrest as last resort' policy, and the policy was 'published' in the local paper, as well as, obviously, being published internally in the department and included in the annual in-service training. Mr Andersen is aware of the policy, since his youth-services agency had a hand in developing it with the PD. He's also aware of the scenarios that the department issued with the policy. One of them could have been written about his situation.

Internal affairs is also aware of the 'arrest as a last resort' policy, and, as part of the investigator's annual in-service training, they reviewed and 'worked through' the scenarios that the department provided to them – and to the public – with the new policy. One of them could have been written about Mr Andersen's situation. Further, the IA investigators are aware that several precinct captains have retrained and/or disciplined officers for similar actions, because these incidents were 'written up' as part of the department's 'open precedents' process, in which officers' actions are analyzed and critiqued by management (non-attributionally, of course), and 'open findings' are posted on the department's public web site and its internal training and policy web site.

The IA investigation 'sustains' one count of violating the 'arrest as last resort' policy against each officer, and indicates to Mr Andersen, both in writing and by a follow-up telephone call, that, although they could not sustain his allegation of racial intolerance, the officers were both counseled and retrained in the 'arrest as last resort' policy, as well as in verbal de-escalation, the 'rule of law', and cultural diversity. Both officers were also disciplined for failure to appear at his trial. They also informed Mr Andersen that, since the compliant was sustained, it would be kept in the officers' files until they retired or resigned from the police department.

---

4.  Numerous American police agencies have articulated such policies. The San Antonio Police Department, in Texas, has had such a policy for more than five years, even though it has not been officially announced to the public.

The officers' sergeant also called Mr Andersen and explained to him that the neighbourhood council that advises the police department on public safety issues in his neighbourhood had requested extra patrols in the immediate vicinity of Mr Andersen's block for 'loud and obnoxious parties and under-aged drinking', and that the two officers who arrested him had been assigned to that neighbourhood council complaint. He explained that, as a result of Mr Andersen's complaint to IA, he (the sergeant) had met with both officers and explained alternative ways they might have responded to the incident. He explained that both officers had been assigned to the training academy for one day for refresher training in verbal de-escalation, cultural diversity, the 'rule of law', and the 'arrest as last resort' policy. He also noted that each officer was disciplined for failure to appear at his trial.

In addition, he referred Mr Andersen to the department's public web-site, where he could review the synopsis of his encounter with the police, along with a 'best practice' statement from the chief of police concerning how the incident should have been handled. A week later, Mr Andersen received a 'customer satisfaction' survey from the police department, asking him to rate the department's overall performance. The cover letter was signed by the chief of police.

In the second example, the department used open policies (everyone knew or could have known about the 'arrest as last resort' policy), open precedents (training scenarios had been developed about situations similar to the one in question), and open informal proceedings (a letter and a telephone call from IA, a telephone call from the sergeant, a write-up on the web-site, and a letter from the chief of police). Even though Mr Andersen may still be angry about his arrest, he certainly can't say the department did nothing about it. The department's responses, all documented in the agency's early warning system, place them in a much stronger position to combat civil suits for 'pattern and practice' allegations, and everyone, the officers, their peers, and the community, learned something from the incident. Even though Mr Andersen's guilty plea stands, the odds of another similar incident are greatly reduced. Openness has stood the test against unbridled discretion and arbitrariness.

Davis' work, combined with a liberalized civil litigation process, offered a small opportunity to effect change in American policing. Visionaries, like G. Patrick Gallagher (1992) and others, including me, began arguing that change must occur to blunt the attack of the plaintiff's bar. The role of 'outsider' was blunted somewhat by the field's need to resolve the issues of civil litigation generated by (perceived) improper police behavior.

As my career shifted yet again, this time from college professor to consultant, other works became important, chief among them section 1984 of the US Code, which all of us involved in American policing found, gave plaintiff's attorney's ample access to redress for perceived police impropriety. That redress came in the form of, at times, large jury awards for damages suffered due to poor police tactics, lax supervision, bad or non-existent policy, ineffective discipline, or poor leadership.

The threat of large civil awards opened a small level of interest in 'change'. Under the theory that it was better to make change of one's own volition than to have it imposed, organizations committed to change in American policing found their *entre* enhanced. The Police Foundation, a non-profit organization created by the Ford Foundation with the mission to 'improve American policing' found its initiatives, such as the establishment of the Police Executive Institute, directed by G. Patrick Gallagher, more widely accepted by American police leadership. Seats at offerings of the prestigious Southern Police Institute (the equivalent to an American police staff college) became highly sought after by American police managers. I spent time at both institutions in the mid-to-late 1980s, as deputy director of the Police Foundation and as director of the Southern Police Institute. As a part of the natural understanding of the need to somehow control police discretion and as a response to the burgeoning levels of civil litigation, the field had come to rely on 'professionalism' as its mantra. This was almost immediately translated to 'bureaucratic management', which focused on policy, control, discipline, and effectiveness. We all knew something was missing, but many of us were unsure what that missing element was. The uneasy feeling that there was work yet to be done soon became more than a feeling.

**Where Has Bureaucratic Management Taken Us?**

Several texts paint a clear picture of where 35 years of bureaucratic police management – police managerial professionalism – has been allowed to take us, and two others (the consent decrees in Pittsburgh and New Jersey) show us where we need to go. What is missing is a treatment of how to get there, which is the topic for the last section of this chapter.

The Police Executive Research Forum, a national organization with an excellent reputation, both among police managers and organizations representing minorities in the U.S., has published three texts that paint a clear picture of where we've come with managerial professionalism: William Geller and Michael Scott's *Deadly Force: What We Know* (1992), and Geoffrey Alpert and Roger Dunham's *Police Use of Deadly Force* (1995) and *The Force Factor* (1997).

These texts allow us to see where efficiency-focused police administrative bureaucracies have taken us. Deadly force analyses, it could be argued, paint the 'best picture' of police discretion, since these actions tend to be the most closely scrutinized and the least discretion-prone incidents in American policing.

Alpert and Dunham's 1997 work, *The Force Factor*, was a quantitative analysis of the levels of force used by officers from three police agencies in the US. The data analyzed were collected between 1993 and 1995 in Dade County, Florida, and in 1993 in Springfield and Eugene Oregon. The analysis of police application of force was conducted through the calculation of a 'force factor', a mathematical 'balance' of the level of force used by the police *subtracted from* the resistance level offered by the suspect. All data collected were 'self-report' data completed by police officers during the normal course of the business of delivery of policing services. Two findings of *The Force Factor* are critical to our discussion of police discretion:

- First, race and ethnicity appear to be factors in the police use of force, with 'Black suspects receiv[ing] the most force relative to the level of resistance.' (Dunham and Alpert, 1997: 6) when compared to other races and ethnicities, in the Metro-Dade data[5].
- Second, training appears to be an effective method of modifying police application of force, since the officers appear to apply a level of force commensurate with training. Metro-Dade officers' use of force data are 'skewed slightly to the negative side' (*ibid.* 18), reflecting the department's use of force policy and training, which calls for the delivery of less force than that with which the officer is confronted. The Oregon officers' use of force data are 'skewed slightly to the positive side' (*ibid.*), reflecting their departments' use of force policy and training, which calls for the delivery of 'one level' more force than that with which the officers are confronted.

---

5.    The analysis of the Oregon data did not present information concerning race or ethnicity of the offender.

Alpert and Dunham's analysis of deadly force data in Dade County, Florida, *Police Use of Deadly Force,* is less instructive, but still of some utility in assessing the rationale behind the Justice Department consent decrees. While the *Deadly Force* analysis did not 'control' for the racial and ethnic composition of the Metro-Dade Police Department, or for the population it served, one analysis provided is remarkably instructive. In conducting an analysis of the racial/ethnic characteristics of the offenders and the officers, by type of behaviour exhibited by the offender, in the 1988-93 time period, a startling result is reported: Anglo and Hispanic officers, when confronted with black suspects used deadly force much more frequently than any other combination of racial/ethnic characteristics (Dunham and Alpert, 1995: 20).

Differentials are as high as four-to-one, in some cases, of black suspect/anglo officer interactions *(ibid.)*[6] Such gross comparisons are, of course, dangerous. The data do not control for criminal behavior patterns, police deployment practices, crime rates in the areas in which deadly force is used, etc.

Better data are available in Geller and Scott's *Deadly Force* (1992). As the data from which one is able to assess police process improve, conclusions become more sound. Geller and Scott conduct a meta-analysis of prior research, and add original research informing the issue of police use of deadly force in America. Their data, quite literally, are drawn from virtually every police agency in America which files Uniform Crime Report information with the FBI, and, as well, from specific studies of America's major police agencies: New York; Los Angeles; Chicago; Dallas; Kansas City; Philadelphia; Metro-Dade, Florida; Santa Ana, California; Birmingham, Alabama; St. Louis, Missouri, and others.

The data are informative, if one knows where (and how) to look. While Geller and Scott acknowledge the difficulty of controlling police use of deadly force data for obvious intervening variables such as demographics, deployment practices, criminogenic tendencies, willingness to resort to violence and other issues, they do produce data that can inform the debate regarding the 'rule of law' and race and ethnicity in American policing.

In virtually every comparative analysis but two, blacks and minorities experience police deadly force at a disproportionate rate when compared to

---

6      The number of interactions reported for black officers was so small as to make analysis impractical.

whites. In comparative studies analyzed by Geller and Scott, blacks are reported as shot by police at a rate often approaching, and at times exceeding, twice their distribution in the population (Geller and Scott, 1992:149-150). Whites, on the other hand, consistently are shot at by police at a rate well *less than* half their distribution in the population (*ibid.*). Regardless of which of the 24 cities was studied, these findings held. Geller and Scott (1992) point out that researchers, using population figures to standardize the number of civilians shot or shot *at* by police in different jurisdictions (that is, creating rates showing the number of shootings per 100,000 population) have found that:

- Blacks in Chicago were 3.8 times more likely than whites to be shot by the police during the 1970s ... and ... 6.2 times more likely in 1991;
- Blacks were six times more likely than whites to be shot by NYPD officers during the 1970s;
- Blacks were 4.5 times more likely than whites to be shot by police during the 1970s and 1980s in Dallas;
- Blacks in St. Louis were 7.7 times more likely than whites to be shot *at* by Metropolitan Police Department officers during 1987-91...;
- Blacks in Memphis were 5.1 times more likely than whites to be shot fatally by police during 1969-74, 2.6 times more likely during 1980-84, and 1.6 times more likely over the period 1985-89; and,
- Considering only property crime suspects, blacks in Memphis were 9.4 times more likely than whites to be shot at by police during ... 1969-74, 13 times more likely during the period 1980-84, and were the only property crime suspects shot at (in incidents ruled unjustifiable) during the period 1985-89 (ibid. 147-149).[7]

Acknowledging that these shooting rates do not control for a large number of intervening variables, Geller and Scott argue that shooting rates should also be calculated by comparing 'such rates as the number of blacks and whites shot per 100,000 residing in the jurisdiction, per 1,000 arrested,

---

7.     In 1984, police use of deadly force to apprehend property crime suspects was expressly prohibited by the US Supreme Court in *Garner v Tennessee* [471, US1 (1985)], a case involving the use of deadly force by Memphis Police Department to effect the arrest of a black juvenile property-crime suspect.

per 10,000 living below the poverty line, and so on' (Geller and Scott, 1992: 148).

The true comparative measure of the viability of the differences in apparent 'shooting rates', however can be calculated by comparing the overall disparities, for example those noted above by Geller and Scott, with the non-discretionary shootings by police at or of blacks and whites. Ideally, when assessing the impact of any police action on various racial or ethnic groups, the comparison would be of police action in discretionary activities *v.* non-discretionary activities. For example, comparing arrests rates for discretionary arrest rates of disorderly conduct, assault on a police officer, resisting arrest, and obstruction of justice for blacks and whites versus non-discretionary arrest rates for offenses such as those with an identifiable complainant: theft, simple assault, and other low-end misdemeanors for blacks versus whites is the most meaningful way to control for intervening variables. The hypothesis behind these discretionary v. non-discretionary arrest comparisons is that the 'control' factor is police discretion, and that officers who are making race- or ethnicity-based decisions will focus more on discretionary areas of law enforcement than on non-discretionary areas.

A comparison of the Geller and Scott data using a discretionary/ non-discretionary filter yields some interesting results. In virtually every overall category analyzed by Geller and Scott, blacks lead whites in the rate at which they are victims of police shootings. When considering only distribution in the population, blacks were the victims of police shootings at rates (on average) nearly eight times higher than whites.[8] When controlling for 'precipitating incident', for example the suspect's use of a firearm, use of other dangerous weapon, or threat to use a dangerous weapon or firearm, blacks were nearly four times as likely to be shot by Chicago police (1974-1978) than whites (Geller and Scott, 1992: 148). Numbers for the same type of 'precipitating incident' analysis in Los Angeles City for the same years were similar: blacks were the victim of police shootings at a rate 2.4 times that for whites. These numbers are roughly comparable with other Geller and Scott shooting rate findings.

When one looks as less discretionary actions of police officers, e.g., shootings which *clearly fit within the acceptable criteria for use of deadly force*, however, the numbers vary dramatically from those analyses which

---

8. Based on the author's analysis of Geller and Scott (1992) data.

include all shootings, both discretionary and non-discretionary. Using unpublished FBI supplemental homicide reports, Geller and Scott identify the nationwide rates at which blacks, whites and Hispanics are killed by police during felony arrest situations in which the suspect attacked a police officer, attacked a civilian, fled, was killed during the commission of a crime, or forcibly resisted arrest. These are clearly incidents in which the police officer tends to have less discretion concerning whether or not to shoot: imminent peril is almost certain in these situations.

Analyzing these less-discretionary shooting data, *blacks are the fatal victims of police shootings less frequently than whites*, by a factor of 1.2, i.e., *whites* are shot and killed by police in less-discretionary situations 1.2 times more often than blacks (Geller and Scott, 1992: 148).

The most frequent reasons police took the life of a white in 1989 was that the white felony suspect attacked the police officer. The most frequent reason a police officer took the life of a black in 1989 was that the black felony suspect was engaged in the commission of a crime  While these analyses do not control for shooting rates, contact rates, demographics, and a host of other possible intervening variables, by comparing the discretionary shooting rates with the less- or non-discretionary shooting rates, one can develop an understanding for the impact of discretionary decisions on the part of the police to shoot or not to shoot under specific circumstances. In situations in which the discretionary decision is available, blacks are shot by the police at rates as much as 13 times higher than the rate at which whites are shot by police. In situations in which discretion is limited, the rate at which police kill blacks is more in line with their distribution in the population, and, in fact, *whites* are killed by the police in less-discretionary situations at a rate 1.2 times higher than blacks[9].

These numbers are clearly disheartening. After nearly five decades of 'reform-minded' policing, it is clear to those looking carefully at American policing that police discretion was simply not equally exercised by all officers at all times. More, apparently needed to be done, but the missing link had yet to be identified.

It became clear to me, and to others on-the-outside looking-in at policing, that what is missing from American policing is a clearly articulated set of values which recognizes the duty to enforce the law, but also recognizes

---

9.      It is important to note that the less-discretionary felony-based shooting statistics reflect citizens *killed* by police, rather than citizens shot by police.

clearly and unequivocally the need to infuse the law enforcement process with an allegiance – in terms of clearly articulated values – to the rule of law. My recent discussions with chiefs of police concerned about issues of racial profiling almost always end in surprise, when, after the chief discusses honesty, truthfulness, ethics, and a host of other 'values' issues, I reply that 'It sounds as if you want to bring your department's "pattern and practice" (a term of art for how and where we police in America) into conformance with the *letter and spirit of the Constitution*'. The reply is almost invariably: 'Exactly! The problem is, how do we do that'.

It occurs to me that we have two choices. We can try to legislate the behavior we want, by recreating and reinvigorating our bureaucratic approach to policing: more policy, more rules, more supervision, more discipline. Or, we can focus on the values that underlie the policing process, the *sin qua non* that makes policing what it is in America: the need to control disorder and crime, and the demand – becoming more clear by the year – that we do so in conformance not just to the letter of the Constitution, but to its spirit as well. Norm Stamper's 1992 work on effective police leadership gives us strong insight into what this process might look like.

## Integrating the Rule of Law Paradigm into American Policing

Bennis' criticisms of managerial bureaucracy in 1965 have proven meaningful for American policing. Over that past 50 years, the professional bureaucratic model of policing has succeeded in implementing an efficiency-based mode of policing nearly devoid of true leadership on the issue of the relationship between policing and the rule of law. As Norm Stamper notes in *Removing Managerial Barriers to Effective Police Leadership*' (Stamper, 1992), in an effort to prevent police abuses, many chief executives exhibit what might be called a 'control' ideology, their principal purpose being the avoidance of poor performance and officer misconduct rather than a pursuit of excellent performance and ethical conduct' (Stamper, 1992: 29). His findings are based on an intensive study of the self-reported behavior of 52 of America's 'big-city' police chiefs.

Thirty-five years of allegiance to the managerial bureaucracy paradigm will be exceedingly difficult to change, if Stamper is correct, and it appears likely that he is. As he notes, 'most of [the] variables that affect [police] behavior are rooted in political, structural, and cultural *systems* of enormous complexity. Police leaders inclined toward significant reform face formidable challenges, first in understanding their complicated world, and second, in changing it' (*ibid., 77)*.

America's big-city police chiefs, according to Stamper, *profess* a commitment to:

> sharing a vision of the future, encouraging and practicing openness and honesty, developing and challenging employees, creating an atmosphere of teamwork and open communication, helping employees get the job done, and recognizing excellence in performance. They also profess a commitment to encouraging questioning and criticism of agency policies, working closely with the communities they serve (which includes a willingness to invite citizen input on policy matters), adopting an intuitive and creative approach to their work, and taking a firm stand against discriminatory practices (ibid. vii).

Yet, the very people who would be required to *implement* those commitments, the chiefs' immediate assistants, observe markedly different *behavior* on the part of the chiefs than that committed to verbally by the chiefs. The big-city chiefs' assistants noted that 'the behavior of chiefs is not consistent with the values they expressed [on Stamper's survey]. This is particularly true on leadership items ... [T]here is still ... a tendency for the chiefs to be much more involved in the technical and procedural aspects [than in the leadership aspects]'(*ibid,* viii*)*. Stamper's final analysis suggests that 'executive leadership has been "structured" out of police administration'(*ibid.* x*)*, just as Skolnick (and Bennis) would have predicted. 'At a time when police executive leadership has never been more demanding – or more important – comes evidence that many of Americas police chiefs are simply not practicing what they preach' (*ibid.*).

What the leaders of America's police agencies have failed to do is to openly and appropriately integrate the rule of law with the rule of efficiency. More importantly, this dichotomy, if anything, has grown worse in recent years with the long-anticipated penetration of information technology into the policing process. Based on this author's personal observations in intensive on-site interaction with scores of police agencies, police administrators have used IT to continue to 'be much more involved in the technical and procedural aspects of the managerial process'(*ibid.,* vii) by focusing on 'efficiency' rather than leadership which 'takes a firm stand against discriminatory practices', by insisting upon a reintegration of the rule of law into American policing practices.

Enter the  US Department of Justice, Civil Rights Division with the most significant pieces of police 'literature' in the 20th century, laying out, as it were, a clear, articulate and demanding statement concerning acceptable methods of police supervision, management and operations in the US in the 21st century. The consent decree is a mechanism which requires selected department's to develop 'good management practices' in an attempt to instill an acceptance of the rule of law into American policing--an acceptance that has been missing in most cases. The consent decree, as a process, however, goes far beyond its impact on a few police agencies. While extant decrees affect the Pittsburgh Bureau of Police, the Steubenville, Ohio Police Department, and the New Jersey State Police, the impact of the decree process will be felt throughout American policing for decades to come. This is true because the consent decrees stipulate standards to which, willingly or not, American police agencies will be held by America's civil courts.

A central component of civil litigation for police negligence in the 1990s, and certainly in the first portion of the 21st century, is a contention that the police failed to follow 'established standards and practices'. In the process of implementing consent decrees related to re-instituting the rule of law in American policing, the US Department of Justice has gone far beyond a simple focus on Pittsburgh, Steubenville, New Jersey, or even the score of other agencies on which it is reportedly focused in 1999-2000. A careful reading of the decrees in Pittsburgh, Steubenville, and New Jersey yields an understanding of the standards to which American policing will be held in the early years of the 21st century.

America's police managers have been placed on undeniable notice by the actions of the US Department of Justice: they will be held accountable for developing systems which reintegrate the rule of law into the policing process. Civil litigation in America has a new set of standards for police management and supervision, which will now be held accountable for developing, implementing and effectively using management and supervisory systems to identify and ameliorate violations of the rule of law in the American system of policing. A careful read of existing consent decrees make it clear that police executives, managers and supervisors will now be held accountable to the standard and practice of developing systems to carefully, thoroughly and effectively review the actions of operational officers for impermissible intrusions into the areas of constitutionally protected rights in the effort to control crime and disorder. Using the extant police consent decrees as a guide, it is reasonable to predict that these systems will include:

- Systems that effectively train operational (line) police officers in acceptable and impermissible intrusions into the areas of constitutionally protected rights in the effort to control crime and disorder, and provide them with the mechanisms that allow them to meet the demands placed on police while enforcing the rule of law within that process;
- Systems that effectively train police executives, managers and supervisors in the process of identifying, analyzing and responding to impermissible intrusions into the areas of constitutionally protected rights in the effort to control crime and disorder;
- Personnel performance systems that support and require police managers' routine monitoring for and responding to impermissible intrusions into the areas of constitutionally protected rights in the effort to control crime and disorder;
- Internal investigations systems that use established standards of proof, effective methods of investigation, and accepted methods of documentation and reporting of the results of investigations into citizens' complaints;
- Specific and effective recruit and in-service training in ethics in policing, alternatives to use of force, use of deadly force, constitutional law, effective supervision and effective management;
- Formal positive discipline systems which use counseling and retraining as effective tools to control impermissible intrusions into the areas of constitutionally protected rights in the effort to control crime and disorder; and,
- Formal discipline systems that use reprimand, suspension and termination to control impermissible intrusions into the areas of constitutionally protected rights in the effort to control crime and disorder.

The consent decree process assumes that modern American police agencies will implement *management processes* designed to blunt Skolnick's prediction that bureaucratic policing systems will not be effective in incorporating the rule of law into the policing process. The process assumes that expanded information technology will address Bennis' contention that bureaucracies have hopelessly outdated systems of control and authority. The consent decree process, in effect, demands a managerial and supervisory approach to a long-standing failure of leadership in American policing.

Despite American police executives' declaration that their roles include 'openness, honesty ... encouraging questioning and criticism of agency policies, working closely with the communities they serve (which includes a willingness to invite citizen input on policy matters) ... and taking a firm stand against discriminatory practices' (Stamper, 1992: 60), with few exceptions, one cannot see those roles operationalized by the leadership of American policing. As Stamper notes, the 'fundamental paradigm shift' from management of America's police agencies to *leadership* of America's police agencies has not been made. Nor has the fundamental paradigm shift been made of practicing a strategy of policing which fully integrates the rule of law into the process of controlling crime and disorder. It is this failure that has led to the Justice Department's *management approach* to integrating the rule of law into policing.

The Justice Department's approach will come to be enforced not only by consent decree on a few police agencies, but by civil litigation holding all American police agencies accountable for the *standard* of integrating rule of law into policing. Police executives are confronted with a choice. They can:

1. Exhibit the type of leadership necessary to stand against impermissible intrusions into the areas of constitutionally protected rights in the effort to control crime and disorder by truly refusing to tolerate it, and by taking reasonable and visionary steps to quash it wherever it presents itself; or they can

2. Invest in expensive managerial and technical systems to monitor for it, and civil processes can ensure that it is appropriately counseled, trained, and disciplined out of existence.

In the spirit of Stamper's paradigm-shifting executives, both approaches are necessary: effective leadership to make it known that the vision of the agency pays allegiance to the rule of law within a framework of effective law enforcement, *and* effective management to put into place managerial and supervisory systems to ensure that the vision is carried out.

This effective management, however, must focus on different criteria than the bureaucratic management that has brought us to this point in American policing. Where bureaucratic management focused on policy, control, discipline, and effectiveness, *values management* must focus on other issues.

As Skolnick reminded us:

> If the police are ever to develop a conception of *legal* as opposed to *managerial* professionalism, they will do so only if the surrounding community demands compliance with the rule of law by rewarding police for such compliance, instead of looking to the police as an institution solely responsible for

controlling criminality. In practice, however, the reverse has been true. The police function in a milieu tending to support, normatively and substantively, the idea of administrative efficiency that has become the hallmark of police professionalism. Legality, as expressed by both the criminal courts community with which the police have direct contact, and the political community responsible for the working conditions and prerogatives of police, is a weak ideal (Skolnick, 1967: 236).

These words were written 34 years ago, yet the institution of American policing has not yet found a way to infuse itself with legal professionalism. In fact, attempts to do so are often met with derision within the field. Many would argue – and have argued – that we do not need policies against racial profiling and other discretionary abuses by police, since such things are already covered in the law enforcement code of ethics!

What is required is strong values management in American policing. Creation of a values management system will be the core of the next 35 years of development in American policing, as pressure is applied to bring policing's pattern and practice into conformance with both the letter and the spirit of the Constitution. The consent decrees in Pittsburgh, Steubenville, and New Jersey are managerial approaches to revising the existing bureaucratic professionalism in order to *require* conformance with the letter of the Constitution. The transformational step, one requiring bold vision, exceptional leadership, courage and commitment, is to transform bureaucratic professionalism, to leave behind the focus on control and discipline based on policy, procedure, rule and regulation, and to pick up the mantel of values-based professionalism.

During the late 1980s and early 1990s, in training police managers, as I would broach the topic of values-based decision making in policing, the idea appeared so radical that it was nearly universally discounted by my audiences. How can we – given existing administrative systems – promote people for fostering attainment of something so vague as a 'value'? Conversely, how could we ever discipline someone – and have it hold up in arbitration – for an action that ran counter to our 'values'? The answer is at once simple and complex:  first, we must ensure that our values are in alignment with our constituencies' values (the values of the Constitution, the communities we serve, the political community, and the courts), and second, we must ensure that these values infuse our agencies at every level, that they control our decision making regarding selection, training, policy development, discipline, management and leadership.

After 50 years, O.W. Wilson's model of policing, the bureaucratic professionalism model (Wilson, 1950), has outlived much of its utility. The 'community policing' model, given much attention since the late '80s in America, can be viewed in the long-term as nothing more than a transitional phase in the history of policing, a transitional phase that stood between bureaucratic professionalism and values-based policing. After observing American policing over four decades, we know this change will not be easy, nor will it be rapid. The catalysts, however, are 'in the mix'. Public demand for police accountability will not be changed by a change in the American White House. While the interpretation of the Constitution may change with the appointment of new US Supreme Court justices, the spirit of the Constitution will be with us for decades to come. Access to civil penalties will continue to militate for change in policing. Demand for change will continue to be made by those who perceive a style of policing focused so adamantly on crime control, with too little allegiance to the spirit of the Constitution. More of the same will not suffice. A shift to a new paradigm, the paradigm of values-based professionalism in policing will make these factors manageable.

## References

Adams, T.F. (1963). Field Interrogation, *Police*, March-April, 1963, 21-38.

Alpert, G., and Dunham, R. (1997).*The Force Factor: Measuring Police Use of Force Relative to Suspect Resistance.* Washington DC: Police Executive Research Forum.

Alpert, G. and Dunham, R. (1995). *Police Use of Deadly Force: A Statistical Analysis of the Metro-Dade Police Department.* Washington, D.C.: Police Executive Research Forum.

Baldwin, J. (1962). *Nobody Knows My Name* .New York: Dell Publishing Company.

Bennis, W. (1965). Beyond Bureaucracy, *Trans-action*, 2 (July-August), 30-39.

Bittner, E. (1970).*The Functions of Police in Modern Society.* Chevy Chase, Maryland: National Institute of Mental Health.

Davis, K. (1969). *Discretionary Justice: A Preliminary Inquiry.* Urbana: University of Illinois Press.

Davis, K. (1975). *Police Discretion.* St. Paul, Minnesota: West Publishing Co.

Fyfe, J. (1981). Race and Extreme Police-Citizen Violence. In R.L. McNeeley and Carl E Pope (eds), *Race, Crime and Criminal Justice.* Beverly Hills: Sage.

Gallagher, G.P. (1992). *Risk Management Behind the Blue Curtain: A Primer on Law Enforcement Liability.* Arlington, Virginia: Public Risk Management Association.

Geller, W. and Karales, K. (1981). *Split-Second Decisions: Shootings of and by Chicago Police.* Chicago: Chicago Law Enforcement Study Group.

Geller, W. and Karales, K. (1981). Shootings of and by Chicago Police: Uncommon Crises. *Journal of Criminal Law and Criminology,* 72 (4): 1813-1866.

Geller, W. and Scott, M. (1992). *Deadly Force: What We Know.* Washington, D.C.: Police Executive Research Forum.

Skolnik, J. (1967). *Justice Without Trial: Law Enforcement in a Democratic Society.* New York: John Wiley.

Sparger, J., and Geocapassi, G. (1992). Memphis Revisited: A Re-examination of Police Shootings After the Garner Decision. Excerpted in *Crime Control Digest,* 1, 7-8.

Spitzer, E. (1999). *The New York City Police Department's 'Stop and Frisk' Practices: A Report to the People of the State of New York from the Office of the Attorney General.* New York: Office of the Attorney General.

Stamper, N.H. (1992). *Removing Managerial Barriers to Effective Police Leadership: A Study of Executive Leadership and Executive Management in Big -City Police Departments.* Washington DC: Police Executive Research Forum.

*United States of America v. The City of Pittsburgh,* Pittsburgh Bureau of Police and Department of Public Safety, Federal District Court for the Western District of Pennsylvania, Civil Number 97-0354,1997.

Van Maanen, J. (1978). The Asshole. In P.K. Manning and John Van Maanen (eds), *Policing: A View from the Street.* Santa Monica: Goodyear.

Wilson, O.W., (1950). *Police Administration.* New York: McGraw-Hill.

# PART 3

# THE POLICE ROLE

# 6. Reinventing Governance: The Case of Private Policing

LES JOHNSTON

## Introduction

*The Dilemmas of Selection*

Commencing this chapter, one is reminded of the long-running British radio programme, *Desert Island Discs*. In the programme, a shipwrecked 'castaway' is asked to choose the eight gramophone records (sic) which he or she would take to a hypothetical desert island. The island is equipped only with a record player, a bible and a copy of the collected works of Shakespeare, though guests are also permitted to select a further book and a single (inanimate) luxury item to help them through their ordeal. Castaways are invariably asked by the presenter to outline the principles behind their record selection. Some invoke nostalgia (e.g. '"The Birdie Song", reminds me of my holiday in Ibitha'). Others rely on musical form, some opting for the classical route (Vivaldi's *Four Seasons*), others for the popular one (Frankie Valli's *Four Seasons*). Despite obvious differences between the programme and this book – no bible, no Shakespeare, no luxury item, and a maximum of six choices – contributors to this volume will have experienced similar selection dilemmas to castaways. Some may even have deliberated on the relative merits of classical and popular authors: whether to opt for Nils Christie or for Agatha Christie.

     Selection of items for a project of this sort is, therefore, fraught with difficulty. This is no less true for the present writer whose specialist field, though having a smaller body of literature than 'mainstream' areas of criminal justice, such as penology and criminal law, remains sizeable. To begin with, therefore, it will be useful to give a short resume of the literature on private policing as it has developed in Britain and the USA during the post-war period. This will help to place the selected items in a broader context and will also indicate some categories of material which have been excluded from consideration.

## British and North American Literature on Private Policing

In Britain, as elsewhere, significant expansion of private security began in the 1960s. However, analysis of the industry was slow to develop and, with the exception of occasional journalistic forays (e.g. Clayton, 1967), coverage remained thin. Despite occasional contributions from academics (e.g. McLintock and Wiles, 1972; Flavel, 1973), little systematic study was undertaken during the 1970s, though there was some criticism of private policing from those concerned about civil liberties and the rule of law (Bunyan, 1977; Bowden, 1978). Though Draper's (1978) socio-legal analysis of the industry was one of the earliest academic books on the subject it was not until a decade later that South (1988) considered the topic from the sociological and criminological perspectives. Over the next decade interest grew with the publication of several books (e.g. Johnston, 1992; McManus, 1995; Jones and Newburn, 1998) and an increasing number of journal articles (e.g. George and Button, 1998 on regulation, Gill and Hart, 1997 on private detectives, Loader, 1997 on governance and ethical propriety). More recently, a number of doctoral theses, wholly or partly devoted to the subject, have been completed (e.g. Noaks, 2000; Singh, 2000).

Though security companies were established in North America during the mid-19th-century (Pinkerton was founded in 1850, Wells Fargo in 1852, and Brinks in 1859), there was little analysis of their activities until the 20th century. Indeed, with rare exceptions (Burns, 1913; Siringo, 1915; Shalloo, 1933) it was not until the middle of the century that commentators began to address the significance of the industry. During the 1950s and 1960s several volumes appeared devoted to the examination of particular security organisations. One of these was Dewhirst's (1955) book on *The Railroad Police*. Another was Horan's (1968) work on *The Pinkertons*. At this time, the rapid growth of commercial security led to the publication of a number of national reports assessing the causes, rates and implications of expansion. An early and influential example was *The Rand Report* (Kakalik and Wildhorn, 1972). Similarly large-scale research was undertaken in each of the following decades under the auspices of the Hallcrest Corporation (Cunningham and Taylor, 1985; Cunningham, Strauchs and van Meter, 1990). On the academic front a number of sociologists and historians, some of them from the radical and revisionist schools, began to address the issue of private policing during the 1970s (Becker, 1974; Spitzer and Scull, 1977). However, the main thrust of academic research emanated from the Centre of Criminology at the University of Toronto, led by Shearing and Stenning (see, for example, Stenning and Cornish, 1975; Farnell and Shearing, 1977; Freedman and Stenning, 1977; Jeffries 1977; Stenning and Shearing, 1979; Shearing *et. al.,* 1980; Stenning, 1981; Shearing, Stenning and Addario, 1985 (a), (b), (c); Shearing and Stenning, 1987). Two other areas of research are worthy of note. First, given America's long-standing 'vigilante tradition' (Brown, 1975) there has been some interest in autonomous citizen action as a form of private policing (Marx and Archer, 1981; Pennell *et. al.,* 1985). Second, the segmentation of US housing into ghettoised areas located alongside wealthy ones has encouraged the development of 'gated communities' to a much greater extent than exists in Britain. Recently, this has been the object of increased analysis (Davis, 1990; Blakely and Snyder, 1997). As in Britain several doctoral theses concerned in part (Wood, 1999) or in whole (Rigakos, 1998) with private policing have recently appeared.

*A Personal Note*

Before outlining the structure and rationale of this chapter it is necessary to say a few words about my own intellectual history since this obviously has a critical bearing on the items selected for analysis. To begin with, it should be said that my interest in private policing was an almost accidental by-product of earlier doctoral research concerned, in large part, with theories of the capitalist state (Johnston, 1982). When this research was first initiated in the mid-1970s my aim was to develop, within a British context, theoretical concepts deployed by a number of contemporary European Marxist writers. The most notable of these, Nicos Poulantzas, had formulated a theory of the 'relative autonomy' of politics and the state vis-à-vis the interests of capital (Poulantzas, 1973, 1975, 1978). The concept of relative autonomy had been intended to provide a corrective to the so-called problem of 'reductionism' within the Marxist analysis of capitalism, many Marxists propounding the erroneous view that socio-cultural, political and ideological phenomena could be reduced (or 'read off') as more or less complex reflections of dominant class interests. In developing the concept of relative autonomy, Poulantzas aimed to give due recognition to the irreducibility of politics and, by so doing, to provide the theoretical basis for an effective (albeit class-based) socialist politics. For reasons that need not be pursued here, I soon abandoned the conceptual apparatus of Marxism, arguing it to be theoretically incoherent and an obstacle to socialist political thinking. By contrast, I argued that class-based conceptions of politics were unsustainable and that socialist theory had to develop along pluralist lines, recognising the varied forces and interests which constituted 'the left' (Johnston, 1982, 1986).

Up until the early 1980s I had no particular interest in policing. Like all sociologists familiar with Weber's classic definition of the state, I knew the police to be a fundamental agent of the state's authority. Yet, the preoccupation of police researchers with issues of crime seemed to assign policing to 'criminology' rather than to 'social theory'. Thatcherism undermined that assumption by mobilising the police as agents of government during a period of 'state-legitimation crisis' (Habermas, 1975). At the same time, 'New Right' philosophers such as Hayek (1960) and Nozick (1974) were providing an intellectual justification for the privatisation of state services.

The first of these developments led me towards a research interest in the governance of public police. The second led me to focus attention on the extent to which the growth of private policing was indicative of a more fundamental reconfiguration of governance and the state.

Since that period, my work has been informed by several key assumptions:

- That policing should be addressed through the lens of governance, rather than merely through the lens of criminology;
- That, so conceived, policing is about the provision of security more than it is about the enforcement of law and the control of crime. In the contemporary period, the provision of security may be combined, more and more, with the delivery of justice;
- That defining policing as an act of governance does not mean it is the prerogative of the state. Policing may be delivered – and should be delivered – through a plurality of formal/informal and public/private means; and,
- That such diversity of provision reflects the fragmented nature of governance in the contemporary period and calls into question traditional assumptions about the sovereignty of the state and the ubiquity of social control.

The items selected for analysis in this chapter all reflect these theoretical concerns. As a result, many important aspects of the debate on private policing have been excluded from consideration. These include questions about the size of the private security industry in Europe and North America, the reasons for the industry's post war expansion, the varied functions it undertakes in different jurisdictions, the question of its adequate regulation, the powers of its personnel, and the implications of its increasingly transnational character. Instead, the items considered are chosen for their ability to link the issue of private policing to debates on the changing character of contemporary governance. Given the relatively recent growth of private policing, and the fact that theoretical analysis of its importance has been of even more recent origin, all of the items discussed here were written during the last twenty years.

## Private Policing and Governance

*Private Policing and Social Control*

- Shearing, C.D. and Stenning, P.C. (1983), 'Private security: implications for social control', *Social Problems,* vol. 30, no. 5, 493-506.

The first item to be considered was written by Clifford Shearing and Philip Stenning, the initiators of systematic research on private policing, and still its most influential figures. Their research was first developed in Toronto, a city undergoing massive change during the last quarter of the twentieth century. Like many other North American cities Toronto's expansion involved the building of condominiums, shopping malls, banks, sports stadia, health and educational facilities. What was particularly striking in Toronto, however, was that much of this expansion took place underground, with urban and suburban locations being linked by a vast network of subterranean 'streets' and railway stations. These developments had a major impact on Shearing and Stenning's thinking. This article, published in 1983, but representing and refining ideas which they had been developing since the late 1970s, considers the implications for social control of the rapid growth in N. American private policing. Though drawing upon research undertaken with colleagues at the Centre of Criminology over the previous decade (see previous section), the article is less important for its empirical content than for its conceptual and theoretical insights.

The first of these concerns the authors' observation that 'most studies of formal social control ... have focused on systems of state control' (Shearing and Stenning, 1983, p. 494). As a result, even those researching private systems of order maintenance may regard them as 'little more than a private adjunct to the public criminal justice system' (Shearing and Stenning, 1983, 494). This view, the authors argue, is particularly common amongst those who define private police as the 'junior partners' of the public criminal justice system (Kakalik and Wildhorn, 1977; Cunningham and Taylor, 1985). Shearing and Stenning criticise this view because it fails to account for important differences between private and public police, as well as for the different contexts within each operates. Distinguishing between these contexts is particularly important, they argue, since contrary to the 'junior partner' view, private security operates within the domain of 'private justice' (Henry, 1978). Here, Shearing and Stenning accept the position of legal pluralists that the number of legal systems found in a society will mirror its number of functioning social units.

Their contention that private policing represents a specific mode of social control, rather than a mere adjunct of public policing, is linked to a second factor: the emergence of 'mass private property'. Mass private property is a key element in Shearing and Stenning's explanation for the growth of private policing. Rather than seeing that growth as a mere by-product of the state's fiscal crisis, they link it to emergent changes in the organisation of private property and public space. Mass private property, exemplified in airports, office complexes, industrial sites, residential estates and shopping malls, comprises space which, while privately owned, is routinely occupied by the public. The policing needs of such 'privately owned public places' (Shearing and Stenning, 1983, p. 496) are not met by public police for two reasons. First, resource limitations, combined with the police's view that their role is an essentially public one, restricts police activity to the public domain. Second, those who own mass private property prefer to control the manner in which it is policed, something which encourages commercial solutions. However, the commercial policing of mass private property leads private police to encroach, more and more, on to the traditional terrain of public police. As a result, an area of life which was hitherto under state control is brought under the influence of private corporations.

Thirdly, Shearing and Stenning note that where the authority and legitimacy of public police usually depends on statutory powers, private security merely invokes the normal rights of property ownership. This means that while the formal powers of private police are minimal, their real ones are considerable. Citizens may only be allowed access to the 'public/private places' in which they live, work and play if they accede, voluntarily, to random searches, routine surveillance, or the disclosure of personal information. Ironically, they suggest, it may no longer be the state which threatens the liberty of North American citizens, but a private sphere which had traditionally been regarded as the realm of freedom.

Fourthly, Shearing and Stenning maintain that private policing organisations exhibit different philosophies and working practices from public criminal justice institutions. Whereas the criminal justice system divides its personnel on the basis of specialised functional roles, private security personnel play overlapping roles. Security is, thus, seen as most effective when it is 'embedded in other functions' (Shearing and Stenning, 1983, p. 499) and a key task for the security officer is to ensure that personnel fulfil their routine security responsibilities by locking doors and windows and by informing others of potential security risks or breaches. Furthermore, unlike its public counterpart, private security is a form of 'victim controlled policing' (Shearing and Stenning, 1983, p. 500). Here, client interests are maintained by closing security loopholes rather than by calling upon a public justice system whose concern is with the apprehension and punishment of offenders. In accordance with this, the focus of private security is on the application of instrumental sanctions rather than penal ones.

Finally, the authors contend that the growth of mass private property has facilitated an ongoing privatization of social control with the result that 'North America is experiencing a 'new feudalism': huge tracts of property and associated public spaces are controlled – and policed – by private corporations' (Shearing and Stenning 1983, p. 503). Moreover, it is claimed, since private security redefines both deviance (a deviant is anyone who creates opportunities for loss) and the nature of sanctions (deviants, so defined, may legitimately be subjected to instrumental sanctions) 'the reach of social control has been extended' (Shearing and Stenning, 1983, p. 504). That extension is further consolidated by the 'embedding' of security in mundane social relations. Shearing and Stenning close by suggesting that these developments cast doubt on contemporary claims that the state had become more dominant in capitalist societies (see Miliband, 1967, Poulantzas, 1973). Rather, the development of private security 'raises the possibility of sovereignty shifting from the state directly to private corporations in both their national and ... international guises' (Shearing and Stenning, 1983, p. 504). This theme is developed further in a paper by Shearing (1992) to be discussed later.

**Fragmented Governance: An Historical Example**

*   McMullan, J.L. (1987) 'Policing the criminal underworld: state power and decentralized social control in London 1550-1700', in Lowman, J.Menzies, R.J. and Palys, T.S. (eds), *Transcarceration: Essays in the Sociology of Social Control,* Gower, Aldershot, 119-38.

Shearing and Stenning's use of an historical analogy ('new feudalism') to depict the present state of social control opened up several avenues of thinking. For one thing, it suggested the need to consider private (and public) policing within the wider history of governance. In Britain, conventional police histories had regarded 1829 (the date of the formation of the 'new police') as the 'year zero' from which 'real' history began. Considered in the broader historical context, however, it became more plausible to argue that the state police's relative monopoly of policing (dating from about the mid-nineteenth century to the last quarter of the twentieth) was the historical exception rather than the historical rule (Johnston, 1992). Secondly, the concept of 'new feudalism' emphasised the conditional and problematic nature of state sovereignty. This second theme is the subject of John McMullan's chapter in the edited collection *Transcarceration.*

In this chapter McMullan examines the coercive capacity of the Absolutist State in England, focusing on crime control in sixteenth and seventeenth century London. The formation of population settlements in England had given rise to a disparate system of social control where responsibility for law enforcement lay with decentralised, voluntary, communal bodies. These patterns of social control reflected the political and economic fragmentation of the country into independent shire-states. Though different, London displayed its own specific form of fragmentation. Being a preferred centre for labour migration during the transition from feudalism to capitalism, it had a growing and mobile population, many of whom were masterless men and women. It was also developing as a centre for crime, growing consumption having increased the quantity of cheap goods available amongst the various social strata. Added to that, the proliferation of nobility, gentry and professionals in the city opened up new criminal opportunities for pickpockets, cheats and swindlers. Yet, despite its expansion as a centre of commercial capitalism, London also possessed a number of unregulated spaces, the residue of previous 'feudal territorial customs'(McMullan, 1987, p. 121):

Ancient boundaries marked off various living spaces, and the city was a myriad of diverse social worlds ... Aside from the anonymity that the city afforded by virtue of its size, social density and heterogeneity, crime was further enhanced by traditions of territoriality that offered social protection in unregulated areas (McMullan, 1987, p. 121)

These 'wayward districts' often took the form of medieval 'liberties' (places deemed to be independent of city or state control by virtue of having been ecclesiastical franchises). In some of these areas law breakers were protected under feudal rights of sanctuary which, though having formally been terminated in the sixteenth century, sometimes persisted until the eighteenth. While these *de facto* practices persisted, the Elizabethan and Stuart state showed a singular lack of capacity to eradicate them. On the contrary, such areas extended their borders, displaying considerable organisation and stability and becoming 'an archipelago of crime sanctuaries' (McMullan, 1987, p. 122).

Opportunities for crime were, therefore, exacerbated by the inability of enforcement agencies to penetrate wayward areas. Worse than that, there were serious gaps in the coercive capacity of the Absolutist State itself. Here, the absence of either a professional army or a paid bureaucracy, meant that the imposition of state power depended upon complex networks of patronage, with formal state control being 'an elaborate, negotiated and tenuous artifice' (McMullan, 1987, p. 123):

Patronage was especially pervasive as a system of government. Political order was effectively mediated by elaborate webs of affiliation and parochial hierarchies which developed around semi-autonomous centres of influence ... [This] fluid system of patron-client power blocks [was] capable, at times, of formidable competition to central government (McMullan, 1987, p. 123).

Under these circumstances policing was both uncoordinated and open to purchase or negotiation. Watch and ward policing lacked any central command structure being an 'amalgam of disjointed bodies with an array of heterogeneous rules' (McMullan, 1987, p. 125). Yet, any attempt at central coordination met with local resistance. Financially better off citizens found ways of exempting themselves from their constabulary responsibilities and 'a market in the speculation of policing offices and duties emerged' (McMullan, 1987, p. 126). In time, a body of full-time constables and watchmen emerged who were paid to act as proxies in the hire of others, local ward officials being able to procure a secret income in the process. In due course, both the quantity and quality of police declined and the state sought to bolster social control through other means. Such means included Privy Council policing and the creation of the city marshalry, neither of which was particularly effective and each of which created new jurisdictional complications:

> Crime control in London comprised welters of competing jurisdictions, authorities and agencies. The major tiers of city policing organization – watch and ward, privy council messengers and city marshalmen – overlapped uncertainly, and often pulled in contrary directions' (McMullan, 1987, p. 133).

Such diversity and disorganisation, coupled with the corruption arising from a speculative market in police services, led the city to encourage self-policing on a greater scale. Citizens were encouraged to spy on one another for reward and to inform on accomplices when arrested. Informers and thief-takers were 'recruited from the criminal worlds and sent back to survey them' (McMullan, 1987, p. 134). Justices of the peace encouraged victims to seek out intermediaries in order to recover their stolen property and the state's trade in warrants and pardons linked the judiciary to the commercial thief-taking sector. In effect, these practices exerted a degree of centralisation and coordination over policing since the state authorised the activities of those whom they employed to deliver justice, albeit in a commercialised form.

In this account, McMullan describes a situation where the sovereignty of the Absolutist State is far from absolute, something which is partly due to the continued efficacy of feudal territorial relations under conditions of developing capitalism. Moreover, the state, far from being an unambiguously 'public' institution, is penetrated by a network of commercial interests. Indeed, the minimal degree of coordination which the state achieves is precisely the result of compromises and trade-offs struck between these cross-cutting interests. There are striking parallels here between McMullan's historical account and Shearing and Stenning's contemporary one. For, in each case, territories beyond the direct control of the state (whether 'wayward districts' or areas of 'mass private property') are subjected to commercialised forms of (residual-feudal or neo-feudal) social control. Indeed, the parallel goes further than that. Though the commercial solution described by McMullan had only limited efficacy – achieving enhanced coordination but little more – by the eighteenth century commercialisation had secured an effective monopoly over policing:

> ... one can see, in the period from 1550 to 1700, a confederation of theft networks tending towards the more administratively-centred system of the

eighteenth century, in which thief-takers were to monopolize not only market circumstances, but also police work and the entire fate of thieves who worked for them (McMullan, 1987, 137).

By the eighteenth century, then, it was not the sovereign state that dominated policing but the commercial market. The extent to which this historical outcome might be repeated in the twenty-first century is one of the issues raised by Shearing (1992) whose paper is considered later.

*The Critique of Social Control*

- Cohen, S. (1989), 'The critical discourse on "social control": notes on the concept as a hammer', *International Journal of the Sociology of Law*, 17, 347-57.

So far, each of the items reviewed has been concerned with the issue of social control, taking that concept to be unproblematic. Though by no means averse to using the term, Cohen subjects the concept of social control to critical analysis in this article, casting particular doubt on the way in which it has been deployed by Marxist sociologists, radical criminologists and revisionist historians – all exponents of what he terms 'the critical discourse'. Though the paper does not address the subject of policing – let alone private policing – directly, it is included here for two reasons. First, it expresses in a succinct manner (the article is only ten pages long) a number of my own early concerns about the shortcomings of Marxist and radical state theory (Johnston, 1982, 1986); Crucially – though Cohen does not express it as such – one of these shortcomings is the tendency for radical theorists to perceive the problem of governance as a problem of (social) *control*. Secondly, this argument (in which the *control* element of social control is considered problematical) may usefully be contrasted to an alternative view in which the *social* element of governance is also subjected to criticism (Rose, 1996). Rose's argument is discussed in the final section.

Cohen, himself a leading writer within the critical tradition, argues that exponents of the critical discourse have wielded the concept like a hammer:

> In sociology – as elsewhere – concepts are used like hammers. A formless and recalcitrant reality is banged into shape, rendering it manageable and comprehensible. This is both necessary and inevitable ... Sometimes, though, the project gets out of hand. The concept/hammer is wielded with much

imagination and inventiveness, but without much attention to consequences (Cohen, 1989, p. 347).

Cohen outlines ten features of the critical discourse where, he claims, this tendency is evident:

1. Revisionist histories of policing, the prison or the asylum adopt essentialist principles. While aware of the fact that social control occurs in a variety of specific contexts, they invariably see particular cases as 'manifestations of a common essence' (Cohen, 1989, p. 348), thereby denying the specificity of those particular forms.
2. Critical writers elevate social control to an independent process with its own trajectory. Thus, for example, rather than seeing social control as a reaction to deviance, deviance may be seen as the mere artifact of social control.
3. There is a concomitant refusal to analyse ideologies and structures of social control in their own terms. Rather, these are traced back to essential social interests, themselves located within certain master processes (e.g. the dominant class interests said to be associated with the capitalist mode of production).
4. This refusal to accept ideology on its own terms leads to a 'hermeneutics of suspicion' (Cohen, 1989, p. 350), the aim of which is to demystify the pretensions of social control professionals.
5. As a result social control is stripped of any benign meaning, being conceived as invariably malignant.
6. Critical theory favours historical, not to say, historicist theories and research techniques. As a result, revisionist histories of policing and the prison have become models for the critical explanation of contemporary reality.
7. Critical analysis gives a privileged role to the modern state and pays little attention to informal or commercial control mechanisms. Thus, the market is only considered as a mechanism of social control insofar as it takes over existing state systems (privatisation) or mimics them (private policing).
8. The trajectory of social control is assumed to be driven by some inner logic (e.g. the interests of capital).
9. It is also assumed that there is an overriding tendency towards 'more' social control (as seen, for example, in the proposition that de-

institutionalisation within criminal justice merely precipitates 'net-widening').

10. Accordingly, critically theory is partisan, challenging traditional structures of social control with demands for decarceration, decriminalisation, anti-psychiatry and abolitionism.

Cohen admits that this critique is, partly, a caricature since, at the time of writing, there is already evidence of a 'revision of revisionism' (Cohen, 1989, p. 352). This is exemplified in a wide variety of ways: from the emergence of left-realist criminology; to the various 're-readings' of Foucault which gave rise to a decentred image of power, quite at odds with the earlier, monolithic, one which had been attributed to him. Cohen's point is merely that, by subjecting the concept of social control to critical consideration, it is possible to raise important issues. Of those raised in the article (Cohen, 1989, 353-5), three are worthy of brief note. First, he suggests, there is a need to move away from the assumption that social control is synonymous with state control. Secondly, he questions the assumption that the state always acts in its best interests, a view which leaves 'too little room for cracks in the system, irrationalities, random innovations, trial and error' (Cohen, 1989, p. 355). Thirdly, he draws attention to the problem which subsumes all others – that of specificity. How, in other words, can one register the importance of the specific while also being mindful of the influence of the general? These observations cast doubt on the view that (social) control is a universal, ubiquitous and unconditional force, capable of securing its own conditions of reproduction. By contrast, Cohen's final comment suggests it to be of a variable, contingent and conditional nature:

> to hammer reality with the concept of 'social control' will produce neither the coherent social essence nor the unambiguous political messages that were once promised. It will reveal fragments – shifting strategies and alliances, unconnected zones of power, changing vocabularies of intervention – which cannot be reassembled by conventional means (Cohen, 1989, p. 356).

### Taking Stock: Private Policing: Risk, Security and Governance

- Shearing , C.D. (1992) 'The relation between public and private policing', in Tonry, M. and Norris, N. (eds), *Modern Policing: Crime and Justice. A Review of Research,* Volume 15. Chicago: University of Chicago Press: 399-434.

Shearing's contribution to the 1992 edition of *Crime and Justice* focuses on the relationship between public and private policing. In so doing, it makes a number of important conceptual advances, and draws attention to the connections between policing, risk, security and governance. Shearing begins by defining policing in terms of those activities which aim to provide assurances of 'peace' or 'security' to subjects:

> [P]olicing, understood as the preservation of peace, refers to activities through which an assurance or guarantee is realized or, more accurately, to activities intended to promote such realization (Shearing 1992, p. 401).

This definition implies three things. First, the provision of security guarantees involves not just the presence of protection, but the promise of some future absence of (or reduction in) risk. Secondly, guarantees of peace do not merely 'happen' but are the product of strategic thinking and action by those who police. Thirdly, policing is by no means the prerogative of public police. In respect of this last point, Shearing notes that while nation states have claimed supremacy over the provision of security during the modern era, corporate entities have always played – and continue to play – a major role in policing.

Shearing's aim in this chapter is to account for the evolution of private policing by examining three different conceptions of its relationship to public policing. In the first of these ('state-centred policing') he describes how the formation of the 'new police' in 1829 was seen as a symbolic turning point in the gradual transfer of responsibility for policing from private to public hands. Nedelsky's comment captures how this view was held in North America:

> Modern America is characterized by the expanding scope of state power. More and more areas of life once left to the 'private' ordering of individual choice are now considered properly matters of collective control, regulation and amelioration (cited in Shearing 1992, p. 404).

This conception shaped governmental attitudes to private policing for most of the twentieth century. In the USA, Senate and Congressional reports castigated railroad and mining companies for employing their own 'private armies', and for contracting the service of Pinkerton 'mercenaries' to promote 'private orders' which were, allegedly, at odds with the public interest. Such was the force of this view in liberal democracies, Shearing notes, that by the middle of the twentieth century, private policing was regarded as an historical anachronism. Indeed, even Marxist scholars who questioned the authority of western capitalist states, shared the liberal view of policing as an inherent state monopoly.

During the 1960s, while scholars and policy makers continued to operate within this framework of thinking, private policing was, in fact, expanding dramatically. When the US Department of Justice commissioned the Rand Corporation to explore this development in the early 1970s the ensuing report (Kakalik and Wildhorn, 1972) 'developed an influential policy stance that directly challenged the earlier conception of corporate police as "private armies"' (Shearing, 1992, p. 409). As Shearing notes, the Report's view that private police were the legitimate 'junior partners' of public police in the fight against crime was indicative of an emerging 'laissez-faire' conception of the relationship between the two. This transformation of private policing from 'threat' to 'asset' was given further credibility by various follow-up studies commissioned by the US government (Cunningham and Taylor, 1985; Reiss, 1988; Cunningham, Strauchs and van Meter, 1990). By the early 1990s Rand's laissez-faire position, articulated two decades before, had become conventional wisdom in North America and throughout much of Europe. Now, it was argued, security was a partnership between public and private sectors, the state – as 'senior partner' – retaining ultimate sovereignty over the determination of policing policy.

However, as Shearing notes, the laissez-faire position is an unstable one. For one thing, partnership implies a fractured conception of security which, by denying the state its privileged position, challenges the idea of continued state sovereignty over policing. For another, partnership demands such a level of integration between public and private security that the distinction between two mutually exclusive spheres becomes untenable. As the two become fused, however, the demand for state sovereignty over policing is rendered increasingly meaningless. Recognition of these tensions has given rise to a 'pluralist perspective' whose proponents consider power to be 'dispersed' (and security to be 'embedded') throughout the entire social fabric, rather than to be concentrated in the state . The idea of power as dispersed, harks back to our previous references to policing under 'old' (McMullan, 1987) and 'new' (Shearing and Stenning, 1983) feudalism. For as Shearing argues, the privatisation which has accompanied new feudalism produces 'a fundamental shift in responsibility for policing, from state to corporate hands, that is challenging state power and redefining state-corporate relationships' (Shearing 1992, p. 422).

Unlike advocates of laissez-faire, however, pluralists regard privatisation as more than the mere technical transfer of risk from one sector to another.

> [There is] a fundamental shift in the location of responsibility for guaranteeing and defining the peace from state to corporate entities. Together with the state, these corporations constitute a field of interpenetrating and loosely coupled entities that negotiate territories and spheres of autonomy … Pluralists dispute a conception of the political and legal spheres as organized vertically with the state at the apex (Shearing 1992, p. 425).

For Shearing, this development raises two issues. First, will the state's loss of sovereignty lead to the greater empowerment of communities or merely to the renewed domination of corporations? Secondly, how will these changes impact on the conventional distinction between 'public' and 'private' spheres which has underpinned liberal conceptions of governance? Here, Shearing leaves the reader with an intriguing possibility:

> What we recognize now as blurring may prove in retrospect to be the earliest stages of a very different conception of social space in which the public realm may come to be equated with the corporate realm. Such a development may well have implications far beyond policing (Shearing 1992, 428-9).

This possibility is examined in the concluding section where I make some general observations about factors to be considered when addressing the problem of governing plural policing systems.

*Future Considerations in the Governance of Policing*

My aim in this chapter has been to consider policing, in general, and private policing, in particular, in the context of debates about the changing character of governance. A prominent theme within these debates has been the growing diversity of governance functions. This process is exemplified by the dispersal of such functions from the central state to various 'peripheral' arenas – the market, corporations, voluntary bodies, non-governmental agencies, community organisations, groups of active citizens, and the like. The expansion of private policing is, thus, part of a wider shift towards plural, diverse, risk-based forms of governance which feature loose 'partnerships' between public, commercial, voluntary and other bodies. In the case of security, this process creates both opportunities and risks. Diversity may offer enhanced choice to consumers of security services. Yet, it may also compromise effectiveness and threaten equity unless subjected to 'good governance'.

## *The Ambiguous Implications of Risk-Based Policing and Justice*

The double-edged character of diversity may be illustrated with respect to risk. Shearing and Stenning's (1983) article demonstrated that there is a difference between the respective philosophies and working practices of public and private police. Historically, public policing has been reactive, enforcement-based, crime-focused and offender-oriented. Private policing, by contrast, has been proactive and preventative, has focused on the minimisation of loss, and has been oriented towards the needs of the victim-client. This distinction corresponds to two different systems of justice, the first being concerned with the apprehension, conviction and punishment of offenders, the second with the application of anticipatory, informal and instrumental sanctions to those whose action (or inaction) might increase risks and, thereby, compromise security. Of course, these different mentalities are neither mutually exclusive nor mutually incompatible. On the contrary, public police nowadays think and act more and more like private security. This point is well-illustrated in the case of Zero-Tolerance policing (ZTP). On the one hand, ZTP applies traditional enforcement-led techniques against those who perpetrate so-called 'quality of life' crimes. On the other hand, one of its objectives is to collect street-level information which can be transformed into intelligence for proactive policing purposes. Despite the force of its rhetoric, therefore, ZTP is neither solely nor primarily concerned with policing mere 'incivilities'. It is also linked to a variety of risk-based techniques, including the targeting and profiling of offenders, crime pattern analysis and geographical information systems.

This example confirms that public police, like private police, are more and more concerned with the collection, collation, analysis and dissemination of information for risk management purposes (Ericson and Haggerty, 1997).

However, it is also the case that police will be expected to engage in acts of informal ('anticipatory') justice that were hitherto, the preserve of commercial or state security personnel. (Doubtless, police have administered informal justice in the past – as evidenced by historical and sociological accounts of 'cuffs and capes' – but the administration of justice has never been implicit in the police role). For example, under the terms of the Security Services Act 1996, MI5 agents may work alongside police to tackle serious crime and terrorism. Some years ago, an unnamed 'Home Office source' suggested that 'disrupting the activities of organised criminals may be a desirable role if MI5 is unable to bring them to justice' (cited in Gibbons and Hyder, 1996, p. 5). The police's delivery of justice through the application of 'techniques of disorganisation' (Johnston, 2000) raises obvious ethical questions. How, for example, can we be sure that those subjected to anticipatory and informal sanctions are 'deserving' rather than 'undeserving' targets? More generally, the combination and recombination of proactive, risk-based, anticipatory techniques with reactive, enforcement-based, disciplinary ones casts doubt on our traditional conceptions of policing and justice. For when police deploy techniques to disrupt the activities of alleged criminals they impose sanctions which are neither reactive nor based upon due process.

The fact that risk-based ('actuarial') practice undoubtedly poses ethical, practical and conceptual problems explains why criminologists have taken a negative view of the shift towards 'actuarial justice' (see, for example, Feely and Simon, 1994; Hudson, 1996). However, blanket rejection of actuarialism should be avoided for two reasons. First, much of the criminological critique of actuarial justice replicates the failings of the 'critical discourse on social control' identified by Cohen (1989). (See, for example, Simon's (1988) claim – both functionalist and teleological – that actuarial techniques have replaced disciplinary ones because they are both more efficient and less likely to provoke political resistance). Secondly – obvious dangers notwithstanding – it is important to consider whether actuarial techniques can be deployed in a manner which enhances, rather than detracts from, justice. It is striking that the features of commercial security practice identified by Shearing and Stenning (1983) – proaction, prevention, risk-minimisation, victim-orientation and the like – fit much more comfortably with restorative conceptions of justice than with punishment-based ones. This raises the question of whether, under the right political conditions, the risk-based approach can be integrated effectively into community-based restorative justice programmes rather than merely contained within existing managerialist parameters. (These issues are discussed more fully in Johnston and Shearing forthcoming.)

*From Social Control to Plural Governance*

In the previous section I drew attention to Cohen's (1989) critique of the 'critical discourse on social control'. Cohen identified three problems with the critical position: that it over-emphasised the role of the state and under-emphasised the role of alternative control agencies; that it exaggerated the capacity of control agencies to act consistently in their own interests; and that, consequently, it represented social control as an all-pervasive force, capable of reproducing its own conditions of existence. Cohen (1989) demanded that due recognition be given to the conditional nature of power and control, something which has, subsequently, been explored by others. (See, for example, O'Malley's (1992; 1999) discussion of this issue in the context of risk-based approaches to crime prevention and punishment).

Cohen's analysis implies that the concept of *social* control is salvageable once due attention is paid to the conditional nature of *control*. Recently, however, Foucauldian critics have cast doubt on *the social*, itself, as a contemporary locus of governance. Contrary to critical theorists, who conceive governance as a process of (primarily state) control of the social realm, proponents of this view deny the primacy of the social as a site of governance. Ewald (1991), for example, argues that governance during the 20th century has become preoccupied with the management of risks through the application of actuarial and insurential techniques, a process which has undermined state-led conceptions of social governance. In the same vein, Rose (1996) claims that recent governing discourses – such as communitarianism, associationalism, consumer sovereignty, and civic republicanism – have dispensed entirely with the aim of 'governing through society'. The social, he argues, is no longer regarded as the objective of strategies of government. Accordingly, the state's capacity to rule in the name of the social – by invoking social justice, social planning and social rights, or by employing a public police force with responsibility for the provision of social protection – is less and less meaningful. In Rose's (1996) view state governance gives way to a plurality of community-oriented modes of governance. However, community is no longer the singular, homogenising force of the past. On the contrary, the singularity of 'community' is displaced by the plurality of 'communities' (corporate communities, virtual communities, ethnic communities, religious communities, communities defined by gender or sexual orientation, etc.) which often have incommensurable or incompatible interests. One implication of this approach is that political programmes constructed through the problematic of 'the state and social control' (such as radical agendas about police accountability) are no longer salient to the governance of plural policing systems. The governance of policing can no longer rely on the certainties of control but must, instead, find ways of addressing the complexity inherent in pluralism and diversity.

## Governing Diverse Policing

Diverse policing, if left unchecked, may give rise to a fragmented security system which combines the worst of all worlds: ineffectiveness (due to lack of coordination between the elements) and injustice (due to inequity in the distribution of services). In addition, increased preoccupation with risk – coupled with an uncritical adoption of the assumption that every identifiable risk justifies a security response – could lead to an over-invasive system of policing linked to what one writer has termed a 'maximum security society' (Marx, 1988).

However, this pessimistic outcome is far from inevitable. There is no inherent reason why diverse policing cannot be subjected to 'good' (effective, just and democratic) governance. The problem is that conventional control solutions are inadequate to the task. While the British Government's current proposals to subject private security to statutory regulation are undoubtedly justified, statutory regulation does not, in itself, amount to a coherent theory of governance under present conditions. There are two reasons for saying this. First, the imposition of state control over a single element within a security network leaves unresolved the question of the relationship between all of the elements in that network. The project of good governance demands that security be understood as a relationship between commercial, state and voluntary elements. Secondly, the project of state control is problematical for the simple reason that the state – as a unified, authoritative, exclusively public body, with an in-built capacity to exercise sovereign control – is becoming an historic relic.

This means that while diversity is the site of several problems (over policing, invasive policing, inequitable, uncoordinated and unaccountable policing), in the absence of sovereign authority it provides the context in which these problems have to be resolved. Elsewhere (Johnston, 2000) I have proposed a model of 'optimum policing', the object of which is to secure public interests within diverse security networks. Optimal policing may be defined as a system of security which is neither qualitatively excessive (to the detriment of social values and objectives other than security) nor qualitatively invasive (to the detriment of public freedoms) and which satisfies conditions of public accountability, effectiveness and justice. One of the aims of optimal policing would be to develop security as a public good. In the past, the state ('the public sphere') was conceived as the sole repository of the public good. Yet, with its declining sovereignty and increased penetration by commercial interests, it is difficult to defend this position. Nowadays, the state is one player – albeit an important one – in a complex network of governing agencies. The challenge for democratic governance is to ensure that the actions of those commercial bodies which participate in security accord, as much as possible, with the public good.

That is a difficult challenge to meet since, behind it, lies the implication that there is no *immutable* contradiction between commercial and public interests. Yet, that is precisely the implication behind Shearing's suggestion that, in future, a different conception of social space may need to be devised 'in which the public realm may come to be equated with the corporate realm' (Shearing, 1992, p. 429). Some commentators reject this view entirely. Loader, for instance, contends that private security is a contradiction in terms: 'an oxymoronic way of thinking about and delivering community safety' (Loader, 1997, p. 155). Yet there is no necessary reason why, in a market economy, governmental mechanisms cannot be put in place to ensure that public interests are effectively represented in security networks composed, in part, of commercial elements. Interestingly, Shearing's (1996) discussion of developments in New York and Kempa *et al's* (1999) account of North American 'business improvement districts' suggest that commercial security can, under appropriate governmental conditions, begin to provide the rudiments of accountable, just and democratic policing. That outcome, is by no means certain, but the alternative – an implicit demand for the socialisation of security through the establishment of a state monopoly over policing – is an impossible one.

## References

Becker, T. (1974). The place of the private police in society: an area of research for the social sciences. *Social Problems*, 21, 3: 438-53.
Blakely, E.J. and Snyder, M.G. (1997). *Fortress America: Gated Communities in the United States.* Brookings Institution Press: Washington DC.

156   *Criminal Justice Research*

Bowden, T. (1978). *Beyond the Limits of the Law.* Penguin: Harmondsworth.
Brown, R.M. (1975). *Strain of Violence.* Oxford University Press: New York.
Bunyan, T. (1977) *The History and Practice of the Political Police in Britain.* Quartet: London.
Burns, W.J. (1913). *The Masked War.* Arno Press: New York
Clayton, T. (1967). *The Protectors: The Inside Story of Britain's Private Security Forces.* Oldbourne: London
Cohen, S. (1989). The critical discourse on 'social control': notes on the concept as a hammer. *International Journal of the Sociology of Law,* 17, 347-57.
Cunningham, W.C., Strauchs, J.J. and Van Meter, C.W. (1990). *Private Security Trends 1970 to 2000: The Hallcrest Report II.* Butterworth-Heinemann: Boston
Cunningham, W.C. and Taylor, T. (1985). *Private Security and Police in America: The Hallcrest Report I.* Butterworth-Heinemann: Boston.
Davis, M. (1990). *City of Quartz: Imagining the Future in Los Angeles.* Verso: London.
Dewhirst, H. S. (1955). *The Railroaa Police.* Charles C Thomas: Springfield Illinois.
Draper, H. (1978). *Private Police.* Harvester: Sussex.
Ericson, R. and Haggerty, K. (1997). *Policing the Risk Society.* Clarendon: Oxford.
Ewald, F. (1991). Insurance and risk. In Burchall, G., Gordon, C. and Miller, P. (eds), *The Foucault Effect.* Harvester-Wheatsheaf: London, 197-210.
Farnell, M. and Shearing, C.D. (1977). *Private Security: An Examination of Canadian Statistics 1961-1971.* Centre of Criminology: University of Toronto.
Feely, M. and Simon, J. (1994). Actuarial justice: the emerging new criminal law. In Nelken, D. (ed), *The Futures of Criminology,* Sage: London.
Flavel, W.R.H. (1973). Research into security organisations. Paper presented to the Second Bristol Seminar on the Sociology of the Police (unpublished).
Freedman, D.J. and Stenning, P.C. (1977). *Private Security, Police and Law in Canada,* Centre of Criminology: University of Toronto.
George, B. and Button, M. (1998). Too little too late: a critique of recent policy proposals for the private security industry in the United Kingdom, *Security Journal,* 10, 1, 1-7.
Gibbons, S. and Hyder, K. (1996). MI5 crime fighting role needs tighter control says Sharples. *Police Review,* 19 January, p. 5.
Gill, M. and Hart, J. (1997). Exploring investigative policing: private detectives in Britain. *British Journal of Criminology,* 37, 4, 549-67.
Habermas, J. (1975). *Legitimation Crisis.* Beacon Press: Boston.
Hayek, F.A. (1960). *The Constitution of Liberty.* Routledge and Kegan Paul: London.
Henry, S. (1978). *The Hidden Economy: The Context and Control of Borderline Crime.* Martin Robertson: London.
Horan, J. (1968). *The Pinkertons: The Detective Dynasty that Made History.* Crown: New York.
Hudson, B. (1996). *Understanding Justice.* Open University: Buckingham.
Jeffries, F. (1977). *Private Policing: An Examination of In-House Security Operations.* Centre of Criminology: University of Toronto.
Johnston, L. (1982). *Classes and the Specificity of Politics in Marxism and Sociology.* Unpublished Ph.D. Dissertation, University of Liverpool.
Johnston, L. (1986). *Marxism, Class Analysis and Socialist Pluralism.* Allen and Unwin: London.
Johnston, L. (1992). *The Rebirth of Private Policing.* Routledge: London.
Johnston, L. (2000). *Policing Britain: Risk, Security and Governance.* Longman: Harlow.

Johnston, L. and Shearing, C.D. (forthcoming) *Policing Diversity: Explorations in Governance*. Routledge: London.

Jones, T. and Newburn, T. (1998). *Private Security and Public Policing*. Clarendon Press: Oxford.

Kakalik, J.S. and Wildhorn, S. (1972). *Private Police in the United States*. National Institute of Law Enforcement and Criminal Justice: US Dept. of Justice. Four volumes.

Kempa, M., Carrier, R., Wood, J. and Shearing, C. (1999). Reflections on the evolving concept of 'private policing', *European Journal on Criminal Policy and Research*. 7, 2, 197-223.

Loader, I. (1997). Thinking normatively about private security, *Journal of Law and Society*. 24, 3: 377-94.

McClintock, F. H. and Wiles, P. (eds), (1972). *The Security Industry in the United Kingdom: Papers Presented to the Cropwood Round-Table Conference, July 1971*. Institute of Criminology: Cambridge.

McManus, M. (1995). *From Fate to Choice: Private Bobbies, Public Beats*. Avebury: Aldershot.

McMullan, J.L. (1987). Policing the criminal underworld: state power and decentralized social control in London 1550-1700. In Lowman, J.Menzies, R. J. and Palys, T. S. (eds), *Transcarceration: Essays in the Sociology of Social Control*, Gower, Aldershot, 119-38.

Marx, G. and Archer, D. (1976). The urban vigilante, *Psychology Today*. January, 45-50.

Marx, G. (1988). *Undercover: Police Surveillance in America*. University of California Press: Berkeley.

Miliband, R. (1967). *The State in Capitalist Society*. Weidenfeld and Nicholson: London.

Nokes, L. (2000). Private Cops on the Block: A Review of Private Security in a Residential Area. Unpublished Ph.D. Dissertation, University of Cardiff.

Nozick, R. (1974). *Anarchy, State and Utopia*. Blackwell: Oxford.

O'Malley, P. (1992). Risk, power and crime prevention. *Economy and Society*. 21, 3, 252-75.

O'Malley, P. (1999). Volatile and contradictory punishment. *Theoretical Criminology*, 175-96.

Pennell, S., Curtis, C. and Henderson, J. (1985). *Guardian Angels: An Assessment of Citizen Response to Crime*. US Dept. of Justice, Washington: Government Printing Office.

Poulantzas, N. (1973). *Political Power and Social Classes*. New Left Books: London.

Poulantzas, N. (1975). *Classes in Contemporary Capitalism*. New Left Books: London.

Poulantzas, N. (1978). *State, Power, Socialism*. New Left Books: London.

Reiss, A. (1988). *Private Employment of Public Police*. US Dept. of Justice, National Institute of Justice: Washington DC.

Rigakos, G. (1998). The New Parapolice: Risk Markets and Commodified Social Control., Ph.D. Dissertation, York University: Toronto.

Rose, N. (1996). The death of the social? Re-figuring the territory of government. *Economy and Society*, 25, 3, 327-56.

Shalloo, J. P. (1933). *The Private Police*. American Academy of Political and Social Science.

Shearing , C. D. (1992). The relation between public and private policing. In Tonry, M. and Norris, N. (eds), *Modern Policing: Crime and Justice. A Review of Research*, Volume 15. Chicago: University of Chicago Press, 399-434.

Shearing, C. D. (1996). Public and private policing. In Saulsbury, W., Mott, J. and Newburn, T. (eds), *Themes in Contemporary Policing,* Independent Committee of Inquiry into the Roles and Responsibilities of the Police: London,  83-95.

Shearing, C. D. and Stenning, P. C. (1983). Private security: implications for social control. *Social Problems,* vol. 30, no. 5,  493-506.

Shearing, C.D. and Stenning, P.C. (eds), (1987). *Private Policing.* Sage: California.

Shearing, C.D., Farnell, M. and Stenning, P.C. (1980). *Contract Security in Ontario.* Centre of Criminology: University of Toronto.

Shearing, C.D., Stenning, P.C. and Addario, S. M. (1985a). Police perception of private security. *Canadian Police College Journal,* 9,  127-52.

Shearing, C.D., Stenning, P.C. and Addario, S. M. (1985b). Public perception of private security. *Canadian Police College Journal,* 9,  225-53.

Shearing, C D., Stenning, P.C. and Addario, S.M. (1985c). Corporate perception of private security. *Canadian Police College Journal,* 9,  367-90.

Simons, J. (1988). The ideological effects of actuarial practices. *Law and Society Review,* 22: 772.

Singh, A.M. (2000). *Governing Crime in Post-Apartheid South Africa.* Unpublished Ph.D. Dissertation, University of London.

Siringo, C. (1915). (1968). *Two Evil 'Isms' Pinkertonism and Anarchism,.* Steck-Vaughn Company: Austin, Texas.

South, N. (1988). *Policing for Profit.* Sage: London.

Spitzer, S. and Scull, A. (1977). Privatization and capitalist development: the case of the private police. *Social Problems,* 25: 1,  18-29.

Stenning, P. C. and Cornish, M. F. (1975). *The Legal Regulation and Control of Private Police in Canada.* Centre of Criminology: University of Toronto.

Stenning, P.C. and Shearing, C.D. (1979). Search and seizure: powers of private security personnel. Study paper prepared for the Law Reform Commission of Canada. Ministry of Supply and Services, Ottawa.

Wood, J. (1999). *Reinventing Governance: A Study of Transformations in the Ontario Provincial Police.* Unpublished Ph.D. Dissertation, University of Toronto.

# 7. Community Policing: The US Experience

HAROLD K. BECKER AND DONNA LEE BECKER

## Introduction

This chapter is the product of a partnership of over 40 years. Our research and writing collaboration is a fusion of risk taking and inquisitiveness from one partner to sensitivity and social awareness with the other partner. What started as an informal sharing, observing manuscript preparation, and discussion of ideas has evolved into a formal consensus of selecting evaluation and research projects. Our research and writing partnership has matured to the collective authorship of the ideas and issues, which are contained in this chapter.

This introduction is our summary of what this chapter will cover. The road to community policing in the US has been a difficult journey that is not yet completed and the weary traveller may not even arrive at the desired destination.

We have observed bumps in the road; e.g., the bureaucratic bulwark of the traditional police organization, the failure in developing an acceptable community-relations program, and the lack of a working definition and strategy for community policing.

The resistance to community policing reflects an earlier time during the development of policing in American cities. The traditional policing style was characteristic of political control, police violence, and corruption from the inception of modern policing in the US in the 1840s to the 1950s.

There was a second wave of concentrated change, that included community relations beginning in the 1960s, for police reform in response to public riots and civil disobedience, the passage of federal civil rights legislation, and a political mentality to view the enforcement of federal and state laws as a war on crime. However, this kinder, gentler, sensitivity phase had as a primary objective to generate two-way communication between the police and the public with the hope to prevent further civil hostility and civil unrest that dominated in the 1960s and 1970s.

*A personal view of the influence of traditional policing, community relations, and community policing*

The principal author of this chapter, Harold K. Becker, was introduced to the writings of Weber's bureaucracy, and Frederick Winslow Taylor's and Frank B. Gilbreth's scientific management in the graduate program in public administration at the University of Southern California in 1960. He had joined the Los Angeles Police Department in 1959 with a baccalaureate degree in economics and co-workers looked upon him as a curiosity. The question, sometimes spoken but most often presented with a raised eyebrow or some other display of body language by supervisors, was, 'Why are you wasting your college degree being a policeman?' He did not have a ready response to this question. He went to graduate school part time and learned a great deal about scientific management.

In the Los Angeles Police Department, as well as other bureaucratic city organizations, Taylor and others had influenced many persons at the middle management and executive levels on management principles and efficiency. However, this was also a transition period with the introduction of the behavioral sciences with Douglas McGregor's (1960) *The Human Side of Enterprise* which described the contradictions of efficiency and human behavior by developing two models, Theory X, which expressed many principles of the scientific management, and Theory Y, which introduced the ideas of behaviorism and the human side of organization. It was difficult for quasi military police departments to accept the human side of organization.

Harold was offered and accepted a professorship at California State University Long Beach in 1963. All the books he wrote, revised, and co-authored were about the police in the US or in other countries. He was still influenced by the traditional aspects of policing. In 1971 he completed his D.Crim from the School of Criminology at the University of California, Berkeley in the program that had been started by Vollmer.

Our academic research became more influenced by President Johnson's *Commission on Law Enforcement and Administration of Justice* (Task Force Report, 1967) and our interest included more aspects of crime prevention. We began to observe that community relations was not successful because police departments retained their traditional attitudes and alienated a significant portion of the community. We felt that most police departments used community relations as an alternative for police relations.

It was not until community policing was attempted in Chicago did we believe there was an alternative to civil unrest, police and military control of metropolitan areas, and the accompanying waste of human lives. Our research and evaluation of criminal justice related projects, both domestic and foreign, have expanded into studies of gangs, drug use, community policing, and crime prevention.

The good news for us, and for all Americans, is that the US Constitution is the energy core that keeps the police in the US democratic society moving forward. We select the Constitution as our first influential document. It is for Americans, our navigational instrument allowing us to maintain a balance of equality and order between individuals, states' rights, and centralized government; e.g., it describes the power and responsibility of the legislative, judicial, and executive branches of government. As Americans, we revere our Constitution as the foundation of our rights and criminal law. The US Constitution has lasted longer than 200 years and has been tested many times. It remains as one of our most important documents. The Constitution was ratified in 1787 and begins with the following brief paragraph:

> We the people of the United States, in order to form a more perfect union, establish justice, insure domestic tranquillity, provide for the common defense, promote the general welfare, and secure the blessings of liberty to ourselves and our posterity, do ordain and establish this Constitution for the United States of America.

When socioeconomic and political groups malfunction the Constitution allows room to restore or invent remedies. In 1791, four years after ratification adjustments were made with the first ten amendments being added to the Constitution. The first ten amendments are known as the Bill of Rights. Further amendments have been added over the years. Most of the amendments have added to the durability and resilience of 'We the people of the United States'. However, in retrospect, some changes now seem illogical; e.g., the Second Amendment which gives the right of the people to keep and bear arms and the Eighteenth Amendment which in 1920 prohibited the manufacture, sale, and transportation of intoxicating liquors. The Eighteenth Amendment was not reversed until 1933. These two amendments have directly contributed to the role of law enforcement and the type and amount of crime in the USA.

Four other amendments from the original ten describe how police are to conduct enforcement of criminal laws:

- The First Amendment deals with religious freedom and freedom of speech and the press, and the right of the people to peaceably assemble and to petition the government for a redress of grievances;
- The Fourth Amendment which states the right of the people to be secure in their persons, houses, papers, and effects against unreasonable searches and seizures shall not be violated, and no warrants shall be issued but upon probable cause supported by oath or affirmation and particularly describing the place to be searched and the persons or things to be seized;
- The Fifth Amendment, which in part states that no person be subject for the same offence to be twice put in jeopardy of life or limb or be compelled in any criminal case to be a witness against one's self or be deprived of life, liberty, or property, without due process of law; and
- The Sixth Amendment states that in all criminal prosecutions the accused shall enjoy the right to a speedy and public trial by an impartial jury of the state and district wherein the crime was committed and to be informed of the nature and cause of the accusation and to be confronted with the witnesses against the defendant and to have compulsory process for obtaining witnesses in his favor and to have the assistance of counsel for defence, and neither excessive bail nor fines will be imposed nor unusual punishments inflicted.

These amendments continue to be debated by the judicial branch of government and at times adjusted by the nation's highest court – the US Supreme Court. The US Supreme Court consists of nine justices appointed to lifetime positions by the President with the approval of Congress. A primary responsibility of the Court is to interpret the Constitution.

The Constitution of the United States, with its various amendments, presents the foundation of this chapter on community policing and has been briefly summarized as a force in guiding public policy. In addition, we have selected three publications of the 20th century that have had an impact on our research and writings. They have made a significant influence on the police and we will describe them in detail under the subheadings of *Traditional Policing, Traditional Policing Versus Community Relations*, and *Traditional Policing Versus Community Policing*.

**Traditional Policing**

The early beginnings of the US police reflect, in part, England's Metropolitan Police Act of 1829, which established a civilian police force with a military hierarchy, twenty-four hour prevention patrol by uniformed personnel, and a non-uniform group of detectives who dealt with the most serious crimes. The police in England were held individually accountable for their professional actions beginning in 1829 but the US police were more susceptible to political patronage.

This modern police idea moved west from the metropolitan cities on the Atlantic east coast of the US, such as the New York City Police Department in 1844 (Clift, 1956) and the Boston Police Department in 1855 (Lane, 1971) and continued north and south and to the then developing communities in the west towards the Pacific Ocean. Twenty-six (52 per cent) of the present 50 states had not been admitted to the Union in 1829 and of these, five states entered the Union in the 20th century. In 1829 the US had only been an independent country for approximately 50 years.

*The First Half of the 20th Century.* The first 50 years, after the turn of the century, introduced a myriad of practical mechanical and electronic devices, scientific discoveries, and social changes that seem to have placed the 'Industrial Revolution' at a crossroads - nothing was impossible for mankind.

Many thought that the pinnacle for research and development had been achieved. Work organizations, both private and public, were becoming more complex and researchers set about to discover the most efficient means to economize man's interaction with the machinery of production and the administration of organization itself.

*Scientific Management.* Prior to the development of scientific management the US Congress had passed the Pendleton Act of 1883 that created a competitive civil service examination process to select the best available person for a public job. The civil service idea was not quickly implemented but a continued increase in public corruption made the idea of competitive selection a preferred alternative to one of nepotism and government inefficiency.

Max Weber (1864-1920) had described bureaucracy as an ideal model (Blau and Meyer, 1956) with emphasis on form of organization with specific and regular activities (Pfiffner and Sherwood, 1960); e.g., hierarchy, lower organizational units under the control of higher units; specialization of task, individuals are selected on the basis of merit and ability to perform; a specified sphere of competence that comes from specialization; established norms of conduct that influences predictability; and the recording of organizational activities. But, we believe, it was the Scientific Management writers, led by Frederick Winslow Taylor in 1911 with his publication of *The Principles of Scientific Management* that introduced the idea of efficiency and maximum organizational effort into US governmental and private organizations.   Other contributors to the philosophy of increasing administrative output were Frank B. Gilbreth (1914), Henry L. Gantt (1916), Clarence B. Thompson (1917), and the consolidated papers on administration by Luther Gulick and L. Urwick (1937), and observations by many other writers.

Within this idealism of public efficiency, honesty in government, and the application of science to public administration, August Vollmer became a natural candidate to apply these new ideas to policing, police management, and police organization.

*Police Corruption and Reformation.* The police idea in the US was, in part, further defined by August Vollmer (1876-1955) with his innate curiosity and sensitivity for experimentation with his early study and reorganization of the San Diego Police Department in 1915. During 1923-24, while on a leave of absence from the Berkeley Police Department, he became Chief of the Los Angeles Police Department where he conducted surveys and prepared a plan for departmental reorganization. His Report on Police Conditions in the United States in 1931 for the National Commission on Law Observance and Enforcement (also known as the Wickersham Report) was submitted to the administration of President Herbert C. Hoover (1874-1964). Donal E.J. MacNamara in 1977 wrote a chapter in Philip John Stead's *Pioneers in Policing* describing August Vollmer as a '...police pioneer who, more than any other, dragged American law enforcement, protesting and resisting all the way, into the twentieth century'.

Vollmer's major contribution was the development and pursuit of police professionalism. He started his law enforcement experience in 1905 as a town marshal in Berkeley, California and, after a municipal reorganization, he became Chief of Police of Berkeley in 1909. This was the same year that construction of Sather Gate at the University of California at Berkeley was underway, which was to become an important symbol for US student protests in the 1960s and 1970s at the University of California at Berkeley. Vollmer was an innovator in the policing of the city of Berkeley and introduced motorcycle patrols in 1913, automobile patrols in 1914, and placed radios into patrol cars in 1921. He  reorganized the police training curriculum and in

1922 introduced a single-fingerprint classification, developed a department planning and research unit, as well as conducting department reorganization, including arrest-record keeping and the gathering of crime statistics.

During his active police career he became president of the California Police Chiefs Association in 1907, president of the International Association of Chiefs of Police in 1922, and was one of the founders in 1941 of the American Society of Criminology and became its first president. He remained Chief of the Berkeley Police Department until his retirement in 1932.

Vollmer was a professor of police administration at the University of Chicago and in the early 1930s joined the University of California at Berkeley as a professor to teach a few courses in police administration. From this humble beginning, these few courses evolved in the 1950's into the University of California at Berkeley's School of Criminology. Over the years he conducted numerous surveys of domestic and foreign police departments.

*National Commission on Law Observance and Enforcement.* The national government became concerned with police corruption and police reorganization and established the *National Commission on Law Observance and Enforcement* in 1929. The Commission was originally created to study the national prohibition laws which were a result of the Eighteenth Amendment; but, soon widened its scope and became the most extensive documentation at that time of US law enforcement problems, practices, and procedures. The *Report on Police Conditions in the United States*, written under the supervision and influence of Vollmer, was submitted to President Hoover in 1931.

For approximately two years the Wickersham Commission conducted surveys, reviewed law enforcement and other relative literature, interviewed persons, and collected statistical and written data to be summarized and presented in 14 reports. Each report dealt with a particular topic: e.g., No. 1, Preliminary Report on Prohibition; No. 2, Enforcement of the Prohibition Laws of the United States; No. 3, Criminal Statistics; No. 4, Prosecution; No.5, The Enforcement of the Deportation Laws of the United States; No. 6, The Child Offender in the Federal System of Justice; No. 7, Progress Report on the Study of the Federal Courts; No. 8, Criminal Procedure; No. 9, Penal Institutions, Probation and Parole; No. 10, Crime and the Foreign Born; No. 11, Lawlessness in Law Enforcement; No. 12, Cost of Crime; No.13, Causes of Crime, Volume I and Causes of Crime, Volume II; and No.14, Police.

Although other reports dealt directly or indirectly with the topic of police, this section of the chapter will deal with the limited interaction of community policing as shaped by Vollmer in Report No.14 and helped shape our interest and understanding of US policing.

The Wickersham Commission wrote a preface to the police report stating that 'The general failure of the police ... has caused a loss of public confidence in the police of our country' and then described what was considered to be the primary police problems:

- A major problem, '... in our opinion, lies in the insecure, short term of service of the chief or executive head of the police force and in his being subject while in office to the control by politicians in the discharge of his duties.' The report then describes the control that politicians had over the appointment and conduct in office of the chief and that, 'The chief knows perfectly well to whom he owes his appointment ...' and the results of a questionnaire that was sent to 745 city police forces indicated that the average term of chief of police was five years;

- A second problem '... is the lack of competent, efficient, and honest patrolmen and subordinate officers ... Even where there are civil service examinations, the hand of the politician is all too plainly visible';

- A third problem was the lack of modern technology, in that, 'To serve the community effectively the policeman should be fully equipped with the tools of his profession';

- A fourth problem in producing police inefficiency is the result of political corruption;

- A fifth problem is the increasing immigrant and foreign born in the nation's cities that '... requires a higher degree of executive ability, talent, and management of the police force and in the patrolmen that we have now ... more police officers should be on each force who are of such races and familiar with their language, habits, customs, and cultural background';

- A sixth problem is 'As the urban population increased, no diversification was made in the duties of officers or patrolmen. Numbers were added to the force as the exigencies of the time required without changing the duty of the officer to watch for breaches of all laws and ordinances ... It gives opportunity for graft and oppression which a different system, created and maintained in consonance with modern conditions and needs, would have avoided'; and,

- In summary, 'This commission has no authority to make recommendations to city officials as to how they shall reorganize or remodel their police forces to bring them into line with present day conditions of efficiency in the discharge of their duties to keep the peace and protect the lives and property of its citizens. It can but state the facts as they have been developed in many surveys and the study wherewith submitted. The facts largely speak for themselves. We do, however, commend to city officials and the intelligent public generally desirous of police betterment, the conclusions formulated by Mr Vollmer ...' and other members of the research team supervised by him.

Vollmer, writing in a separate preface restates some of the previous observations of the Commission but adds a paragraph describing the prevention of crime to be '... one of the newly recognized obligations of the policemen ... especially with regard to its dependence upon cordial relations with public and private agencies which may be involved ...' is the addition of female police and their distinctive contribution to crime prevention. A brief description of juvenile delinquency is then presented.

*Report on Police Conditions in the United States*

The Police Report devotes Chapter VII to crime prevention and states that

> Police departments in the United States have not been long familiar with crime prevention as a distinct function of the police organization ... Much of the reluctance of departments to assign separate standing to this activity has possibly been due to the absence of any clearly defined field in which such unit should operate, as well as to the habit of preserving the status quo. In the hard school of experience the police have learned that 'let well enough alone' is usually the safest path.

> It has so far been tacitly assumed that some adequate definition exists for the term crime prevention. This is not true. Indeed, we should have difficulty in fixing even the meaning of crime in a manner satisfactory to any considerable number of thinkers. By repeated reference to crime prevention we may have created the impression that the causes of crimes are known, and this is also untrue.

There follows a further discussion of the causes of crime with the conclusion that there is probably not any one condition but many. The text includes a reference to a 1930 State of New York crime commission report which notes that within some environments of large cities the '... areas of excessive juvenile delinquency and crime are geographical and ecological areas of transition or isolation, otherwise known as city slums.' The report adds that 1927 data from 'State prison reformatories and five Federal penal institutions' indicated that 23.4 per cent of the prisoners were less than 21 years of age and 44.8 per cent under 25. The argument is then made that a prevention program by police departments, cooperating with community welfare agencies, could reduce crimes: 'No city of considerable size can afford to be without a unit which will devote its whole time to crime prevention. Such a unit must receive official recognition in large enough measure to command respect from the members of the force and other community agencies.' The need for community collaboration is discussed suggesting that it is desirable to have 'an advisory committee on which are represented the agencies and institutions which will furnish their main contacts.   The school, church, welfare societies, associated charities clearinghouse ... and probation officers are represented. The cooperation of other groups may be secured from time to time by direct representation or special invitation. It is of particular importance that the support of the press be obtained; a general community understanding of the aims of the unit is essential to any large success.'

It is recommended that female officers, in some situations, will be more adequate in dealing with youth prevention problems: 'Women police have been especially successful in handling cases involving women and children, where their sex has opened avenues of approach which are normally closed to men. Actual street patrol by women police has been found to provide a better perspective of the problem by furnishing practical examples upon which effective techniques must hinge.'   Vollmer's experience in the Berkeley Police Department is cited by describing the need to organize 'community work, serving on committees developing a rather extensive volunteer service from the university and other sources, and fostering activity in connection with juvenile delinquency work.'

There is a need, according to the report, for experimentation in regards to crime prevention 'before a crime prevention unit can settle down to a comfortable place as a member of the police family.'   In a nation where the cost of crime is high 'it would not seem unreasonable to spend a few hundreds of thousands on crime prevention.'

As researchers and writers, we have been influenced by Vollmer's direction in the Wickersham Report in that we continue to observe police departments, based on his recommendations, as we conduct research on community policing.

It is extraordinary that Vollmer, as part of an official government publication in 1931, was discussing the following ideas on crime prevention:

- Police departments will be reluctant to accept crime prevention concepts;
- There is an absence of a clear and acceptable definition of crime prevention;
- There is probably not any one contributing factor to crime – but many;
- Areas of excessive juvenile delinquency and crime are geographical with ecological areas of transition or isolation;
- It can be assumed that a prevention program by police departments and community agencies can reduce crimes;
- No city of considerable size can afford to be without a unit which will devote its whole time to crime prevention;
- A crime prevention unit must receive official recognition in large enough measure to command respect from the members of the force and other community agencies;
- The need for community collaboration is desirable;
- Community collaboration should include the school, church, welfare societies, community based organizations, probation, etc;
- Community understanding of the aims of crime prevention is essential to be successful;
- It is recommended that female officers patrol the streets;
- There is a need for experimentation in regard to crime prevention; and,
- Money should be made available to facilitate crime prevention.

## Traditional Policing Versus Community Relations

Vollmer's understanding that the nation's police departments would be 'reluctant' to accept new ideas seemed to be correct and not many of his suggestions in the 1931 Wickersham Report were implemented and had to wait over 30 years to be revisited.

The 1950s introduced the duality of the police myth as opposed to the police reality – the two were not compatible. The myth of police efficiency, police fairness to all people, and police professionalism was offset by an increasing crime rate, accusations of police brutality, and racial discrimination. Like two gigantic glaciers, two US populations – one white, the other nonwhite – were starting to rub against each other and the friction was producing mass violence in the form of riots.

By the 1960s, the FBI's *Uniform Crime Reports* indicated that major crimes against the person and property were increasing and that a series of riots that had been occurring in the USA from the 1900s into the 1960s was now being concentrated in metropolitan areas with approximately 20 riots occurring in cities during the summers of 1964, 1965, and 1966.

Typical reasons for the riots were many; but, as in the Los Angeles Watts riot in 1965, major issues were unfair police practices, racial targeting, political disenfranchisement, and economic issues. A precursor of unfair police practices to the Watts riot was identified in a 1963 *Commission on Civil Rights Report on California: Police-Minority Group Relations*, but was ignored.   The California Advisory Committee to the United States Commission on Civil Rights held meetings in two major metropolitan areas of California: Los Angeles in 1962; and, also in San Francisco and Oakland in 1963. The meetings focused specifically on police and minority relations. In Los Angeles, testimony was given by African-Americans and Mexican-Americans who accused the Los Angeles Police of using excessive violence in effecting arrests, that they were arrested for acts ignored when committed by whites, and that they were harassed in a discriminatory manner. The police and other city officials denied these allegations. The meetings reflected testimony from the police and the minority groups that was deeply emotional, accusatory, and with no apparent room for conciliation. One of the five recommendations that were presented indicated that 'the United States Commission on Civil Rights consider the availability of scheduling a hearing in Los Angeles to investigate the allegation that officers of the Los Angeles Police Department use excessive force in many of their contacts with Negroes.' This was not done.

The Watts Riot lasted six days with 34 people killed and over 1,000 people wounded.  At times there were 10,000 rioters in the city streets, and ended the trouble ended with the commitment of approximately 14,000 military equipped personnel of the California National Guard.

Soon after the riot, the Governor of California formed a commission, chaired by former CIA Director John A. McCone (1965), to investigate the incident. The Commission's report, *Violence in the City – An End or a Beginning?* was presented to the Governor in December of 1965 with an horrific warning:

As a Commission, we are seriously concerned that the existing breach, if allowed to persist, could in time split our society irretrievably. So serious and so explosive is the situation that, unless it is checked, the August riots may seem by comparison to be only a curtain-raiser for what could blow up one day in the future.

One of the major recommendations of the Commission was that 'The Police Department should institute expanded community relations programs.'

*Commission on Law Enforcement and Administration of Justice*

In 1965 President Lyndon B. Johnson (1908-1973) established a Commission on Law Enforcement and Administration of Justice (Task Force Report, 1967) which was chaired by Nicholas deB. Katzenbach who was Attorney General of the United States from 1965-1966. The primary Commission Report was entitled The Challenge of Crime in a Free Society and was published in 1967. Nine additional reports were topic specific and called Task Force Reports on; The Courts, Corrections, Juvenile Delinquency and Youth Crime, Organized Crime, Science and Technology, Assessment of Crime, Narcotics and Drugs, Drunkenness, and The Police. These reports were published in the 1960s and a number of research studies and selected consultants' papers were published at various times. Nineteen commissioners, 63 staff members, 175 consultants, and hundreds of advisers supported the Commission. It is apparent that the output of this Commission was designed and generated by a committee.

*The Challenge of Crime in a Free Society*

When describing the willingness of the criminal justice system to change, it was stated,

> The inertia of the criminal justice system is great. More than 30 years ago the Wickersham Commission described the scandalous way in which justice was being administered and in attempting to understand the cost of crime and how this may influence decision making and public policy. 'It is surprising that the cost information on which they are based is as fragmentary as it is. The lack of knowledge about which the Wickersham Commission complained 30 years ago is almost as great today.

Our evaluation of law enforcement became more focused at this time and our standards for comparison reflected Vollmer's 1931 Report and attempts in the 1960s and 1970s to perform crime prevention and community relations. It remains clear that the police and the minority communities did not understand each other's needs or how to correct the impasse.

The Commission's summation of crime is stated clearly: 'Despite the seriousness of the problem today and the increasing challenge in the years ahead, the central conclusion of the Commission is that a significant reduction in crime is possible if the following objectives are vigorously pursued:'

1. *Preventing Crime.* 'The prevention of crime covers a wide range of activities: eliminating social conditions closely associated with crime; improving the ability of the criminal justice system to detect, apprehend, judge, and reintegrate into their communities those who commit crimes; and reducing the situations in which crimes are most likely to be committed.'

2. *New Ways of Dealing with Offenders.* 'The Commission's second objective – the development of a far broader range of alternatives for dealing with offenders – is based on the belief that, while there are some who must be completely segregated from society, there are many instances in which segregation does more harm than good. Furthermore, by concentrating the resources of the police, the courts, and correctional agencies on the smaller number of offenders who really need them, it should be possible to give all offenders more effective treatment.'

3. *Eliminating Unfairness.* 'The third objective is to eliminate injustices so that the system of criminal justice can win the respect and cooperation of all citizens. Our society must give the police, the courts, and correctional agencies the resources and the mandate to provide fair and dignified treatment for all.'

4. *Personnel.* 'The fourth objective is that higher levels of knowledge, expertise, initiative, and integrity be achieved by police, judges, prosecutors, defense attorneys, and correctional authorities so that the system of criminal justice can improve its ability to control crime.'

5. *Research.* 'The fifth objective is that every segment of the system of criminal justice devote a significant part of its resources for research to insure the development of new and effective methods of controlling crime.'

6. *Money.* 'Sixth, the police, courts, and correctional agencies will require substantially more money if they are to control crime better.'
7. *Responsibility for Change.* 'Seventh, individual citizens, social-service agencies, universities, religious institutions, civic and business groups, and all kinds of governmental agencies at all levels must become involved in planning and executing changes in the criminal justice system.'

## Task Force Report: The Police

One chapter out of nine chapters in this report deals in a meaningful way with the community and the police.

Chapter 6, entitled The Police and the Community, describes the importance of police community relations; e.g., 'The need for strengthening police relationships with the communities they serve is critical today in the nation's large cities and in many small cities and towns as well ... Police community relationships have a direct bearing on the character of life in our cities, and on the community's ability to maintain stability and to solve its problems ... Indeed, no lasting improvement in law enforcement is likely in this country unless police community relations are substantially improved.'

When describing the effect police community relations has on the police department as an organization and on police operations, it was stated that the

> Hostility, or even lack of confidence of a significant portion of the public, has extremely serious implication for the police ... Perhaps most significant of all, when the police and the public are at odds, the police tend to become isolated from the public and become less capable of understanding and adapting to the community and its changing needs ... and poor police community relations adversely affect the ability of the police to prevent crime and apprehend criminals – people hostile to the police are not so likely to report violations of law, even when they are the victims.

When discussing police community relations and the effect on community stability the report says

> poor police community relations has contributed to the disturbances and riots which have increasingly afflicted our cities for the last 3 years ... poor police community relations, together with poor housing, unemployment, and oppressive commercial practices were basic underlying factors in these riots. In addition, more often than not, riots were set off by some quite ordinary and

proper action by a policeman. Some riots, however, started after improper or at least unwise police conduct.

In describing the role of police programs that are directly related to community relations it was observed that 'Unless, however, the legitimate grievances relating to the police are confronted frankly and effectively, improvement of police community relations will be impossible. Modification of police procedures on the street, stronger internal discipline over officers, greatly enlarged and strengthened police community relations units, improved procedures for handling citizen complaints, better screening to eliminate candidates for the police force who are biased, and many other measures deeply affecting police agencies and police work will be necessary ... the primary responsibility for improving police community relations must rest with the police. As a responsible and organized public service agency, they must take the initiative in making good police community relations a reality.'

It is suggested that to develop successful community relations it is essential to establish a special responsible community relations unit:

> If community relations units are to be successful, they must clearly have prestige and authority. Consequently, responsibility for community relations must be placed at the highest possible level ... Community relations programs cannot be effective if responsibility is split between various police units. In one large city, for instance, a public information division handles press relations, speeches, tours, and citizen crime prevention programs; a human relations section working out of the field services division investigates incidents with religious, racial, or ethnic overtones and gives advice concerning high-tension situations; and, a community relations coordinator, in the office of the chief of patrol, coordinates neighborhood police community workshops ... A commonly accepted function of community relations units is working with citizen groups.

We feel that the stated position is correct, but nevertheless, most police departments failed to incorporate community relations into the police organization.

The report further recommended that police department policy should reflect community needs and expectations indicating that 'in most police departments the problems of community relations are rarely translated into policies except under public pressure. It is essential that police community relations units have a formal role in formulating policies affecting community relations' and emphasising the need to track the progress of community relations by conducting evaluation and research.

A community relations unit must constantly evaluate its own programs. New ideas are frequently tried, but the programs have rarely received sufficient professional evaluation ... One means of evaluation is through attitude surveys conducted among residents. Such surveys can indicate how residents view the police, where community relations programs have succeeded and where they have failed, and what areas need concentrated effort. Similar evaluation should be conducted of ... the police.

In conclusion of this section, several observations are given. Those, which appear to be the most relevant, are the following:

- Police officials and officers often adopt a defensive attitude toward those who criticize and are hostile to them. Many of the people most hostile to the police are ordinary citizens acting honestly out of firm belief. It is therefore essential that the police explore problems openly – that, indeed, the police seek out their critics so that problems can be met together;
- The police must be willing to adapt to change;
- The problem, particularly between the police and minority groups, is a deep and complex one involving many other issues and institutions of our society; and,
- Finally, 'much has been said about the ineffectiveness of existing community relations programs ... Unfortunately, however, progress is not nearly fast enough. Impatience, frustration, and now violence are growing quickly in minority communities and these trends are likely to accelerate. Consequently, if the problem is not to get worse, to the serious detriment of both the police and the community, drastic and creative action is urgently needed.

## Traditional Policing Versus Community Policing

Kelling and Moore (1988) described the difficulty of *The Evolving Strategy of Policing*, suggesting that the police 'like all professions, learn from experience'. However, they continue,

The difficulty is that police history is incoherent, its lessons hard to read. After all, that history was produced by thousands of local departments pursuing their own visions and responding to local conditions ... the classical theory of organization that continues to dominate police administration in most American cities is alien to most of the elements of the new strategy [community policing]. The new strategy will not accommodate to the classical theory ... Organizational theory has developed well beyond the stage it was during the early 1900s, and policing does have organizational options that are consistent with the newly developing organizational strategy ... It is overthrowing a strategy that was remarkable in its time, but which could not adjust to the changes of recent decades.

Successes in this new community strategy '... are broad: quality of life in neighborhoods, problem solution, reduction of fear, increased order, citizen satisfaction with police services, as well as crime control.' Four, of several elements of community strategy, would include:

* Community support;
* Crime control and crime prevention through collaborative problem solving;
* Organizational decentralization; and,
* Quality of life and citizen satisfaction.

By 1993, community policing had attracted many labels, some of which were identified by Edwin Meese III (1993), a former Attorney General of the United States in *Community Policing and the Police Officer*. Meese suggested that this new concept has '... a variety of names – strategic policing, problem-solving policing, neighborhood-oriented policing ... and others – police agencies are developing new concepts to better satisfy the demands and needs of the citizens they serve.' As this new concept develops, he observed, '... the emphasis and methods of policing change, the position of the police officer in the organization changes also. Instead of reacting to specified situations, limited by rigid guidelines and regulations, the officer becomes a thinking professional, utilizing imagination and creativity to identify and solve problems.'

Also, in 1993, Herman Goldstein, writing in *The New Policing: Confronting Complexity*, stated, 'The downside of this new-found popularity is that 'community policing' is widely used without any regard for its substance. Political leaders and, unfortunately, many police leaders latch onto the label for the positive images it evokes but do not invest in the concept itself.' Goldstein suggests that a possible response to this problem '... is to press for definition and simplification, to seek agreement on a pure model of community policing.'

He does, however, indicate that some changes to community policing are being implemented 'for example, the permanent assignment of officers to specific beats with a mandate to get to know and relate to the community.' Goldstein argued that there is now growing and persuasive support for decentralization, permanent assignment, and the development of partnerships between the police and the community. But that these changes represent only 'a fragment of the larger picture.'

> Policing in the United States is much like a large, intricate, complex apparatus with many parts. Change of any one part requires changes in many others and in the way the parts fit and work together.'

Goldstein indicated that change is occurring in the following areas:

*Refining the police function and public expectations.* 'The new forms of policing expand the police function from crime fighting, without any abdication of that role, to include maintaining order, dealing with quality-of-life offenses ... now recognized as being much more important than previously believed.'

*Getting involved in the substance of policing.* 'A common theme in initiatives under the community policing umbrella is the emphasis on improving relationships with the citizenry. Such improvement is vital in order to reduce tensions, develop mutual trust, promote the free exchange of information, and acquaint officers with the culture and lifestyle of those being policed.'

*Rethinking the relationship between the police and the criminal justice system.* 'Buried in all of the rhetoric relating to community policing is the fact that, with little notice and in subtle ways, the longstanding relationship between the police and the criminal justice system is being redefined. This is a radical change, but it is given scant attention in the literature on community policing.'

*Searching for alternatives.* 'The diversification of policing – the move from primary dependence on the criminal law to the use of a wide range of different responses – is among the most significant changes under the community policing umbrella ... These may include informal, common sense responses used in the past but never formally authorized.'

*Changing the working environment in a police agency.* 'If new forms of policing are to take hold, the working environment within police agencies must change. Much has been written about new management styles supportive of community policing.  But with a few remarkable exceptions relatively little has actually been achieved.'

In 1993, a random, stratified sample of 2,314 municipal and county police and sheriff's departments was sponsored by the National Institute of Justice in association with Mary Ann Wycoff of the Police Foundation and presented in *Community Policing Strategies, Research Preview* (1995). It was reported, that 'Almost half (47 per cent) of the police chiefs and sheriffs were unclear about the practical meaning of community policing.  Forty-eight percent agreed that implementation would require major changes in organizational policies or goals, and 56 per cent anticipated that rank-and-file employees would resist such changes.'

A 1996 the National Institute of Justice Journal devoted its entire edition to 'Against Crime, Making Partnerships Work' and described in a series of articles the expanded role of community into the various components of criminal justice; e.g., community prosecution, community courts, community corrections, and community justice.

*Community prosecution.* Barbara Boland (1996) answers the question What is Community Prosecution? by indicating that neighbourhood district attorney's are relocated into identifiable communities and in general, they '... work with citizens and police to help come up with ways to control the types of street behavior and low-level disorder that threaten neighborhood safety ... by devising alternative responses.' And that '... solutions arrived at by informal negotiations ... need to be solidly grounded in the law.' This redirection in prosecution is seen as an approach, not as a program.

*Community courts.* '... in response to pressures to provide better service, courts are decentralizing facilities,' is reviewed by David B. Rottman (1996) in Community Courts: Prospects and Limits. 'A community-focused court is a more expansive effort still, requiring ongoing collaboration between a trial court and one or more community groups either for a specific purpose or in a major aspect of the court's adjudicator scope ... Survey research reveals a judiciary that has great confidence in the courts but a public that consistently rates them lower than other public institutions. The potential exists for community-focused courts to offer a means to improve the performance of judicial institutions, respond to concerns about racial and ethnic bias, and increase public trust. Ultimately, the challenge of creating community-focused courts may lie with communities themselves ... organized community interests need to view the courts as a resource and as a vehicle for change.  In other words, if there are to be community-focused courts, there must be court-focused communities.'

*Community corrections.* In the article Toward a Corrections of 'Place': The Challenge of 'Community' in Corrections by Todd R. Clear (1996), it is stated that community corrections has been operational for some time, but, in '... corrections, the term 'community' does not stand for the problem-solving focus but instead often merely indicates that an offender happens to be living outside a correctional facility.' The idea of place related to corrections '... depicts local corrections systems in which all offenders who come from one community would be dealt with in that place.' High risk offenders will continue to require greater control.

*Community justice.* The article Community Defense and the Challenge of Community Justice by Christopher Stone (1996) describes a neighbourhood defence approach that tests '... new ways of organizing and deploying public defenders that can solve problems of justice in the community while providing high-quality representation at a cost government can afford.' The approach is client based and like community policing focusing '... on the underlying problems in communities that generate high crime. If prosecutors, judges, and corrections officials do the same, they will find opportunities to forge alliances with defenders whose clients share an interest in eliminating problems that produce crime.'

However, for all the attempts to introduce community into all forms of criminal justice, in 1992 the City of Los Angeles exploded into another struggle between the police department and minority community members, which has become known as the 'Rodney King Riot.' Rodney King, an African-American, was arrested by Los Angeles Police officers for driving an automobile at excessive speeds and operating an automobile while intoxicated; but, in the process of the arrest several police officers struck him on his shoulders and head with police batons. The incident took place at night but was captured on videotape by a local resident and was repeatedly displayed on television. Four police officers were put on trial for using excessive force and on April 29, 1992 were found not guilty. Within an hour of the verdict, looting, violence, and fires were being set to buildings and a riot erupted which lasted for six days.

An inquiry report called *The City in Crisis: A Report by the Special Advisor to the Board of Police Commissioners in the Civil Disorder in Los Angeles* was completed on October 21, 1992. The report indicated that, 'In the end, during the six days of the disturbance, at least 42 people lost their lives, more than 700 businesses were burned, and some $1 billion in property was damaged or destroyed.'

Over the six days of rioting, 5,002 persons were arrested, over 7,000 California National Guard military troops were deployed into the city and 3,500 federal (US Army and Marine Corps) military troops were brought into the city in addition to Los Angeles Police personnel, Los Angeles County Sheriff's personnel, and other law enforcement personnel acting under mutual assistance. The Report states 'The toll of death, destruction and human misery left this time compels us to recall another such tragedy – one that scorched the ground of the City and its people just over a quarter of a century ago.

To read the report of the Governor's Commission empanelled to study that tragedy, causes us to experience a profound sense that, while much has changed since 1965 [in particular since the Watts Riot], much remains the same.

## Community Policing in Chicago

Chicago is the nation's third largest city with a population of nearly 2.8 million and a police force of approximately 13,500 personnel. In 1993, after a year of planning, a new type of policing was being created, tested, modified, and implemented. It is called the Chicago's Alternative Policing Strategy (CAPS). The city is divided into 279 beats, each staffed by a group of officers called a beat team. Approximately 5,000 residents a month attend their beat community meetings with the police beat teams.

Local politicians and the police department were motivated to bring about a positive change in the citizens expectations of an increasing crime problem but also in the actual reduction of the crime problem by forming community partnerships. In 1993 the Mayor's Office and the Police Department produced a 29-page brochure entitled Together We Can: A Strategic Plan for Reinventing the Chicago Police Department, which was made available to the public and police personnel. This publication discussed the limitations of traditional policing, in that 'National research conducted during the 1970s and early 1980s exposed, and for the first time quantified, many of the limitations of the traditional policing model, in particular its ability to impact levels of crime.' Then, a discussion of the limitations of traditional policing was given emphasising the following statements:

•     We learned that citizen fear, not just index crime rates, is important in measuring levels of neighborhood safety and public satisfaction with the police;

- We learned the limitations of preventive patrol using the automobile (a linchpin of the traditional model);
- We learned the limitations of rapid response to calls for service (another linchpin of the traditional model, especially here in Chicago);
- We learned that citizen information, as much as forensic technology, was the key to identifying offenders and solving crimes; and,
- Finally, we learned that continually arresting and incarcerating offenders had little deterrent effect in the long term.

Perhaps more than anything else, this research revealed a fatal shortcoming of the traditional model: the forced isolation of the police from the community prevented police from meeting their expectations of preventing (or at least controlling) crime. 'The challenges facing Chicago demand new approaches that target neighborhood problems with a partnership of government and community resources delivered at the neighborhood level.' Thus, part of the strategy is that the police department will be reinvented: 'We are embarking upon a major strategic change with the Police Department. The implications of these changes will touch every management, operational, and administrative entity within the organization.'

It was stated that 'solving crimes is, and will continue to be, an essential element of police work. But preventing crimes is the most effective way to create a safer environment in our neighborhoods.'

- The corporate culture of the Department must be redefined to emphasize and reward organizational and individual behavior that makes a real difference in fighting crime and helping to solve other neighbourhood problems;
- Crime control and prevention must be recognized as dual parts of the fundamental mission of policing;
- The principles of customer service and problem solving must be incorporated into all organizational entities of the Department;
- The organization must reinforce integrity and ethical behavior among our members at all times; and,
- The isolation between the police and the community must be broken down, and responsibility for the safety of Chicago's neighborhoods must be shared by police and citizens alike.

Some additional requirements shared with the public and the police are:

- All parts of the Department, including investigative, management, and support functions, will act in a unified manner to support the efforts of the beat officer;
- New technologies must provide the information and analytical capabilities that help police officers and the community identify and solve problems; and, therefore, prevent crimes;
- All of our training curricula must be retooled to emphasize and reinforce our law enforcement role and the skills that will be critical to our future success;
- Whereas in the past we have measured primarily activities, our new strategy demands that we evaluate results as well;
- Our beat boundaries should be made more compatible with the strong and natural neighborhood boundaries that already exist in Chicago;
- Sharing of useful information must be a pervasive value throughout the Department. The intentional withholding of information from one another for selfish purposes is a dangerous practice that will not be tolerated; and,
- Every Department member – but especially those at the most basic operational levels – must see community outreach as an important and ongoing element of their jobs.

The project was field tested in five selected districts before being implemented on a citywide basis. The program was designed to increase the responsiveness and effectiveness of police problem solving by linking these efforts directly to a broad range of city services involving the public in identifying and seeking solutions to neighborhood problems. If CAPS is to be successful, it will be because of the strong encouragement by local elected officials and ranking police administrators and the development of a workable relationship between the police and residents of the city. In *Community Policing, Chicago Style* in (1997) Skogan and Hartnett state that there are four general principles of community policing:

- Community policing relies on organizational decentralization and a reorientation of patrol in order to facilitate communication between police and the public;
- Community policing assumes a commitment to broadly focused problem solving;
- Community policing requires that police respond to the public when they set priorities and develop their tactics; and,

- Community policing implies a commitment to helping neighborhoods solve crime problems on their own, through community organizations and crime prevention programs.

We believe that the Chicago community police program reinvented policing in one of the largest police departments in the US (See Skogan and Harnett (1997), CCPEC (1995); CCPEC (1996); CCPEC (1997) for more complete details of the initiatives). This is probably the most important advancement to modern policing since the establishment of the Metropolitan Police in 1829. Other police departments in the US have attempted community policing, but have failed. The government, citizens, and police of Chicago were committed and made it work. Skogan and Hartnett, (1997) ask what the implications are of Chicago's experience for the remainder of the country? Their answer is 'We think there are two: It is hard to get community policing off the ground, but it can be made to work ... the first challenge to police and municipal executives is to get something concrete to happen on the street ... Community policing has to be the community's program, representing a commitment by the city's political leaders and taxpayers ... Learning from the successes and failures of other cities should be part of the process. A related problem is sustaining commitment to the enterprise ...[and] requires something that many cities have too little of – patience.' It may take years.

**Final observations**

We make these final observations on the basis of our examination of the key literature we have examined above.

- Community policing requires total commitment by police department personnel. Traditional police behaviors and attitudes must be replaced with real 'community collegiality and trust.' Many times the police stress ideas of community empowerment without the transfer of community decision making to residents. We were disappointed to find that not many police departments share decision making within their own ranks. They are retaining the traditional bureaucratic style of policing;
- New departmental policies and procedures must reflect a dedicated community policing effort. Resources must be made available for enforcement and prevention. The department must have a stated plan

with goals and objectives, and the means to evaluate the process of the plan. Community collaboration must start with the department plan and be a joint development with the community. Community and police creativity must be allowed to formulate new policies and procedures;

- The police and the community must be briefed as to what community policing is all about. We found that a large number of police agencies indicate their lack of understanding as to what community policing is about. The National Institute of Justice has developed an abundance of written material on community policing. There are numerous books, studies, and articles on the subject. Researchers and practitioners are discovering underlying principles of community policing. Police departments can no longer claim that there is a lack of understanding of community policing, they can only claim a total lack of motivation to process the current level of knowledge;

- The physical reorganization of the police department is critical to the success of community policing. We, and other researchers, have observed that small departments, because of necessity, have unconsciously been doing community policing and large departments have more difficulties in performing community policing because of their bureaucratic shape. Through reorganization, big departments must become responsive small departments;

- Officer recruitment must be changed to include skills related to community policing and currently serving officers must receive community policing training. We firmly believe that all personnel must receive, and then be held accountable to, the requirements of community policing. Department assessment and promotion of personnel must reflect community policing standards; and,

- The role of policing will reflect behavioral skills as well as law enforcement skills. We believe that community policing is a new concept and requires new thinking. Community policing is not a public relations advertisement. It is an honest attempt to improve the quality of community life and, in the long run, to prevent crime. New skills must be acquired, taught, and reinforced to make all of this possible.

**Where do we go from here?**

It is difficult to predict the future – to separate the wish from the reality. All the indicators of the past tell us that police departments will not change and, at best, change slowly. We can look back over 100 years of policing and feel the anguish for the many lives that have been shattered, the many commissions that have conducted inquiries, and the many recommendations that have been ignored. We can read the good intentions of good people who attempted to make good improvements – but were not totally successful. The reality reduces our expectations and hardens us to the failures. It is an impossible task to move the police from their war on crime, war on drugs, and the next war on whatever the new target may be. Or is it?

As we have shown, a major city in the US, the City of Chicago, with a very large police department and diverse ethnic population, has made a commitment to community policing that is redefining the idea of policing. The program is thoughtful, it is a collaboration of community and police, and it is committed for more than a quick fix. If communities wish to truly make a significant change in their crime problem they should look at Chicago for planning, evaluation, and collaboration styles; but, above all, they must be committed.

## References

A Report by the Governor's Commission on the Los Angeles Riots (1965). *Violence in the City: An End or a Beginning?* Los Angeles: Jeffries Banknote Co.

Berson, L.E. (1966). *Case Study of a Riot: The Philadelphia Story.* New York: Institute of Human Relations Press.

Blau, P.M. and Meyer, M.W. (1956). *Bureaucracy in Modern Society.* New York: Random House.

Boland, B. (1996). What is Community Prosecution? in Communities: Mobilizing Against Crime, Making Partnerships Work. *National Institute of Justice Journal,* US Department of Justice. Washington D.C.: Government Printing Office.

California Advisory Committee to the United States Commission on Civil Rights (1963). *Report on California: Police-Minority Group Relations in Los Angeles and the San Francisco Bay Area.* Washington DC: Government Printing Office.

CCPEC (1995). *Community Policing in Chicago, Year Two: An Interim Report,* June, The Chicago Community Policing Evaluation Consortium :The Illinois Criminal Justice Information Authority.

CCPEC (1996). *Community Policing in Chicago, Year Three,* November, The Chicago Community Policing Evaluation Consortium. The Illinois Criminal Justice Information Authority.

CCPEC (1997). *Community Policing in Chicago, Year Four: An Interim Report,* November, The Chicago Community Policing Evaluation Consortium. The Illinois Criminal Justice Information Authority.

City of Chicago (1993). *Together We Can: A Strategic Plan for Reinventing the Chicago Police Department.* Chicago: The City of Chicago.

Clear, T.R. (1996). Toward a Corrections of 'Place': The Challenge of 'Community' in Corrections in Communities: Mobilizing Against Crime, Making Partnerships Work. *National Institute of Justice Journal,* US Department of Justice. Washington, D.C.: Government Printing Office.

Clift, R.E. (1956). *A Guide to Modern Police Thinking,* Cincinnati: The W.H. Anderson Co.

Community Policing Strategies. (1995). *National Institute of Justice, Research Preview,* US Department of Justice. Washington, DC: Government Printing Office.

Gantt, H.L. (1916). *Industrial Leadership.* New Haven: Yale University Press.

Gilbreth, F.B. (1914). *Primer of Scientific Management.* New York: D.Van Nostrand Co.

Goldstein, H. (1993). *The New Policing: Confronting Complexity.* National Institute of Justice, US Department of Justice. Washington DC: Government Printing Office.

Gulick, L. and Urwick, L. (1937). *Papers on the Science of Administration.* New York: Institute of Public Administration, Columbia University.

Kelling, G.L. and Moore, M.H. (1988). *The Evolving Strategy of Policing.* National Institute of Justice, U.S. Department of Justice, and the Program in Criminal Justice Policy and Management, John F. Kennedy School of Government. Boston: Harvard University.

Lane, R. (1971). *Policing the City: Boston 1822-1885.* New York: Atheneum.

MacNamara, D.E.J. in Philip John Stead, ed. (1977). *Pioneers in Policing.* Montclair, New Jersey: Patterson Smith Publishing Corporation.

McCone, J.A. (1965). *Violence in the City: An End or a Beginning?* A Report by the Governor's Commission on the Los Angeles Riots. Los Angeles, Jeffries Banknote Co.

McGregor, D. (1960). *The Human Side of Enterprise.* New York: McGraw-Hill Book Company.

Meese III, E. (1993). *Community Policing and the Police Officer.* National Institute of Justice, US Department of Justice, and the Program in Criminal Justice Policy and Management, John F. Kennedy School of Government. Boston: Harvard University.

Pfiffner, J.M. and Sherwood. F.P. (1960). *Administrative Organization.* Englewood cliffs, N.J.: Prentice-Hall, Inc.

Rottman, D.B. (1996). Community Courts: Prospects and Limits in Communities: Mobilizing Against Crime, Making Partnerships Work. *National Institute of Justice Journal,* U.S. Department of Justice. Washington DC: Government Printing Office.

Skogan, W.G. and Hartnett, S.M. (1997). *Community Policing, Chicago Style.* New York: Oxford University Press.

Stone, C. (1996). Community Defense and the Challenge of Community Justice in Communities: Mobilizing Against Crime, Making Partnerships Work, *National Institute of Justice Journal,* US Department of Justice. Washington DC: Government Printing Office.

State of New York, Legislative Document, No. 98. (1930). Reprint of the Crime Commission.

Task Force Report (1967). *The Police. A Report by the President's Commission on Law Enforcement and Administration of Justice.* Washington D.: Government Printing Office.

Taylor, F.W. (1911). *The Principles of Scientific Management.* New York: Harper and Brothers.

The Challenge of Crime in a Free Society (1967). *A Report by the President's Commission on Law Enforcement and Administration of Justice.* Washington DC: Government Printing Office.

The City in Crisis: A Report by the Special Advisor to the Board of Police Commissioners in the Civil Disorder in Los Angeles (1992). Los Angeles: Special Advisory Study.

Thompson, C.B. (1917). *The Theory and Practice of Scientific Management.* Boston: Houghton Mifflin Co.

Vollmer, A. (1931). *Report No. 14: Police* (prepared and written in part under the direction of August Vollmer).US National Commission on Law Observance and Enforcement (Wickersham Commission). Washington DC: Government Printing Office.

# PART 4

# CRIME INVESTIGATION

# 8. The Story of Criminal Proceedings: From Fact-finding to Police Decision-making[1]

PETER J. VAN KOPPEN

## Introduction

My first study in the field of law and psychology was on decision-making by judges in civil cases, done together with Jan ten Kate (ten Kate and van Koppen, 1984; van Koppen and ten Kate, 1984). We asked a large number of Dutch judges to decide on the same nine civil disputes and had them fill out a number of personality questionnaires. They key question was how personality characteristics of the judges might influence their decisions. To reach maximum probability that we would find any relation in our study, we carefully – with the aid of a group of judges and attorneys – designed the nine cases such that the arguments in favour of the position of both the plaintiff and the defendant were equally strong. So, we could expect half of the judges to decide in favour of the plaintiff and the other half in favour of the defendant. In the study two nasty things happened. First, the decisions by the judges were not equally divided; in all nine cases more than 80 per cent chose one party and a meagre number, less than 20 per cent, the other. Second, we found no relationship between our personality characteristics and decision-making by the judges. Our conclusion was that apparently judges are socialized to such an extent that they are able to minimize differences in decision-making and thus individual differences do not play a role in the run-of-the-mill cases.

Our study on individual differences in judicial decision-making fitted nicely into the tradition that had grown up by then, especially in political science (for a recent overview, see Baum, 1997). And this tradition fitted nicely into the dramatic changes that took place in the 20th century in the

---

1.    I wish to thank Jan de Keijser for valuable comments on an earlier draft.

views on legal decision-making. In the19th century, Netherlands legal decision-making was modelled as à rather straightforward process. Statutes were supposed to be clear and the only task of the judge was to render the one and only right application of the law. This 19th century ideology was drawn from Montesqiueu (1748-1834) who, within the division of powers, envisaged the role of the judge as nothing but being the *bouce de la loi*. The judge's decision had the form of a simple syllogism. Starting from a sharp division of general rules and the facts of a case to which the rule was to be applied, the judge's decision was supposed to be the only right conclusion from a *major* (rule) and a *minor* (facts). In the days of old, rules were rules, and facts were facts, and all were out there just to be found. Interpretation of facts or of rules was a very limited process indeed.

Now, views of legal decision-making have changed dramatically. I have always found these changes fascinating, not just because they lead to a changing role for judges and the judiciary as a whole, but also because they affect the behaviour of attorneys, prosecutors and the police and principally because they emphasize the peculiar dual nature of decisions in a legal context. Unlike many other decisions, legal decisions are both descriptive and prescriptive. Judges, for instance, try to establish what happened but at the same time they append values to these facts. These are intertwined processes, as I shall discuss below. The study of legal decision-making thus goes beyond much of the research in the field of psychology of law, where the main focus – with the exception of jury research – is on contributions to evidence, especially as far as witnesses are concerned (see for overviews Bull and Carson, 1995; Roesch, 1999; Wójcikiewicz, 2000 ; Traverso, 2000; Milne, 1999; Horowitz, 1998; Boros, 1998; Ainsworth, 1998; Kapardis, 1997).

I have been working in the field of criminal law for the last 15 years. In this chapter I shall discuss the changes in legal doctrine, the present state of affairs in the theories of legal decision-making, and some possible future directions. I limit the discussion to a consideration of facts in criminal cases. Not because interpretation of rules and especially the interactions of rules and facts are not of interest, but because, limiting the discussion to facts brings in the authors who form the central focus of this chapter: Reid Hastie and Nancy Pennington. Their work has been and still is a major input to the work I have done, for a large part in collaboration with Hans Crombag and Willem Albert Wagenaar.

## Changes in decision-making

Nineteenth and early 20th century life seemed simple for Dutch judges. They followed a four step procedure: find out what the facts are, take the law out of the bookcase and find the relevant rule, apply the rule to the facts found, and decide what consequences this should have for the future. Now we know that these steps cannot be distinguished from each other. For instance, the relevant rule of law can only be found after interpretation of the facts and facts can only be interpreted in light of the relevant rule.

The attack on a mechanical view of legal decision-making started a little earlier in the USA than on the European continent. Holmes (1881; 1897) considered law nothing more than what a judge in fact does: 'The prophecies of what the courts will do in fact, and nothing more pretentious, are what I mean by the law' (Holmes, 1897, p. 43). Roscoe Pound (see the discussion by Grossman, 1935) – together with Cardozo (1921) exponent of the so-called *sociological jurisprudence* – then gave the judge a central role in the law. The judge is, according to Pound, the really creative element in the law, the one who takes care that the law can keep the pace of modern times. This line of reasoning was continued by proponents of the legal realists as Karl Llewellyn (1960; Llewellyn and Hoebel, 1941) and Jerome Frank (1950). They asked attention for the more pragmatic aspects of legal decision-making (see for German and Dutch lawyers in this area Esser, 1970; Scholten, 1974). This has led to extremes as some lawyers consider the legal decision as a highly individual creative act by the judge (for instance Van Dunné, 1974).

This line of legal thinking fits neatly with an interest in research on social and psychological influences on legal decision-making (see for some early attempts Herzog, 1917; Schröder, 1918; Sturm, 1910) both in the Western (see for instance Hogarth, 1971; ten Kate and Van Koppen, 1984; De Keijser, 2000) and Non-Western world (Fallers, 1969; Gluckman, 1967; Von Benda-Beckmann, 1984).

Two general conclusions can be drawn from all these studies on court behaviour. First, legal decisions have a principled open character; facts and rules can be interpreted in many differing ways. Second, at the same time, interpretations of facts and rules are limited as well. Judges in bench trials are, for instance, limited in their decisions by the opinions of their colleagues and, moreover, their anticipation of what the superior court may do if one of the parties appeals. Juries, to give another example, are limited in their freedom of decision-making because they have to come to a shared decision.

## Psychological models of legal decision-making

As said, psychological models of decision-making in criminal cases share a characteristic that is peculiar in the field of psychology: all are both descriptive and prescriptive in nature. The mixed nature of these models is derived from the mixed nature of law itself. Law is a 'social system created with a view of regulating the conduct of members of a community' (Blackman, Müller, and Chapman, 1984, p. 3). Thus, law is a behavioural technology and law and the legal system can be judged by the extent to which they successfully serve that purpose (Crombag and Van Koppen, 1991). At the same time, however, the law is an expression of a social philosophy in which, depending on place, time and circumstances, an ideal state of affairs is described; one for which society at large should strive (Crombag, 1982; Van Koppen and Hessing, 1988). As a consequence, the study of decision-making in criminal cases has always been a mixture of prescriptive and descriptive theories. This has been most prominent in research on decisions about the guilt or innocence of the suspect – the subject of the present chapter – but also in research on sentencing and in research on distributive and procedural justice. In sentencing studies, the assumption always has been that disparity between sentences in comparable cases is evil and should be removed as much as possible (see for instance Berghuis, 1992; Homel and Lawrence, 1992). The psychological study of justice considerations by individuals draws on the same mixture of prescription and description (Adams, 1965; Deutsch, 1975; Lerner, 1975, 1980; Tyler, 1994; Walster, Walster and Berscheid, 1978) I will limit myself, however, to the decision on guilt and innocence.

In each legal system the decision on guilt or innocence, for instance, is governed by a set of legal rules that prescribes how the fact-finder – court or jury – is to handle the evidence. To me, these rules appear to emerge from the common understanding that without them too many innocent citizens might be convicted or too many guilty suspects might be acquitted. That, in itself, is an understanding that is descriptive in nature. But, the social philosophic character of law is also reflected in rules of evidence. Some of these rules, for instance, may serve to control police behaviour, by declaring evidence inadmissible if it is generated by police practices that are unwanted for whatever reason. Other pieces of evidence are inadmissible because they are considered biased against the defendant, even though they might be highly relevant for the decision on guilt or innocence; for example, in some legal systems, the prior criminal record of the defendant.

The above was necessary to argue that a valid theory of decision-making in criminal cases needs to account both for the empirical reality and for the normative elements involved. In this chapter I will discuss the models that are most widely used in the psychological study of decision-making in criminal cases. As I shall discuss below, some of these models are, in my modest opinion, too far away from how reasoning is done psychologically. It should be noted, however, that I found, for instance, the Bayesian model very enlightening in discussing individual pieces of evidence. This framework, however, never appealed to me as one that could in any way produce a model that comes near to anything a judge is, in practice, doing. The 'story' model comes much closer to that. It also accords much more with my experience in teaching in the law school in Rotterdam for some 12 years. Dutch law students do learn the law, but they get much more excited when they discuss Supreme Court cases. These stories are, in the Dutch legal mind, used to investigate and define the boundaries of the law and its application. Moreover, these are considered the heart of law, where law gets its shape. Supreme Court cases and the stories from these cases, however, are anomalies. After the selection process in the inferior courts these are cases in which both parties still think they have good arguments for their position. That is far away from normal legal life, where usually one of the parties – both in civil and in criminal cases – just is dead wrong. In this sense, law is the science of anomalies and it teaches its students to be more attentive to the exception than to the average.

For empirical psychologists, who are much more concerned with averages and group differences, this is a weird experience. I later found out that in teaching or lecturing for lawyers, a well chosen example is much more convincing to them than any sound or hard empirical data. Among psychologists carefully chosen examples are considered cheap argumentation tricks; among lawyers it appeals to the heart of their trade. That very mechanism makes the presentation of evidence by the prosecution from the case file, which is not more than well chosen examples of what might have happened, so dangerous. How these dangers can be tackled, is the subject of the rest of my chapter.

## The logic of evidence

It would be most appealing if the evaluation of evidence in a criminal case could lead to a decision through a strictly logical process of consecutive steps. Such a process would require that the facts presented as evidence to the court or jury can be established in some objective manner. Then some inferential process almost automatically and inescapably would lead to the conclusion on guilt or innocence of the suspect.

The possibility of such a process is debatable both on philosophical and on practical grounds, because it assumes that there are facts 'out there' which can be known with certainty if we just look hard enough. It has long been established that each of these individual steps in such a logical process needs some form of interpretation (in law, for instance, by Cueta-Rua, 1981, p. 133 ff.; Scholten, 1974, p. 11 ff.). At the same time, lawyers often behave as if such process is possible. Wigmore (1937), for instance, described this process as a regression by which the *probandum* is specified into a large number of *facta probanda*, which are at some point matched with *facta probantia*. He appears to assume that the *probandum* can be specified as much as we want, which implies that legal proof can attain any required degree of precision. This conclusion does not follow. The regression to conditions of conditions *postpones* the problem without *solving* it. In the end the evidence must be matched with conditions and it is far from obvious that any degree of specification will make this matching less problematic. It seems that only a solid match would allow a perfectly *safe* conclusion that the condition is met. Such a conclusion can only be safe when the evidence allows just one interpretation. In reality there are always more interpretations.

Not only are the individual steps to be taken in such a logical process impossible; also the structure of the process as a whole poses problems. Any process of logical inference is a bottom-up process: one starts with the facts – the evidence – and infers conclusions from these facts. But how do we know which facts are relevant for the decision and which are not? We only know which facts are relevant if we anticipate the decision. But, at the same time, we only know which decision is anticipated, if we know the facts of the case. This circular problem can only be solved by taking a decision first and working back to the facts. Such a decision needs not to be final but can take the shape of a working hypothesis. In criminal cases this working hypothesis is splendidly provided for by the prosecution.

Together, these problems shape the manner in which the decision is made into a top-down process, in which the hypothesis (of theft, rape or murder) comes first, and the fact-finding is derived from it. Intent is not inferred from facts that happened to be presented, but the other way around: certain facts are sought and presented because they may serve to prove intent. This way of describing the process comes closer to what appears to be actually happening during the trial. The trial starts with a presentation of the indictment, i.e. before facts are presented. The charge is not inferred by the judge or jury from the evidence, but the other way around. Basically, this is a process in which the evidence is used to *verify* the indictment; not one in which the innocence of the defendant is falsified. Again, this is a gruesome way of reasoning for psychologists, but to a large extent it seems to be inevitable in legal proceedings.

## Hypothesis testing

If decision-making in criminal cases is not a logical bottom-up process, one might turn to Hart's conclusion that courtroom decision-making comes closer to rhetoric than to reason (1961, p. vii). In psychology, two alternative paths have been chosen to model judicial decision-making. One draws upon the analogy to typical scientific top-down reasoning: a hypothesis is tested against evidence, as is done in most empirical sciences. The reverend Thomas Bayes gave us a mathematical formula for this process; one that has become quite popular in modelling decision-making in criminal cases (Edwards, 1988; Finkelstein and Fairly, 1970; Goldsmith, 1980; Saks and Kidd, 1980; Schum, 1994; Tribe, 1971). This model has never appealed to me. It is a fine and elegant model when used to structure scientific decision-making, but is in my opinion too far from how real people reason. It does not accord with the mixed prescriptive and descriptive nature of law, since it assumes the 'evidence' used as input is value free. I simply do not like this model, but let me first explain it and then give some more fundamental objections to it.

The principle is simple. It is assumed that the decision maker has a certain *prior* belief in the truth of the hypothesis. This degree of belief is mathematically expressed by odds, i.e. a number between zero and infinity. These odds are obtained by dividing the probability that the hypothesis is true, $P_{true}$, by the probability that it is false, $P_{false}$. The prior belief or the prior odds, then, are expressed by:

$$\text{Prior} \quad \text{odds} \quad = \quad \frac{P_{true}}{P_{false}}$$

For instance, when $P_{true}$ is .80, and $P_{false}$ is .20 (the hypothesis is either true or false), then the prior odds are .80/.20 = 4.0. In a criminal trial the two mutually exclusive hypotheses are 'guilty' or 'innocent'. New evidence offers the opportunity to revise the prior belief, and turn it into a *posterior* belief. This is achieved by multiplying the prior odds by the *diagnostic value* ($D$) of a piece of evidence:

$$\text{Posterior odds} = \text{prior odds} \cdot D_i$$

After this piece of evidence the prior odds – whatever they were – are adjusted to become posterior odds that may serve as prior odds for the next piece of evidence. With $n$ pieces of evidence, the initial prior odds are turned into final posterior odds as follows:

$$\text{Posterior odds} = \text{prior odds} * D * D_2 * \Lambda * D_i * \Lambda * D_n$$

If the final posterior odds surpass a preset level of confidence, the defendant can be convicted. This Bayesian approach thus seems an elegant model of decision-making. I will argue, however, that modelling decision-making in criminal cases as hypothesis testing is the right solution to the wrong problem. I will discuss four defects of this approach: (1) setting the initial probability; (2) determining the diagnostic value of evidence; (3) revision of the probability; and (4) taking the final decision (the arguments advanced here are more fully discussed in Wagenaar, Van Koppen and Crombag, 1993).

The presumption of innocence assumes that the defendant is innocent until proven guilty.[2] This would require the decision maker to give a prior probability of zero to the hypothesis that the defendant is guilty. Then, of course, evidence of whatever quality cannot change the odds to anything higher than zero – the result of a multiplication with zero is always zero – and the Bayesian model would be useless. A solution might be to keep the initial

---

[2]  I am not quite sure if this sentence is correct. I have participated in a lot of criminal trials, not as a suspect, but as an expert witness. My experience is that a court can either start from a high prior odd of guilt or from a low prior odd and that does not make much of a difference for the end result. Having a trial starts from the assumption that the suspect may be guilty as hell. In fact, questioning the suspect in court is only possible if the court assumes guilt, at least during the interrogation. To me it seems that the presumption of innocence is much more relevant for the manner in which a suspect is treated prior to his conviction than as an element of judicial decision-making.

probability 'very, very low' (proposed by Wagenaar, 1988, p. 149), say at 0.0001, or give it the value of the base-rate of guilty defendants, say 0.95. For both levels – and many more levels – arguments can be given. This problem is avoided in a variation of the model, proposed by the Swedish psychologist Goldsmith (1980). He suggests that it is possible to leave the prior odds of guilt before the presentation of evidence undetermined. But his 'Evidentiary Value Theory' still suffers from the drawbacks listed below.

On a theoretical level the initial probability of guilt is not of overwhelming importance, since it can be shown that during the process of adjustment of odds, the influence of the initial value becomes less and less. However, in real life, as I know from the courts, the initial probability of guilt can be of decisive importance to the final decision. This was demonstrated by Schünemann and his co-workers (Schünemann, 1983; Schünemann and Bandilla, 1989). In one of their experiments, professional judges who had read the file of the case before the trial all convicted the defendant, while only 27 per cent of the judges who had not read the file beforehand convicted. Reading the file before the trial – as is common in most inquisitorial systems – apparently introduces a prior belief in guilt of the defendant which subsequently requires less evidence to come to a conviction at trial. Schünemann's results are confirmed in research by Koehler, who concluded that any task 'that prompts a person to temporarily accept the truth of a hypothesis will increase his or her confidence in that hypothesis' (Koehler, 1991, p. 502).

In the Bayesian model – or in any quantitative approach to evidence in criminal cases for that matter – it is a *conditio sine qua non* that the value of evidence can be quantified in some way. Sometimes this can be done. An example is the identification line-up in which a witness recognises the suspect (see Cutler and Penrod, 1995; Wells *et al.*, 1998). If a line-up in a case proved positive, the diagnostic value of such evidence is known. That is, it is known if certain conditions are met. We at least must have empirical facts or research before we can give a fair estimate of the diagnostic value of some specific piece of evidence, provided that the research is of decent quality and the facts are close to the evidence at hand. But, usually research is scarce and the facts are difficult to assess. Research on identification line-ups, for instance, has shown that the diagnostic value of a splendidly performed line-up exceeds 15 (compare the formulas above, see Wagenaar and Veefkind, 1992), but what if not all the requirements are met to call it a very good line-up? And even then, some argue, the present tradition of laboratory research does not apply to forensic practice (Bekerian, 1993; Egeth, 1993; Wells, 1993; Yuille,

1993). So, even with well researched kinds of evidence we usually know much about what problems and pitfalls can be encountered, but the effect on the diagnostic value of such evidence remains an enigma. With other kinds of evidence, we are much more in the dark. How to assess, for instance, the diagnostic value of the testimony of a witness who might have an interest in the outcome of the trial?

In the absence of robust figures on the diagnostic value of pieces of evidence, judges and juries cannot but step in and guess. It would be most appealing if they could be helped in decision-making with at least some indication of the lower and upper limit of the diagnostic value of evidence. The theory of anchored narratives, discussed below, provides for such a decision aid.

The process of revision, as described by the Bayesian model, assumes a number of properties that are, in fact, quite unrealistic. One of these properties is *compensation*: one very diagnostic piece of incriminating evidence can be cancelled out by a number of facts that point in the opposite direction through the multiplication operation. Then, a very strong piece of evidence favouring the defendant – for instance he or she was in prison at the time of a crime that was committed elsewhere – can be compensated by a large number of fairly weak pieces of evidence against him or her. Or the other way around: the fingerprints of the defendant found at the scene of the crime – often decisive evidence for a conviction – can be cancelled out by a good explanation which places the defendant at the scene at some other time. A sufficient number of 'facts' of low diagnostic value may, in the end, compensate for a fact that might be considered as decisive evidence.

Another problem is the *independence* of the supposed diagnostic values. All sorts of interactions cannot be represented in the Bayesian model. The same is true for contradictions. The Bayesian model, however, has no provision for such dependencies among pieces of evidence and would lump their diagnostic values together (see Cohen, 1977; Wagenaar, 1991).

Finally there is the problem of the decision criterion. When are the odds in favour of guilt high enough to convict? The model does not explain how such a criterion is chosen, or even whether the criterion is constant or variable. For instance, should the criterion be the same in the case of a traffic violation, for which only a fine can be given, as in the case of a capital crime? One could argue that the fact-finder should take fewer risks of a wrongful conviction in the latter case. Should a court or jury in a case of multiple rapes put the criterion on a lower more risky level, since after a wrongful acquittal, the criminal may rape again? Does consideration of consequences justify variations in the decision criteria? The Bayesian model does not answer such questions.

Taken together, the problems faced by the Bayesian model of legal decision-making are overwhelming. The most important argument against the use of models of hypothesis testing for decision-making in criminal cases, however, is that judges and juries do not argue and decide in that way. In fact, hypothesis testing is so far off from what actually happens in court that it is not only unsuccessful as a descriptive model, but also too alien to the legal tradition to be of use as a prescriptive model as well. That does not mean that models of hypothesis testing might not be useful to discuss certain individual pieces of evidence or might not apply to some – but atypical – cases. The Collins case (*People v. Collins*, 68 Cal.2d 319, 1968) is such a case, and has been analysed many times (for instance Edwards, 1991). But, the hypothesis testing models will not hold in most cases – and indeed in most cases with problems of evidence. Thus, these models are the right solution to the wrong problem.

**The story model**

For the reasons discussed above, the hypothesis-testing model of legal decision-making seems a less plausible model. Rather, a story model seems to come closer to what actually happens in the courtroom. 'The criminal trial is organized around story telling', Bennett and Feldman (1981) wrote in a book that set the tone for my research in decision-making in criminal cases: *Reconstructing Reality in the Courtroom*. Story models are based on the notion that stories give meaning to behaviour of individuals, or as Bruner (1984) puts it, are 'concerned with the explication of human intentions in the context of action.'

Scientists in many disciplines have tried to establish what makes a story believable. Rumelhart (1975), Robinson (1981), and Van Dijk (1980) all designed *story grammars*; sets of rules to which a well-formed story must obey. The story grammar proposed by Bennett and Feldman (1981) was designed specifically for judicial contexts (comp. Jackson, 1988). The manner in which they obtained their grammar is quite interesting. They asked 58 students to tell a story; half of them were asked to tell a *true* story, the other half to *invent* a story. Every time a story had been told, the others were asked to guess whether this was a true or an invented story. The guesses were not better than chance. But stories that were *accepted* as true shared some properties that the rejected stories were lacking. In short these properties were: (1) A readily identifiable central action and (2) a context (setting) that provides an easy and natural explanation of why the actors behaved in the way they did.

In a good story all elements are connected to the central action; nothing sticks out on its own. The context provides a full and compelling account of why the central action should have developed in this particular manner. If the context does not achieve that effect, then the story is said to contain *ambiguities*. Authors of detective fiction will recognize this, as I have described elsewhere (van Koppen, 1991).

Nancy Pennington and Reid Hastie extended the analysis of what makes stories plausible in a series of subsequent publications (Hastie and Pennington, 1991; Pennington and Hastie, 1986, 1988, 1991, 1992, 1993a, 1993b, 1993c). Indeed, using a story model was not new. Their approach was new, however, because for the first time a rigorous application was given to decision-making in a legal context, which resulted in a remarkable precision of claims and hypotheses. Pennington and Hastie focus on jury decision-making but there is no reason why judges or panels of judges would behave differently, as far as interpretation of the facts of a case is concerned.

Pennington and Hastie propose that the central cognitive process in jury decision-making is based on the construction of a story. They distinguish three component processes: (1) evidence evaluation through story construction, (2) representation of the decision alternatives by learning verdict category attributes, and (3) reaching a decision through the classification of the story into the best fitting verdict category (an overview of their theory and experiments is given in Pennington and Hastie, 1993b). Their main thesis is that the story constructed by a juror *determines* the juror's decision. Their story model is based on the hypothesis that jurors impose a narrative story organisation on trial information. In the story three types of knowledge are used: (1) case-specific information acquired during the trial, (2) knowledge about events similar in content to those that are the topic of dispute, and (3) generic expectations about what makes a complete story. This three-step activity results in an interpretation of the evidence in narrative form. As a consequence, different jurors will construct different stories of the same criminal case. These differences arise from differences in world knowledge among jurors.

In the whole process, the structure of the story is of paramount importance. Without going into too much detail, it can be said that, according to Pennington and Hastie, all actions are explained in good stories by factors of three kinds: physical conditions, psychological conditions, and goals. Gaps in the story are filled with inferences made by the jurors themselves. In one study, for instance, they found that of the references in protocols made by their subject-jurors, 55 per cent consisted of information that was actually included in the trial presented to them, while an amazing 45 per cent referred to *inferred* events, consisting of actions, mental states and goals that filled in the story (Pennington and Hastie, 1981).

Of course, Pennington and Hastie acknowledge that jurors can entertain several competing stories before a decision is reached. The processes by which the story that in the end is considered the 'best' story, is called *certainty principles*. They propose three of these principles: *coverage*, *coherence* and *uniqueness*. Coverage refers to the extent to which a story accounts for the evidence presented at trial. Coherence is considered to be based on three principles: consistency, plausibility and completeness of the story. Finally, uniqueness, or better lack of uniqueness, refers to the extent to which different competing stories are judged to be coherent.

The second component of jury decision-making consists of representation of the decision alternatives by learning verdict category attributes. Pennington and Hastie propose that this is a quite difficult one-time learning task, usually centred around the instruction to the jury. Since this part is typical for jury systems, I will not discuss it here. But, please note that in the discussion of anchored narratives below, this component returns in a different fashion, namely as the *anchoring* of evidence. The third component is reaching a decision through the classification of the story into the best fitting verdict category. Pennington and Hastie give, I think, a rather optimistic view of how juries handle this component. Pennington and Hastie, for instance, argue that jurors will only accept a story if its quality surpasses the 'beyond a reasonable doubt' criterion, assuming that juries entertain such a rigorous decision criterion. I am quite sure they are wrong here. I must admit I am biased because I do not like the jury system for many reasons, one being the list of described miscarriages of justice in countries with a jury system (see for instance Bedau and Radelet, 1987; Belloni and Hodgson, 2000; Borchard, 1932, 1970; Brandon and Davies, 1973; Callaghan, 1994; Carrington, Dever, Hogg, Bargen, and Lohrey, 1991; Chamberlain, 1990; Crispin, 1987; Dennis, 1993; du Cann, 1960; Engelmayer and Wagman, 1985; Floriot, 1972; Folsom, 1994; Frank and Frank, 1957, 1971; Frasca, 1968; Gardner, 1952; Greer, 1994; Gross, 1987, 1996, 1998; Hale, 1961; Hill, Young and Sergeant, 1985; Huff and Rattner, 1988; Huff, Rattner and Sagarin, 1986; Huff, Rattner and Sagarin, 1996; Karp and Rosner, 1991; Kee, 1986; Mullin, 1989; Nobles and

Schiff, 1995; Radelet, Bedau and Putnam, 1992; Radin, 1964; Rattner, 1988; Rose, 1996; Sharlitt, 1989; Sotscheck, 1990; Subcommittee on Civil and Constitutional Rights of the Committee on the Judiciary, 1994; Thornton, 1993; Tullock, 1994; Wadham, 1993; Walker and Starmer, 1993; Waller, 1989; Walsh, 1993; Woffinden, 1987; Yant, 1991; Young and Hill, 1983; Young, 1989; Zimmermann, 1964). A list that far outnumbers the number of cases described in The Netherlands (see Boumans and Kayzer, 1979; Frieswijk and Sleurink, 1984; Hannema, 1964). But that is a side issue.

The most fundamental claim in the theory of Pennington and Hastie is that the story construction, with all its falters and flaws *causes* the decision by the jury. Pennington and Hastie's story grammar, and their thesis about the importance of stories, was strongly supported by their research. I will not, here, go over all their empirical studies which cover more than a decade, but shall only present what I consider the most telling support for their theory. In an earlier study, Pennington demonstrated that story structures differed systematically for jurors who chose different verdicts (Pennington, 1981). That left open the question whether these story constructions were *post hoc* adaptations to the decisions reached, or that indeed story structure caused the decisions. This question was settled in a study in which Pennington and Hastie (1986) showed that the order in which evidence is presented has a major influence on the judgement. In their study, both the prosecution and the defence could present their evidence in witness order (i.e. a rather random order) or in story order. The combination of these two variables results in four groups. The dependent variable was the answer to the question whether the subjects thought that the defendant was guilty of first-degree murder. Their results are presented in Table 8.1.

**Table 8.1**  **Effects of presentation of evidence at trial: Percentages of subjects choosing a verdict of guilty of murder by prosecution and defence order condition (source Table 4 in Pennington and Hastie, 1988, p. 529)**

| Prosecution evidence | Defence evidence | |
|---|---|---|
| | Story order | Witness order |
| Story order | 59 | 78 |
| Witness order | 31 | 63 |

The data indicate that the party which presents the evidence in story-order was believed more readily, even though the evidence itself was exactly the same in all four conditions. The effect can be as large as changing a 31 per cent chance of conviction into a 78 per cent chance. Clever presentation of the story is half of the work. What is the other half? We tried to answer that question (Crombag, Van Koppen and Wagenaar, 1992; Wagenaar *et al.*, 1993).

## Anchored narratives

The theory of *Anchored Narratives* (Crombag *et al.*, 1992; Wagenaar *et al.*, 1993), discussed here, is strongly influenced by the work done by Pennington and Hastie. Hans Crombag, Willem Albert Wagenaar and I did not start our work on anchored narratives with the intention to contribute to the theory of judicial decision-making. We had started with the intention to write a draft for a Dutch Code of Criminal Evidence. Dutch rules on evidence are very scarce and the reason is simple: in the Netherlands the judge is both gatekeeper for the admissibility of evidence and decides on all issues in a trial. Thus, having rules on evidence serves no purpose. The few Dutch rules therefore are all on how the court can use evidence in its decisions. We felt that the draft code should at least reckon with the problematic cases, where the evidence can be of the essence. Being empiricists, we wanted to start by reading a number of difficult cases. So, we asked a number of attorneys for files of cases in which, in their opinion, their client had been convicted on flawed or absent evidence.

We were shocked by the cases we received. The most notorious example is a case in which the suspect was convicted of sexual abuse on the basis of a police report of an interrogation by a mother who related that her daughter had told her that she had heard from her eight-month-old sister that she also had been abused. For those readers who are not parents: eight-month-old children do not talk at a level that they can discuss sexual abuse. These cases changed our project dramatically to answering the question: how is it possible that a court would convict with such flawed or little evidence? We started with the idea that the work of the fact-finder – judge or jury – consists of determining the *plausibility* of the stories presented by the prosecution and by the defence. Part of this plausibility is found in the quality of a story as described by Pennington and Hastie.

The most important extension we gave to their model is that the story, as presented by the prosecution, needs evidence. How evidence is treated is the anchoring part of anchored narratives. Supporting the story is done with general rules. If a fact-finder accepts a story or part of a story, it always involves the acceptance of a general rule, which is part of the fact-finder's knowledge of the world. If, for instance, a witness statement is accepted as evidence, this can only be done if the rule is accepted that witnesses tend to speak the truth.

Such general rules, however, are seldom true without exception. Witnesses sometimes err or lie. The rules that make evidence prove something should more accurately be phrased: witnesses speak the truth *most of the time*; or pathologists *almost* never make mistakes, to give another example. The possibility of exceptions to rules means that, on a particular occasion, we must show that a possible exception does not apply. This argument, for instance, may call on the general rule that it is very improbable that two lying eyewitnesses come up with the same lie. But, of course, this rule allows exceptions: if witnesses have had the opportunity to confer before testifying, they can easily lie and be mutually consistent at the same time. Hence the prosecution must prove that this exception does not apply, for instance by showing that the two witnesses had no opportunity to confer, or if they had, did not do so.

In a similar manner every piece of evidence needs further support, until it can be safely *anchored* in a general rule that cannot be sensibly contested because all parties acknowledge it to be true. These general rules are usually common-sense facts of life. We often accept an argument because we unwittingly believe the underlying rule that gives it an anchor, even though an explicit formulation of the rule would cause us to protest or even reject it. Cohen (1977, p. 247) calls these generally accepted rules 'common-sense presumptions, which state what is normally to be expected but are rebuttable in their application to a particular situation if it can be shown to be abnormal in some relevant respect.' I shall qualify the role of general rules later but for the time being define them as 'Common knowledge of the world in the form of rules which are usually valid.' A pictorial representation of the anchoring heuristic is presented in Figure 8.1.

At the top of Figure 8.1 there is the story of the original indictment, of which the soundness, in terms of Pennington and Hastie, has already been judged satisfactory. Next comes an ordering of the evidence in such a way that it forms anchors between the story and a 'ground' of generally accepted common-sense rules. At three, detailed evidence is offered, but each piece of evidence forms a *sub-story* in itself, which needs an anchor in the form of further evidence, and which, in turn, forms a sub-sub-story in need of an anchor in the form of further evidence, and which, in turn, forms a sub-sub-story in need of an anchor. Whether a sub-story is safely anchored depends on our willingness to accept as true the common-sense rule of which the sub-story is an instance.

**Figure 8.1    Model of Theory of Anchored Narratives (after Crombag *et al.*, 1992)**

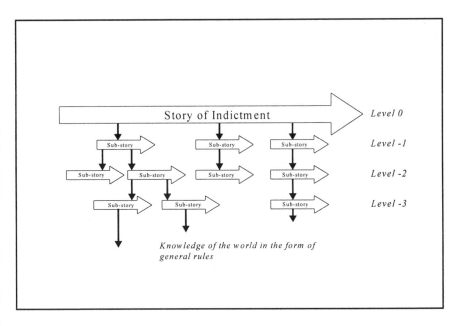

For the first detail of the original story the anchoring is quite complicated, constituting a long anchor chain. Two pieces of evidence are offered, which apparently cannot be safely anchored as such in safe common-sense rules. More evidence is sought, constituting sub-sub-stories. The first of these is anchored on to the ground through a sub-sub-sub-story; the second one is not anchored at all. Hence the anchor chain as a whole is ineffective. The second point in the story is directly anchored on to the ground of some common-sense rule. There is no point in doubting this rule to be generally true and hence no reason to probe deeper for a safer anchor. The third point is anchored through one intermediate story; a police officer's sworn testimony is an example of that sort of anchoring.

Evaluating the story of the indictment and the evidence might seem to be a deductive process: it appears as if the individual case is brought under the general common-sense rule and the reasoning departs from the general rule. It is not. The point of departure is the individual case from which a generalisation is sought to explain the individual story (see Cohen, 1977, p. 247 ff). It is a basic human need to explain the world around us and we are proficient in explaining odd or unexpected occurrences by generating general rules, which might explain them (see Semin and Manstead, 1983).

The Theory of Anchored Narratives is both descriptive and prescriptive, and that is the element I like about it most. This model of decision-making in criminal cases provides a means of describing these decisions, but also can serve as a vehicle to show on what points decisions based on evidence went wrong or are about to go wrong. A detailed analysis of such errors in Dutch cases was presented in Crombag, Van Koppen and Wagenaar (1992) and Wagenaar, Van Koppen and Crombag (1993).

The first task of the prosecutor is to tell a good story; a story with a central action and a context that makes the central action – the crime – so plausible, that judge and jury only will react with 'Aha, of course'. At this point the defence has already lost half the case. And indeed, our study of Dutch cases showed that with a very good story the prosecution could get defendants convicted, even when solid evidence is virtually absent. It is a good story because it readily makes sense and fits expectations. We argue that a good story is independent of the quality of the evidence.

In most cases, however, the prosecutor's narrative needs anchoring in common-sense rules through chains of embedded sub-stories (i.e. pieces of evidence). If a court or jury accepts a piece of evidence without further sub-stories, it can only do so if it accepts one or more common sense rules as valid and applicable to the specific case. Although such acceptance almost always remains implicit, the common-sense rules can usually be reconstructed with some knowledge of the case. If a defendant is convicted on the basis of, among other things, fingerprints at the scene of the crime, the following common-sense rules may implied:

• If someone's fingerprints are found on the scene of the crime, he almost always has been there;
• Technical detectives make small mistakes in securing and comparing fingerprints; and,
• The technique of comparing fingerprints produces small mistakes (in fact this rules is debatable, see Evett and Williams, 1996; Stoney, 1997).

The role of the defence is threefold. First, the defence can challenge the story itself. The defence can either try to introduce information that makes the prosecution's narrative less plausible, or it can try to come with a better, more plausible story. A solid alibi falls in the latter class.

The second role for the defence – anticipating that attacks on the narrative (the prosecution's story) itself almost always fail – is to attack the evidence, the sub-stories. The defence must try to show that acceptance of a specific sub-story proposed by the prosecution would involve the acceptance of a common-sense rule which is silly, not commonly accepted or simply not true. In the latter, expert witnesses sometimes play a role, to demonstrate that commonly held beliefs are wrong. The defence can also try to argue that, although the (implicitly) accepted common-sense rule is true, this case falls under the exceptions. Each common-sense rule knows exceptions, but some have more than others. Identification evidence given by witnesses, for instance, is fairly often not valid, while we know that as a general rule the Dutch National Forensic Laboratory makes few mistakes.

The third tactic of the defence is to come up with sub-stories that falsify the prosecutor's narrative. The way evidence is evaluated in court, however, is most consistent with a system of verification: evidence is used to verify the narrative told by the prosecution. This is at odds with 'beyond a reasonable doubt' standard, as Allen (1991) noted. If the 'beyond a reasonable doubt' standard is taken literally, the doubt should be the focus of attention at trial and the state should suffer the burden of demonstrating that there is no plausible account consistent with innocence (see also Zuckerman, 1989, p. 122 ff). The practice in court is, however, that the prosecution only brings forward verifying evidence and the defence is given an opportunity to bring forward falsifying information. If the defence fails to do so, it is generally seen as evidence that supports the prosecutor's narrative, probably under the general common-sense rule that it is usually easy for innocent defendants to produce exculpatory evidence.

The model we proposed, and daily practice in court, does not guarantee that the decisions of the court or the jury are logically sound. At the same time it must be recognized that the rules of criminal evidence in most civilized countries *usually* produce sound decisions. Judicial errors, wrongful convictions and miscarriages of justice are more interesting to study, because these failures of the system give much more insight into how decision-making operates. A good model of decision-making must therefore provide a framework that can be used to point out where and why decisions in the more 'difficult' cases go wrong.

**Moulding criminal stories**

The work by Pennington and Hastie and our work on anchored narratives take a story as presented by the prosecution as a starting point. Until now I have said little on how this story came about, and indeed the theories have little to say on where the prosecution got its story from or how the police moulds all the data they gathered during an investigation into a story presented at trial.

Some important differences between the police investigation and evidence at trial are obvious. When a criminal offence comes to the notice of the police, their first objective is to find a suspect. In most cases, however, it is not the police, but members of the public who report that a crime has been committed and who point out a suspect to the police (Black, 1970; Bottomley and Coleman, 1976; Erickson, 1981; Greenwood, Chaiken and Petersilia, 1977; Steer, 1980). Professional investigators, who must abide by the rules governing these investigations, perform the gathering of information following such notifications.

Another distinction between investigation and proof is concerned with the level of certainty required for taking decisions. At various stages in criminal procedure, the evidence available must amount to a certain level of certainty to warrant a decision. For instance, 'probable cause', which is necessary before arrest and for searches and seizure are permitted, may require 40 to 50 per cent certainty according to some authorities (Melton, Petrila, Poythress and Slobogin, 1997, p. 27).

Wagenaar, Van Koppen and Crombag (1993) have demonstrated that the roots of many dubious convictions can be found in the police investigation, even in the early stages of investigation (see also, for instance, Belloni and Hodgson, 2000; Gross, 1996; Nobles and Schiff, 1995; Radelet *et al.*, 1992). I shall now briefly discuss some of the mechanisms we identified, namely offence-driven and suspect-driven searches, the problem of verification and falsification, and the so-called trawler method.

One important distinction is between *offence-driven and suspect-driven searches*. This is related to the starting point of the investigation. In an offence-driven search the starting point is the crime and the facts related to the crime. The identity of the culprit, then, is inferred from these facts. In a suspect-driven search someone becomes a suspect for no clear reason, or at least no reason that is explained by the known facts of the crime. Only then is an attempt made at finding evidence which links this particular suspect to the crime. Such a search is limited right from the start. An example of the latter is showing photographs of known criminals to a witness (Wells *et al.*, 1998). The relevance of the distinction between offence-driven and suspect-driven investigations lies in the diagnostic value of the resulting evidence. In an offence-driven search the narrative is the product of an inferential process, based on information. In a suspect-driven search the narrative is the starting point, and the information is its product. In offence-driven search one collects so much information that the search logically excludes all possible alternative suspects. In suspect-driven search one needs only enough information to make the suspect look bad. It can even be argued that one may take any citizen, investigate him thoroughly, and connect him to one of the many unsolved crimes in the police files. This may be done by way of recognition tests, an accusation by another suspect, attributing a motive, identifying some piece of intimate knowledge, forensic analysis of traces, a report by a psychiatrist, the absence of an alibi, or even a confession obtained under prolonged interrogation. Especially the latter in the form of prolonged police interrogations seems prone to produce bad evidence (Gudjonsson, 1992; Van Koppen, 1998).

In many of the cases discussed by Wagenaar, Van Koppen and Crombag (1993) the suspects became suspects because of their criminal records. Gross (1987) reported that in 60 per cent of 92 miscarriages of justice in which a suspect was incorrectly identified by eyewitnesses, the first suspicion was based on outer appearance, while nothing else related the suspect to the crime. This 60 per cent is an extremely high figure, compared to Steer's (1980, Table 4:2 at p. 97) finding that in of all crimes 21 per cent of the suspects are connected to crimes through suspect-driven searches. Suspect-driven searches appear to promote unsafe convictions.

The second mechanism is related to the distinction between *verification and falsification*. Logically, hypotheses are tested by two complementary processes; verification and falsification. An attempt of verification means looking for facts that are predicted by the hypothesis; falsification means looking for facts that are excluded by the hypothesis. To test a hypothesis both processes are necessary. Falsification is not some sort of luxury, in which one only engages when there is an excess of means. As long as alternative hypotheses are not excluded, they may be more likely than the verified hypothesis.

An uncommon example may clarify the distinction between verification and falsification (described by Rossen, 1992, p. 9 ff; Rossen and Schuijer, 1992, p. 437). Some years ago, a twelve-year-old boy called Patrick living in the Dutch town Enschede was accused of sexually abusing about 200 children. The case had started with an accusation made by a single child, but had grown rapidly after the police solicited for more cases in the neighbourhood where the

212 Criminal Justice Research

boy lived. The boy confessed to all cases. One may wonder how a twelve-year-old boy can find the time to abuse 200 children in a time-span of less than one-and-a-half years. Patrick was interviewed as follows: the interviewing policeman showed him a photograph of a child in the neighbourhood and asked whether or not the boy also abused this child. To almost all the pictures presented, Patrick said 'yes'; a verification of the accusation. The police never tried a simple falsification by, for example, showing the boy pictures of children from other towns. The police afterwards said it was not necessary because the boy had a photographic memory.

An attempt at falsification rarely occurs in criminal investigations. As a rule the prosecution limits its activities to verification attempts. In the perspective of research logic this practice is absurd, but it is predicted by the theory of anchored narratives. Anchors are only verifications of the hypotheses included in the indictment's narrative. Falsifications, unless they are definite, do not destroy such anchors, the anchoring structure simply has no place for them. If falsification attempts occur at all, they are most often the initiative of the defence. But even falsifications offered by the defence are rare, probably because the defence realises that falsifications have no place in the anchoring structure, and may therefore not affect the court's decision process; they may easily be considered irrelevant.

Particularly deceptive results may be obtained by means of the third method by which the police investigation may generate miscarriages of justice, which is called the *trawling method*. This method falls into the class of suspect-driven search methods. The term is used for police investigations that start from a generalised and little specified suspicion against a person or, more often, a group of persons, in which a large police force is engaged, investigating every conceivable detail of his or its behaviour until some sort of mischief is discovered. It is like trawling a very wide net in a place where there may not be many fish, but if the net is wide enough one always may be expected to catch some fish.

A less conspicuous but equally misleading set of trawling methods is related to identification procedures. One of these methods is to show a suspect's picture in a nationwide broadcast (such as *Opsporing Verzocht* in The Netherlands, and *Crime Watch* in Great Britain), with the question 'Who saw this person?'. Usually this elicits many responses. It is quite likely that at least one of these will be incriminating for the person shown. Such trawling methods capitalize on chance and are therefore to be avoided if at all possible. While trawling for evidence, one can find enough incriminating facts against virtually anybody.

## The story of the police

The examples of problems in the police investigation I have discussed above all focus on how the investigation may cause wrongful convictions at the trial stage. The construction of proof during the trial will always be suspect-driven, because there is a defendant present right from the beginning. So the question to be answered by the court is not 'Who did it?', but 'Did *he* do it?'. In other words, the objective of the trial is not to uncover the truth, but to evaluate the believability of the indictment's narrative by testing the quality of the available evidence. All parties involved in criminal proceedings, with the possible exception of the defence, have a strong preference for suspect-driven search and verification, both in the investigative stage and during the construction of proof. As a consequence investigation and construction of proof, although essentially different, may become indistinguishable, especially after the investigation did not involve discovery of a suspect, but the construction of sufficient proof against a known suspect. In these cases the investigators become judges, although they were never meant to be so. Judges are doomed to repeat what the investigators have already done, allowing innocent defendants little hope that the outcome of the trial will be anything else than a predictable confirmation of the indictment. Thus, the police have the best opportunities to prevent miscarriages of justice.

My discussion of some characteristics of the police investigation is based on 'looking back' from what happens at trial in difficult cases. We now know a little on how problems in the generation of a story during police investigations may influence what happens at trial. This, however, provides for little information on how the police generate a story during the investigation. We may suspect that the decision that turns an ordinary citizen into a suspect of a criminal offence is taken on the basis of a narrative, in the same manner as at a later stage the decision to convict is to a large extent taken on the basis of a narrative and that any of the problems in court decision-making also apply to decisions of the police.

There are, however, important differences between the story of the police and the story at trial. At an early stage of their investigation the police can probably only work from an incomplete narrative, mostly based on what was found at the scene of the crime. Some elements of the narrative are available from the start, found by accident, by reports from citizens, through combining and verifying facts, or mere guesswork. Other parts of the narrative only emerge during the investigation. From this incomplete story the investigators may work their way up; ambiguities or contradictions are further investigated or put aside as irrelevant. Gradually a coherent and complete story emerges. In the investigation it is hoped that the narrative emerges from the facts.

All these elements, and probably many more, make police work essentially different from the work of fact-finders. How precisely the police build their story of a crime is a virtually un-researched subject (an exception is Binder and Bergman, 1984). Therefore, I consider a thorough study of police decision-making the most important challenge for future research on how stories form criminal proceedings.

## References

Adams, J.S. (1965). Inequity in social exchange. *Advances in Experimental Social Psychology, 2*, 267-299.
Allen, R.J. (1991). The nature of juridical proof. *Cardozo Law Review, 13*, 373-422.
Baum, L.A. (1997). *The Puzzle of Judicial Behavior*. Ann Arbor, MI: University of Michigan Press.
Bedau, H.A., and Radelet, M.L. (1987). Miscarriages of justice in potential capital cases. *Stanford Law Review, 40*, 21-179.
Bekerian, D.A. (1993). In search of the typical eyewitness. *American Psychologist, 48*, 574-576.
Belloni, F. and Hodgson, J. (2000). *Criminal Injustice: An Evaluation of the Criminal Justice Process in Britain*. New York: St. Martin.
von Benda-Beckmann, C.E. (1984). *The Broken Stairways to Consensus: Village Justice and State Courts in Minangabau*. Dordrecht: Foris (diss. Nijmegen).
Bennett, W.L., and Feldman, M.S. (1981). *Reconstructing Reality in the Courtroom*. London: Tavistock.
Berghuis, A.C. (1992). De harde en de zachte hand: Een statistische analyse van verschillen in sanctiebeleid. *Trema, 15*, 84-93.
Binder, D.A., and Bergman, P. (1984). *Fact Investigation: From Hypothesis to Proof*. St. Paul, MI: West.
Black, D.J. (1970). The social organisation of arrest. *American Sociological Review, 23*, 1087-1111.
Blackman, D.E., Müller, D.J. and Chapman, A.J. (1984). Perspectives in psychology and law. In D.J. Müller and D.E. Blackman and A.J. Chapman (eds), *Psychology and Law* (3-15). New York: Wiley.
Borchard, E.M. (1932). *Convicting the Innocent: Sixty-five Actual Errors of Criminal Justice*. Garden City: Doubleday.
Borchard, E.M. (1970). *Convicting the Innocent: Errors of Criminal Justice*. New York: Da Capo.
Bottomley, A.K., and Coleman, C.A. (1976). Criminal statistics: The police role in the discovery and detection of crime. *International Journal of Criminology and Penology, 4*, 33-58.
Boumans, T., and Kayzer, W. (1979). *De Zaak Annie e.* Amsterdam: Bert Bakker.
Brandon, R., and Davies, C. (1973). *Wrongful Imprisonment: Mistaken Convictions and Their Consequences*. London: Allen and Unwin.
Bruner, J. (1984). *Narrative and paradigmatic modes of thought.*: Invited address, Division 1 of the American Psychological Association, Toronto, August 25.

Bull, R., and Carson, D. (eds), (1995). *Handbook of Psychology in Legal Contexts*. Chichester: Wiley.

Callaghan, H. (1994). *Cruel Fate: One Man's Triumph Over Injustice*. Dublin: Poolbeg.

Cardozo, B.N. (1921). *The Nature of the Judicial Process*. New Haven, CO: Yale University Press.

Carrington, K., Dever, M., Hogg, R., Bargen, J., and Lohrey, A. (eds), (1991). *Travesty!: Miscarriages of Justice*. Leichhart, NSW: Pluto.

Chamberlain, L. (1990). *Through My Eyes: An Autobiography*. Port Melbourne, Vic.: Heinemann.

Cohen, L.J. (1977). *The Probable and the Provable*. Oxford: Clarendon.

Crispin, K. (1987). *Lindy Chamberlain: the Full Story*. Boise, ID: Pacific.

Crombag, H.F.M. (1982). Wat is rechtspsychologie? *Ars Aequi, 32*, 237-240.

Crombag, H.F.M., and van Koppen, P.J. (1991). Praktische bezwaren: Psychologie voor juristen. In P.J. van Koppen and H.F.M. Crombag (eds), *De Menselijke Factor: Psychologie Voor Juristen* (1-5). Arnhem: Gouda Quint.

Crombag, H.F.M., van Koppen, P.J. and Wagenaar, W.A. (1992). *Dubieuze Zaken: De Psychologie Van Strafrechtelijk Bewijs*. Amsterdam: Contact.

Cueta-Rua, J.C. (1981). *Judicial Methods of Interpretation of the Law*. Baton Rouge: Louisiana State University, Paul M. Herbert Law Center.

Cutler, B.L. and Penrod, S.D. (1995). *Mistaken Identification: The Eyewitness, Psychology, and the Law*. Cambridge: Cambridge University Press.

Dennis, I. (1993). Miscarriages of justice and the law of confessions: Evidentiary issues and solutions. *Public Law, 1993*, 291-313.

Deutsch, M. (1975). Equity, Equality, and Need: What determines which value will be used as the basis of distributive justice? *Journal of Social Issues, 31*, 137-150.

van Dijk, T.A. (1980). *Macrostructures: An Interdisciplinary Study of Global Structures in Discourse, Interaction, and Cognition*. Hillsdale, NJ: Erlbaum.

du Cann, C.G.L. (1960). *Miscarriages of justice*. London: Muller.

van Dunné, J.M. (1974). *Riskante Rechtsvinding*. Deventer: Kluwer (oratie Rotterdam).

Edwards, W. (1988). Summing up: The society of Bayesian trial lawyers. In P. Tillers and E.D. Green (eds), *Probability and Inference in the Law of Evidence: the Uses and Limits of Bayesianism* (337-342). Dordrecht: Kluwer Academic.

Edwards, W. (1991). Influence diagrams, Baysian imperialism, and the Collins case: An appeal to reason. *Cardozo Law Review, 13*, 1025-1074.

Egeth, H.E. (1993). What do we *not* know about eyewitness identification? *American Psychologist, 48*, 577-580.

Engelmayer, S.D., and Wagman, R. (1985). *Lord's justice*. Garden City, NY: Anchor.

Erickson, R.V. (1981). *Making Crime: A Study of Detective Work*. Toronto: Butterworths.

Esser, J. (1970). *Vorverständnis und Methodenwahl in der Rechtsfindung*. Frankfurt am Main: Athenaeum.

Evett, I.W., and Williams, R.L. (1996). A review of the sixteen points fingerprint standard in England and Wales. *Journal of the Forensic Identification, 46*, 49-73.

Fallers, L.A. (1969). *Law Without Precedent: Legal Ideas in Action in the Courts of Colonial Busoga*. Chicago: University of Chicago Press.

Finkelstein, W.O., and Fairly, W.B. (1970). A Bayesian approach to identification evidence. *Harvard Law Review, 83*, 489-517.

Floriot, R. (1972). *When Justice Falters*. London: Harrap (translated from French by Rayner Heppenstall).

Folsom, J.R. (1994). *Reversible Errors in Federal Criminal Cases: A Digest of Criminal Cases Reversed by the United States Supreme Court and the Circuit Courts of Appeals*. Fort Worth, TX: Knowles.

Frank, J.N. (1950). *Courts on Trial: Myth and Reality in American Justice* (2nd edn). Princeton, NJ: Princeton University Press.

Frank, J.N., and Frank, B. (1957). *Not Guilty*. New York: Doubleday.

Frank, J.N., and Frank, B. (1971). *Not Guilty*. New York: Da Capo (oorspr. 1957).

Frasca, J. (1968). *The Mulberry Tree*. Englewood Cliffs, NJ: Prentice-Hall.

Frieswijk, J., and Sleurink, H. (1984). *De Zaak Hogerhuis: 'Een Gerechtelijke Misdaad'*. Leeuwarden: Friese Pers Boekerij.

Gardner, E.S. (1952). *Court of last resort*. New York: Sloane.

Gluckman, M. (1967). *The Judicial Process Among the Bartose of Northern Rhodesia (Zambia)*. Manchester: Manchester University Press.

Goldsmith, R.W. (1980). Studies of a model for evaluating judicial evidence. *Acta Psychologica, 45*, 211-221.

Greenwood, P., Chaiken, J. and Petersilia, J. (1977). *The Investigation Process*. Lexington, MA: Lextington.

Greer, S.C. (1994). Miscarriages of criminal justice reconsidered. *The Modern Law Review, 57*, 58-74.

Gross, S.R. (1987). Loss of innocence: Eyewitness identification and proof of guilt. *Journal of Legal Studies, 16*, 395-453.

Gross, S.R. (1996). The risks of death: Why erroneous convictions are common in capital cases. *Buffalo Law Review, 44*, 469-500.

Gross, S.R. (1998). Lost lives: Miscarriages of justice in capital cases. *Law and Contemporary Problems, 61*, 125-149.

Grossman, W.L. (1935). The legal philosophy of Roscoe Pound. *Yale Law Journal, 44*, 605-619.

Gudjonsson, G.H. (1992). *The Psychology of Interrogations, Confessions, and Testimony*. Chichester: Wiley.

Hale, L. (1961). *Hanged in Error*. Harmondsworth: Penguin.

Hannema, U.D. (1964). *De Hogerhuis-zaak*. Drachten: Laverman (diss. Amsterdam).

Hart, H.L.A. (1961). *The Concept of Law*. London: Oxford University Press.

Hastie, R., and Pennington, N. (1991). Cognitive and social processes in decision making. In L.B. Resnick and J.M. Levine (eds), *Perspectives on Socially Shared Cognition* (308-327). Washington DC: American Psychological Association.

Herzog, A.W. (1917). A psychology of judges. *Medico-Legal Journal, 34*, 10-12.

Hill, P., Young, M., and Sergeant, T. (1985). *More Rough Justice*. Harmondsworth: Penguin.

Hogarth, J. (1971). *Sentencing As A Human Process*. Toronto: University of Toronto Press.

Holmes, O.W. (1881). *The Common Law*. Boston: Little, Brown.

Holmes, O.W. (1897). The path to law. *Harvard Law Review, 10*, 39-48.

Homel, R.J., and Lawrence, J.A. (1992). Sentencer orientation and case details: An interactive analysis. *Law and Human Behavior, 16*, 509-537.

Huff, C.R., and Rattner, A. (1988). Convicted but innocent: False positives and the criminal justice process. In J.E. Scott and T. Hirschi (eds), *Controversial Issues in Crime and Justice*. Newbury Park, CA: Sage.

Huff, C.R., Rattner, A. and Sagarin, E. (1986). Guilty until proven innocent: Wrongful conviction and public policy. *Crime and Delinquency, 32*, 518-544.

Huff, C.R., Rattner, A. and Sagarin, E. (1996). *Convicted But Innocent: Wrongful Conviction and Public Policy*. Thousand Oaks, CA: Sage.

Jackson, B.S. (1988). *Law, fact and narrative coherence.* Liverpool: Deborah Charles.

Karp, C., and Rosner, C. (1991). *When Justice Fails: the David Milgaard Story.* Toronto: McClelland and Stewart.

ten Kate, J., and van Koppen, P.J. (1984). *Determinanten van privaatrechtelijke beslissingen.* Arnhem: Gouda Quint (diss. Rotterdam).

Kee, R. (1986). *Trial and Error: The Maguires, the Guildford Pub Bombings, and British Justice.* London: Hamilton.

de Keijser, J.W. (2000). *Punishment and Purpose: From Moral Theory to Punishment in Action.* Amsterdam: Thela Thesis (diss. Leiden).

Koehler, D.J. (1991). Explanation, imagination, and confidence in judgment. *Psychological Bulletin, 110,* 173-180.

van Koppen, P.J. (1991). Alleen detectives hebben een happy end, *Misdaad boeit: De crimi belicht* (: 45-57). Den Haag: Nederlands Bibliotheek en Literatuur Centrum.

van Koppen, P.J. (1998). Bekennen als bewijs: Bedenkingen bij het verhoor van de verdachte. *Justitiële Verkenningen, 24*(4), 61-73.

van Koppen, P.J., and Hessing, D.J. (1988). Legal psychology or law and psychology. In P.J. van Koppen, D.J. Hessing and G. van den Heuvel (eds), *Lawyers on Psychology and Psychologists on Law* (: 1-8). Amsterdam: Swets and Zeitlinger.

van Koppen, P.J., and ten Kate, J. (1984). Individual differences in judicial behavior: Personal characteristics and private law decision making. *Law and Society Review, 18,* 225-247.

Lerner, M.J. (1975). The justice motive in social behavior: Some hypotheses as to its origins and forms. *Journal of Personality, 45,* 1-52.

Lerner, M.J. (1980). *The Belief in A Just World: A Fundamental Delusion.* New York: Plenum.

Llewellyn, K.N. (1960). *The Common Law Tradition.* Boston: Little, Brown.

Llewellyn, K.N., and Hoebel, E.A. (1941). *The Cheyenne Way: Conflict and Case Law in Primitive Jurisprudence.* Norman, Oklahoma: Oklahoma University Press.

Melton, G.B., Petrila, J., Poythress, N.G., and Slobogin, C. (1997). *Psychological Evaluations for the Courts: A Handbook for Mental Health Professionals and Lawyers* ( 2nd ed.). New York: Guilford.

Montesquieu. (1834/1748). *De L'esprit Des Lois.* Paris: Lebigre.

Mullin, C. (1989). *Error of Judgment: The Truth About the Birmingham Bombers.* Dublin, Ireland: Poolberg Press.

Nobles, R., and Schiff, D. (1995). Miscarriages of justice: a systems approach. *The Modern Law Review, 58,* 299-320.

Pennington, N. (1981). *Causal reasoning and decision making: The case of juror decisions.* Unpublished doctoral dissertation, Harvard University.

Pennington, N., and Hastie, R. (1981). Juror decision-making models: The generalization gap. *Psychological Bulletin, 89,* 246-287.

Pennington, N., and Hastie, R. (1986). Evidence evaluation in complex decision making. *Journal of Personality and Social Psychology, 51,* 242-258.

Pennington, N., and Hastie, R. (1988). Explanation-based decision making: Effects of memory structure on judgment. *Journal of Experimental Psychology: Learning, Memory, and Cognition, 14,* 521-533.

Pennington, N., and Hastie, R. (1991). A theory of explanation-based decision making. In G.A. Klein, J. Orasanu, R. Calderwood and C.E. Zsambok (eds), *Decision Making in Action: Models and Methods* (188-201). Norwood, NJ: Ablex.

Pennington, N., and Hastie, R. (1992). Explaining the evidence: Tests of the story model for juror decision making., *Journal of Personality and Social Psychology, 62,* 189-206.

218    *Criminal Justice Research*

Pennington, N., and Hastie, R. (1993a). Reasoning in explanation-based decision making., *Cognition, 49*, 123-163.

Pennington, N., and Hastie, R. (1993b). The story model for juror decision making. In R. Hastie (ed), *Inside the Jury: the Psychology of Juror Decision Making* Cambridge: Cambridge University Press.192-221.

Pennington, N., and Hastie, R. (1993c). A theory of explanation-based decision making. In G.A. Klein and J. Orasanu (eds), *Decision making in action: Models and methods* (188-201). Norwood, NJ: Ablex.

Radelet, M.L., Bedau, H.A., and Putnam, C.E. (1992). *In Spite of Innocence: Erroneous Convictions in Capital Cases.* Boston: Northeastern University Press.

Radin, E.D. (1964). *The Innocents.* New York: Morrow.

Rattner, A. (1988). Convicted but innocent: Wrongful conviction and the criminal justice system. *Law and Human Behavior, 12*, 283-293.

Robinson, J.A. (1981). Personal narratives reconsidered. *Journal of American Folklore, 94*, 58-85.

Rose, D. (1996). *In the Name of the Law: the Collapse of Criminal Justice.* London: Jonathan Cape.

Rossen, B.L. (1992). *Children as witnesses/victims in cases of alleged child sexual abuse.* Unpublished paper.

Rossen, B.L., and Schuijer, J. (1992). *Het Seksuele Gevaar Voor Kinderen: Mythen En Feiten.* Lisse: Swets and Zeitlinger.

Rumelhart, D.E. (1975). Notes on a schema for stories. In D.G. Bobrow and A. Collins (eds), *Representation and Understanding: Studies in Cognitive Science* (211-236). New York: Academic.

Saks, M.J., and Kidd, R.F. (1980). Human information processing and adjudication: Trial by heuristics. *Law and Society Review, 15*, 123-160.

Scholten, P. (1974). *Mr C. Asser's Handleiding Tot De Beoefening Van Het Nederlandse Burgerlijke Recht: Algemeen Deel.* Zwolle: Tjeenk Willink (3e druk).

Schröder, T. (1918). The psychological study of judicial opinions. *California Law Review, 6*, 89-113.

Schum, D.A. (1994). *The Evidential Foundations of Probabilistic Reasoning.* Chichester: Wiley.

Schünemann, B. (1983). Experimentelle Untersuchungen zur Reform der Hauptverhandlung in Strafsachen. In H.J. Kerner, H. Kurry and K. Sessar (eds), *Deutsche Forschungen zur Kriminalitätsentstehung uns Kriminalitätskontrolle* (1109-1151). Köln: Heymanns.

Schünemann, B., and Bandilla, W. (1989). Perseverance in courtroom decisions. In H. Wegener, F. Lösel and J. Haisch (eds), *Criminal Behavior and the Justice System: Psychological Perspectives* New York: Springer, (181-192).

Semin, G.R., and Manstead, A.S.R. (1983). *The Accountability of Conduct: A Social Psychological Analysis.* London: Academic.

Sharlitt, J.H. (1989). *Fatal Error: the Miscarriage of Justice That Sealed the Rosenberg's Fate.* New York: Scribner.

Sotscheck, R. (ed),. (1990). *The Birmingham Six: An Appalling Vista.* Dublin: Litereire.

Steer, D. (1980). *Uncovering Crime: the Police Role.* London: Her Majesty's Stationary Office (Research Study no. 7, Royal Commission on Criminal Procedure).

Stoney, D.A. (1997). Fingerprint identification: B. Scientific status. In D.L. Faigman, D.H. Kaye, M.J. Saks and J. Sanders (eds), *Modern Scientific Evidence: the Law and Science of Expert Testimony* (2, 55-78). St. Paul, MI: West.

Sturm, A. (1910). *Die Psychologische Grundlage des Rechts.* Hannover: Helwigsche Verlagsbuchhandlung.

Subcommittee on Civil and Constitutional Rights of the Committee on the Judiciary. (1994). *Innocence and the death penalty: Assessing the danger of mistaken executions (staff report)*. Washington DC: U.S.G.P.O.

Thornton, P. (1993). Miscarriages of justice: A lost opportunity. *The Criminal Law Review, 1993*, 926-935.

Tribe, L. (1971). Trial by mathematics: Precision and ritual in the legal process. *Harvard Law Review, 84*, 1329-1393.

Tullock, G. (1994). Court errors. *European Journal of Law and Economics, 1*, 9-21.

Tyler, T.R. (1994). Psychological models of the justice motive: Antecedents of distributive and procedural justice. *Journal of Personality and Social Psychology, 67*, 850-863.

Wadham, J. (1993). Unravelling miscarriages of justice. *New Law Journal, 143*, 1650-1651.

Wagenaar, W.A. (1988). The proper seat: A Bayesian discussion of the position of expert witnesses. *Law and Human Behavior, 12*, 499-510.

Wagenaar, W.A. (1991). Waar logica faalt en verhalen overtuigen: Een beschouwing over strafrechtelijk bewijs. *Onze Alma Mater, 41*, 256-278 (oratie Katholieke Universiteit Leuven).

Wagenaar, W.A., van Koppen, P.J., and Crombag, H.F.M. (1993). *Anchored Narratives: The Psychology of Criminal Evidence*. London: Harvester Wheatsheaf.

Wagenaar, W.A., and Veefkind, N. (1992). Comparison of one-person and many-person lineups: A warming against unsafe practices. In F. Löse, D. Bender and T. Bliesener (eds), *Psychology and Law: International Perspectives* (: 275-285). Berlin: De Gruyter.

Walker, C., and Starmer, K. (eds), (1993). *Justice in Error*. London: Blackstone.

Waller, G. (1989). *Miscarriages of Justice*. London: Justice.

Walsh, D. (1993). Miscarriages of justice in the Republic of Ireland. In C. Walker and K. Starmer (eds), *Justice in Error* (203-222). London: Blackstone.

Walster, G.W., Walster, E., and Berscheid, E. (1978). *Equity: Theory and Research*. Boston: Allyn and Bacon.

Wells, G.L. (1993). What do we know about eyewitness identification? *American Psychologist, 49*, 554-571.

Wells, G.L., Small, M., Penrod, S., Malpass, R.S., Fulero, S.M., and Brimacombe, C.A.E. (1998). Eyewitness identification procedures: Recommendations for lineups and photospreads. *Law and Human Behavior, 23*, 603-647.

Wigmore, J.H. (1937). *The Science of Judicial Proof As Given by Logic, Psychology, and General Experience* (3rd edn). Boston: Little Brown.

Woffinden, B. (1987). *Miscarriages of Justice*. London: Hodder and Stoughton.

Yant, M. (1991). *Presumed Guilty: When Innocent People Are Wrongly Convicted*. Buffalo, NY: Prometheus.

Young, M., and Hill, P. (1983). *Rough Justice*. London: British Broadcasting Corporation.

Young, N.H. (1989). *Innocence Regained: the Fight to Free Lindy Chamberlain*. Annandale, NSW: Federation Press.

Yuille, J.C. (1993). We must study forensic eyewitnesses to know about them. *American Psychologist, 48*, 572-573.

Zimmermann, I. (1964). *Punishment Without Crime*. New York.

Zuckerman, A.A.S. (1989). *The Principles of Criminal Evidence*. Oxford: Clarendon.

# 9. Applying Psychology to Crime Investigation: The Case of Police Interviewing

RAY BULL

## Introduction

Which aspects of the criminal justice process are among the most deserving of research attention? A majority of people might nominate aspects of court processes such as the finding of guilt/innocent or sentencing decisions. Many others might suggest the police interviewing of suspects (and perhaps of victims and witnesses). While many studies have examined real-life and 'mock' court decisions and numerous others have focused on witness/victim interviewing in the experimental setting, a surprising few have examined real-life police interviews with suspects. Why should this be? Surely how the police, in any country, interview those who may be suspected of crime is important to society, both in terms of detaining the guilty and of freeing the innocent. Interviewing suspects is one of our police services' major activities. Why has it been so little researched?

The major reason for the dearth of research is, of course, gaining access to such interviews. Very rarely have researchers been allowed to sit in on interviews and in most countries these interviews are not audio or video recorded and so there exists no full record of what took place. Notes taken during or made after such interviews have substantial weaknesses (Milne and Bull, 1999) that preclude good research being conducted regarding what actually took place. In the increasing, though still relatively small, number of countries that do audio or video record such interviews, gaining research access to these interviews is a very difficult task. The handful or so published studies based on recordings of interviews with suspects have almost all been part of a government and/or police initiative. Very rarely indeed have researchers outside such initiatives been given access.

I was privileged to have access to several dozen interviews with suspects as part of a Government-sponsored project (Bull and Cherryman, 1996). A few years after this project was completed a student came to discuss with me the possibility of conducting postgraduate research on police interviews with suspects. I strongly suggested that the student think of a 'back-up' programme of research to conduct because I believed it to be very unlikely that we would be given access to real-life tape recorded interviews with suspects as completely independent researchers. I told her to write a literature review on this topic (which wouldn't take too long) while access began to be negotiated and that if after six months we had, as I expected, failed to be given access, she would have to re-focus her research onto experimental studies of interviewing witnesses/victims which present no police access problems.

Within six months (just) we had, to my surprise, successfully negotiated access, in large part due to her skills. I told her that this showed that professors can often be wrong – a good basis for a student/supervisor relationship! At the time of writing this book chapter, we have just begun to analyse many dozens of audio tapes for the procedures and tactics used in the interviewing of suspects and how this relates to officers' interviewing skills.

But what of past publications on the topic of police interviewing? Which are the five which have had the greatest impact on my, and probably other people's, thinking? I have chosen John Baldwin's pioneering early 1990s analysis of audio and video recorded interviews with suspects because his work dispelled many myths about this topic, finding that contrary to popular belief most suspects were cooperative and very few were persuaded during the interview to move from denying the offence to admitting it.

Next I will describe the crucial joint work by Stephen Moston, Geoffrey Stephenson, and Tom Williamson which in the early 1990s not only revealed, like Baldwin, that police interviewing tactics seemed to have little effect on suspects but also that what seemed much more important to suspects was the weight of evidence the police had against them. Then I shall move on to the vast work of Gisli Gudjonsson on how interviewing methods can affect false confessions and/or the admissibility in court of interviews with suspects. I will focus on his 1999 paper with John Pearse which presents one of the best analyses of police interviews for the tactics used.

After that I will change tack a little and focus on the joint work of Frans Willem Winkel and Aldert Vrij concerning how police interviewers may actually create in interviewees the very behaviours the police then take as crucial behavioural signs (e.g. of deception or of suspicion). Finally, I will focus on work designed to assist people to recall in police interviews as much as possible about what has happened. While Professor Ron Fisher's work (some of it with Ed Geiselman) has focused on the interviewing of witnesses, it is also clearly relevant to the interviewing of cooperative suspects. Which brings us back to Baldwin's work which found that many suspects were cooperative.

My own route into the topic of police interviewing probably started in the late 1960s when I was an undergraduate. Though the route I will now briefly describe is, I believe, one as much the result of chance as of planning, when I was an undergraduate I believed that people who had published a lot of work on a topic must have been clever enough to have planned their life accordingly! Hardly anyone seemed then, or even now, to admit in print that it was chance not intellect!

When I was an undergraduate the university's psychology department was still in the centre of town whereas almost all of the other departments had moved to a purposely built campus on the edge of town. In the old Victorian building which housed psychology was also the law department. Those of us who lived on the campus and had to travel into town to our departments got to know each other and this is one way in which I became good friends with some law students. Being undergraduates in the 60s, we rarely devoted our free time to mutual discussion of our two disciplines. We were much more interested in social interactions of other sorts. Nevertheless, this must have been when my abiding interest in the interaction between psychology and law began.

After I graduated I remained at the same university to conduct postgraduate research, not in the psychology-law area but in psychophysiology. Fortunately for this book chapter, the person who provided excellent supervision of my research left the university at Easter time in my first postgraduate year to take up a more senior position elsewhere. We have kept in touch ever since and, somewhat coincidentally, we now work in the same department, each of us having worked separately at several different places in the meantime. (I have partly dedicated this book to him and to another academic who became a good friend that I met as an undergraduate who always honoured me by treating me as an intelligent equal).

At around the time that my supervisor left, the Head of Department kindly invited me to work with him on a completely different topic for a year, by which time the department would have replaced my departing supervisor with someone who had relevant experience. (Two of the lecturing staff were kind enough to say they would take over from my departing supervisor, but they were not psychophysiologists). This new topic related to a (supposedly) short-term research project funded by the Home Office (i.e. the part of Government responsible for policing).

In the early 1970s the Home Office had pioneeringly and wisely made available some funds to support research developments in policing, a practice still current. Our university was at that time the one nearest to a large town in which the police wished to install new technology to assist with the presenting to officers of 'daily operational briefings' at the start of their shifts before they went out on patrol. My Head of Department had been asked by the Home Office to conduct a one-year independent evaluation of this new procedure, given that the new technology was, at that time, rather expensive. The Home Office made available to him funds to employ a research assistant for 12 months. Given that I was short of money, my supervisor was no longer available, and he had, I hope, some faith in my abilities, he offered me the job. This Home Office project was concerned with memory performance in police officers and with their attitudes toward a new way of doing things. How little did I realise at the time that this would be so relevant to my future career!

During the 12 months of this project the Home Office extended it to 24 months. Toward the end of the 24 months my Head of Department and some of his academic colleagues conveyed to me that I was ready to apply for lectureships, having published quite a lot of research work from my year's psychophysiology. I then took up a lectureship in London, and though my application was for a lectureship in physiological psychology I was offered one in general experimental psychology. Thus I never returned to psycho-physiology, though, on occasion in the 70s and 80s I gave lecture courses on it.

A year or so after taking up the lectureship I was approached by the part of the Home Office that funded my research assistantship (which was then called the Police Scientific Development Branch, I think) to write an extensive review of published psychological work on face recognition. Having now lectured on perception (as part of general experimental psychology), I was interested to accept this invitation. Some months later, having written the review, I began discussing with a departmental colleague, with whom I shared an office, some exciting parts of it and he, being a proper cognitive psychologist and a gentleman, expressed interest in what I was saying. To cut a long story short, we decided to publish a book trying to explain why people find person identification difficult (Clifford and Bull, 1978). By now I was 'hooked' on how psychology might contribute to improving policing and the criminal justice system.

Though some senior departmental colleagues warned me not to get too enthusiastic about 'this new, probably short-lived, topic' and to focus my research career on core topics in psychology, I then remembered the discussions I had in fact had (now and again) with some law students when I was an undergraduate, particularly about how their degree course contained very little about psychology.

After the publication of our book we worked together on the ability of humans to recognise strangers by their voice, and I worked on the relationship between facial appearance and criminality. I also began to return to my research assistantship topic of how best to help people remember things. When I left London at the end of 1986 to take up a professorship in Scotland, Dr. Rhona Flin from Aberdeen (who also had an interest in faces) invited me to join with her in a funding application to the Scottish Home and Health Department which related to one of her major areas of expertise, that is child development. This application was concerned with child witnesses in criminal proceedings, in particular how they were questioned in court and their memory performance. Readers will realise the links between this project and my earlier work, but should realise that I then had little experience of developmental psychology. Though I was now a Head of Department I was brave enough (as should be all HOD's!) to acknowledge my weakness and to admit that I needed to learn much more about this very important aspect of psychology. Our two researchers on this two year project ran it so well, and Rhona contributed so much, that I did have time to read.

Subsequent to this project I was fortunate enough to do a lot of work regarding child witnesses. During this Scottish project I became aware of some recent American work on assisting witnesses to recall. Although this work in the USA was on adults, it obviously was relevant to children. This was work on the 'cognitive interview' (see Fisher and Geiselman, 1992). When in 1990 I moved to Portsmouth as Head of Department (HOD) for Psychology, I looked for people with whom I could collaborate on research (being HOD often precludes research other than in collaboration). Fortunately, Amina Memon, an extremely able psychologist who had been a student in my London department when I lectured there, took up a lectureship in the nearby town of Southampton. Also at around the same time a leading German psychology-law researcher (Günter Köhnken) was persuaded to join my department as Reader. We three secured research funds to examine the possible effects of the cognitive interview on children. This led to work relating to police interviews not only of child witnesses but of adults. From this came my interest in the police interviewing of suspects.

There have been several other 'chance' events in my career that I have been able to capitalise on, but space precludes their mention. Suffice it to say that I was wrong as an undergraduate to believe that people succeed in planning their research career. I trust that you, the reader, will not be of the view that it was unwise of me to work in 'this new, probably short-lived topic'. Anyway, it's too late now!

Fortunately for me criminal justice, and therefore policing, research is a topic of fast growing popularity. Though I began this chapter by focusing on why so little research has been conducted on real-life police interviews, I do believe it to be a topic that will more fully be researched in this new millennium. This chapter examines five areas of research publications of great relevance.

## Studying real-life police interviews

Probably the most crucial research paper on police interviewing was published by John Baldwin in the summer of 1993. This paper was based on research he had recently completed for the Home Office and for the Leverhulme Trust. Baldwin had been given access to several hundred audio recorded and video recorded police interviews with suspects. Many readers may already know that since 1986 all police interviews with suspects in England and Wales are required to be audio taped (Zander, 1990). This, along with the research project by Moston, Stephenson and Williamson (1992 – see below), was one of the first major research projects based on tape recorded police interviews. Indeed, since in most countries researchers do not have access to police interviews (either live or recorded) Baldwin's project is still one of the relatively few that are based on real police interviews. Baldwin pointed out that '... little is known about what happens behind the closed doors of the police interview room ... there have been few forays into the interview room itself' (p.326).

Baldwin noted that

> The interrogation of suspects is viewed, both inside and outside police circles, as being at the heart of the police role. Many police officers pride themselves on their skills as interviewers ... officers, in particular detectives, perceive interrogation as the single most important stage in criminal investigations, and almost all suspects arrested for offences of any gravity are routinely interviewed (p. 325).

He also noted that 'The focus of police training courses and manuals has traditionally been upon...individuals who present serious difficulties to interviewers ...'(p. 332), given the belief that '... interviews are complex or difficult encounters with subjects who are likely to prove awkward or aggressive' (p.331).

What Baldwin, in fact, found was that most of the 600 interviews he examined involved 'relatively simple and straightforward interchanges with reasonably compliant suspects' and that 'most were short and surprisingly amiable discussions' (p. 331).

Another important thing that Baldwin found was that very few suspects during an interview changed from denying an allegation to admitting it. Though Baldwin commented that persuading a denying suspect to confess seemed believed to be a major function of police interviews with suspects (this was confirmed later by Plimmer, 1997), this almost never happened. Baldwin found that in less than 4 per cent of interviews did suspects change from denying an offence to admitting it, and in 2 per cent from denial to part admission. In his opinion, in only nine of these 20 interviews was the suspect's '... change of heart attributable to the persuasive skills of the interviewer, and even here only three involved offences of any seriousness' (p. 333). This is one of the most important research findings regarding policing and, especially if replicated, one which could serve to 'change the face' of police interviewing of suspects.

Baldwin noted that 'The great majority of suspects stick to their starting position – whether, admission, denial, or somewhere in between – regardless of how the interview is conducted' (p. 333), and that '... over a third of all suspects admitted culpability from the outset ...' (p. 335).

One possible reason why the interviewers seemed to have little impact on the interviewees' admittance of guilt, apart from the fact that some probably were innocent, is what Baldwin describes as ineptitude. In his opinion

> The most surprising result to emerge from the examination of the tapes used in this study related to the feebleness of many interviews. The image of police interviewers as professional, skilled, and forceful interrogators scarcely matched with reality. More frequently officers emerged as nervous, ill at ease, and lacking in confidence (p. 339).

Many officers seemed to Baldwin to approach the interview anticipating a confession, and when one did not occur they seemed at a loss as to what to do other than to ask a series of leading questions. Baldwin claimed that 'It was apparent in many interviews that crude assumptions of guilt were made from the outset.' (p. 340). This finding was replicated in a field experiment by Anna Mortimer as part of her PhD here at Portsmouth (Mortimer, 1994a). (For more on how such assumptions can profoundly affect interviewing see Mortimer (1994b) and Mortimer and Shepherd (1999).)

Baldwin noted that when, in fact '... an assumption of guilt is not justified, the considerable hazard of false confessions lurks – perhaps the more dangerous because the interviewer does not consider false confession in such cases even as a remote possibility ...' (p. 343). Gudjonsson in his well known and highly regarded 1992 book provides an excellent overview of false confessions – a book that should be required reading for every police officer in the world. This is especially so given that Stephenson and Moston (1994) reported that 80 per cent of the police interviewers they sampled said that obtaining a confession was the main purpose of their interviews with suspects and 70 per cent said that, prior to their interviews, they were already sure of the suspect's guilt.

I have chosen Baldwin's 1993 paper as one of the most important publications regarding police interviewing because it should have dispelled many myths about this topic. Prior to its publication rather little was known about the reality of hundreds of everyday interviews with suspects. (Irving, 1980 and Irving and McKenzie, 1989 had sat in on a much smaller sample of interviews.) Subsequent, to its publication, while there have been substantial training initiatives in the UK, police officers who regularly conduct interviews with suspects do seem to still judge the skills of interviewers in terms of whether a confession was obtained (Cherryman, Bull and Vrij, 1998a), even though many now acknowledge that the aim of interview with suspects is to gather information (Soukara, Bull, and Vrij, in press). In most other countries there has shockingly been almost no recognition of the importance of findings like Baldwin's for their own policing. However, in England and Wales those police officers who train others in interviewing or those who supervise such interviews make judgements about the interviewers' skills which are independent of whether a confession occurred (Cherryman, Bull and Vrij, 1998b).

While Baldwin expressed a concern in his article that his judgements of the interviews were subjective ('there can be no guarantee that different people would reach the same assessments of the quality of any particular interview' (p.329)), we have found researchers experienced with investigative interviewing independently to provide similar assessments of a variety of skills demonstrated in police interviews with suspects (Bull and Cherryman, 1996).

**Strength of other evidence**

Above I stated that one reason why I had chosen Baldwin's 1993 article was because it dispelled some major myths concerning police interviewing. Another article published around the same time also achieved this. It too examined a large sample of taped real-life police interviews with suspects, and it too found little evidence that guilty suspects confess because of police interviewing skill. (In the section after this one I focus on Gudjonsson's work which has shown that suspects, especially psychologically vulnerable ones, may falsely confess due to interview tactics.)

As part of a Home Office project, Moston, Stephenson and Williamson (1992) examined several hundred audio taped interviews with suspects conducted by the London police. They suggested that:

> There are three main sets of factors that may determine the suspect's initial response to an allegation: the background characteristics of the suspect and offence; the contextual characteristics of a case; and an interviewer's questioning techniques. Interviewing techniques are in turn affected by the interviewer's beliefs and attitudes ... (p. 26-27).

They found that 42 per cent of suspects continued to deny the offence they were being interviewed about. Another 42 per cent admitted committing an offence, and the remaining 16 per cent neither denied or admitted the offence. The factor they found to be most strongly related to admission/denial was the case characteristic of the strength of evidence the suspects knew the police had against them. With regard to interviewers' techniques Moston *et al*. noted that their analyses of the tapes

> ... have led us to believe that there were few obvious links between case characteristics and interviewing styles. The only factors that appeared to exert any obvious effect on interviewing strategies were strength of evidence and offence severity. In cases where there was strong evidence against the suspect there was a marked tendency towards accusatorial strategies of questioning ... where the suspect was confronted with the accusation against him or her at the very outset of questioning (p. 38).

Moston *et al*. suggested that '... police officers would probably like to think that suspects make admissions because of skilled questioning techniques. The reality, however, is in all probability quite different' (p. 38). In their study they actually found few interviews in which suspects were persuaded from denial to admission. They noted with regard to admissions that '... these tended to be relatively spontaneous and typically occurred at an early stage of questioning. On some occasions admissions were made to the first question of the interview' (p. 38-39). Of those suspects who at the beginning of the interview denied the offence, in the vast majority of cases they were still denying it at the end of the interview.

A limited amount of flexibility was noted in many interviewers who largely seemed to employ only one strategy in an interview. This strategy often consisted of telling the suspect about the evidence against him/her. If the suspect then admitted the offence, this may be a worthwhile outcome. However, many suspects on hearing about the evidence against them did not admit the offence. When this happened Moston *et al.* noted that the interviewing officers seemed at a loss what to do next, save for merely continuing to allege that the suspect was guilty. One obvious risk with this police strategy is if the evidence against the suspect is revealed as weak, the guilty suspect may decide to continue with denial.

Moston *et al.* noted that relevant legislation (e.g. the *Police and Criminal Evidence Act, 1984*) may have placed, as intended, restrictions on police interviewing techniques, particularly (I might add) with regard to oppression. These restrictions '... appear to have made them wary of using persuasive interviewing techniques ... If this is the case then it is quite encouraging to note that the numbers of admissions arising during police questioning do not appear to have suffered dramatically as a result' (p. 39). They suggested that an explanation of the lack of a link between case characteristics and interview styles (i.e. police inflexibility) could be that most police officers, including those in their large sample, receive no formal training in interviewing. To be added to this crucial point is their suggestion, rather novel at the time, that police officers 'adopt a more information-gathering ... approach ... rather than an approach in which success is defined in terms of admissions obtained.' (p. 39).

Since this 1992 paper was published there have been enormous initiatives within British policing to train offers in interviewing skills largely based on an information-gain perspective (Milne and Bull, 1999). Indeed, the work of Fisher that I review later in this chapter, has been designed largely with this in mind.

The work of Moston and his colleagues, and of Baldwin had a considerable influence on the work Julie Cherryman and I performed later for the Home Office on identifying skills gaps in advanced investigative interviews (Bull and Cherryman, 1996) in which we rated interviews with suspects along several dozen dimensions that included skills relating to information gathering and flexibility.

In a follow up to their 1992 paper Stephenson and Moston (1994) report on their analyses of questionnaires completed by the officers who conducted the interviews mentioned above. They found that a large proportion of these officers reported that obtaining a confession is the main purpose of an interview with a suspect. With regard to the interviews they conducted (in Moston *et al's* sample) '... in 73 per cent of cases the interviewers were "sure" of the suspect's guilt before they interviewed the suspect ...' (p. 152). No wonder they inflexibly displayed an accusatory style of interviewing! Stephenson and Moston also importantly noted that when admissions were made the interviews were often then terminated without further interviewing seeking to establish corroborative information (either to support the confession or to bring it into question).

In recent years it has, at least in some countries, become to be realised that obtaining as full an account as possible from a suspect (as well as a witness) is desirable. Indeed, we have contended (Milne and Bull, 1999) that the 'cognitive interview' (designed for witnesses, see Fisher's work below) be used with cooperative suspects (who, in fact, are a large proportion of suspects), partly in order to assist determine if a confession is false.

**Use of tactics**

I noted above when reviewing Baldwin's seminal 1993 article that he noted the apparent oblivion of many interviewing officers to the possibility of false confessions. There I briefly mentioned Gudjonsson's crucial 1992 book on the psychology of interrogations, confessions and testimony. This book, though it is of unmatched importance, will not be reviewed here because it is so well known to likely readers of the present chapter (see also Gudjonsson, 1999). Instead the publication that I wish to focus on involving Gudjonsson is his insightful 1999 paper with John Pearse.

In this journal article Pearse and Gudjonsson (1999) examine the types of interviewing tactics employed by police officers with resistant suspects. In what seems to be the first published study of police interview tactics Irving (1980) reported upon what he observed while being present at 60 police interviews with suspects in England, as part of a study for the Royal Commission on Criminal Procedure. He noted that the interviewers used a variety of persuasive and manipulative tactics and that in the majority of interviews more than one tactic was employed. These tactics included:

- Pointing out the futility of denial;
- Pretending that the police were in possession of more evidence than was, in fact, the case;

- Minimising the seriousness of the offence;
- Manipulating the suspect's self esteem; and,
- Advising interviewees that it was in their best interests to confess.


In 1989 Irving and McKenzie reported on a similar study conducted after the 1986 introduction of the *Police and Criminal Evidence Act 1984 (PACE)* which provided legislation relating to the police interviewing of suspects (for more on this legislation see Zander, 1990). They found that the frequency of use of such tactics had declined, as had the frequency of repeatedly interviewing suspects. However, they pointed out that the proportion of interviews they observed which resulted in a confession had not decreased, being 65 per cent in their study and 62 per cent in Irving's (1980) study. (However, Wolchover and Heaton-Armstrong (1996) noted that in the Irving and McKenzie study the confession rate for the most serious cases after the introduction of the new law was only half of that which occurred before the new legislation came into force. Whether this difference was due to a reduction in the use of persuasive and manipulative tactics is, unfortunately, impossible to say).

Pearse (himself a police officer) and Gudjonsson open their article by stating that:

> Police officers typically regard the interviewing of suspects as a crucial stage of any investigation, bestowing upon this interaction an elevated status to the detriment of other evidential sources ... (p. 221).

They noted that to date a number of typologies had been provided to categorise tactics employed by the police when interviewing suspects. (For more on these see Memon, Vrij, and Bull, 1998). These tactics largely relate to ways presumed to persuade a reluctant suspect to confess. They also noted that in England and Wales the proportion of interviews that contain confessions seems over the years to have remained fairly stable (at around 50 to 60 per cent) '... despite a marked decrease in the number of manipulative and coercive tactics employed by the police and an increase in the number of suspects receiving legal advice ...' (p. 222). However, they pointed out that this proportion relates to 'run of the mill', general criminal cases where the decision to confess to or deny an offence seemed very largely to have been made prior to the interview. They contended that in more serious cases (such as murder, rape, armed robbery) a different picture might emerge.

They examined in great detail 18 interviews (mean length = 83 minutes) involving allegations regarding serious criminal offences in which the suspects had initially denied the allegations but had then during interview changed their mind and confessed. All the confessions were subsequently retracted.

Each of the audio tape recorded interviews with these suspects was divided up into five-minute segments. From the previous literature and from the authors' own considerable experience a list of 39 tactics was drawn up. Each interview was coded for the presence of these tactics. The resulting data were factor analysed and six factors emerged which Pearse and Gudjonsson describe as

- Intimidation;
- Robust challenge;
- Manipulation;
- Questioning style;
- Appeal; and,
- Soft challenge.

The use of these clusters of tactics was then related to whether the confession in each audio taped interview was deemed admissible or not in the subsequent criminal proceedings. Those interviews which contained 'extreme levels' of the first three tactic factors (above) were ruled not admissible in four cases and admissible in two, whereas those which contained these factors only to a 'marked level' were ruled not admissible in two cases and admissible in ten. This relationship between interview tactics and admissibility was almost significant (p = .057).

Pearse and Gudjonsson suggested that their analytic 'framework has the potential to discriminate between what may be acceptable tactics and ... those that the courts will not approve' (p. 233). This is an important point in any country, not just in one which now has a history of ruling inadmissible interviews with suspects that make undue use of tactics revealed by psychologists to be untrustworthy.

In their conclusion Pearse and Gudjonsson make a crucial point that underlines why their research article is so important.

This study has confirmed that in serious criminal cases, where there is initial resistance to confess, British police officers have resorted to American-style tactics to overcome resistance and secure a confession. Even though in the 18 cases the tactics were successful in terms of obtaining a confession, this was achieved at a considerable risk of the confession being rendered inadmissible by a court and the defendant acquitted (p. 234).

One can hardly think of a more important publication than theirs. It shows an excellent combined contribution of considerable relevant professional experience, an analytic framework clearly based largely on prior research, complex yet comprehensible data analysis, a relationship between police behaviour and court outcome, and recommendations for the future.

The next research work I have chosen also focuses, as did Pearse and Gudjonsson's, on the way in which police officers' interviewing behaviour can affect the behaviour of interviewees (e.g. confessions). However, its focus is from a different perspective.

## Do interviewers cause negative behaviour?

Many years ago now we noted in our book *Psychology for Police Officers* (Bull, Bustin, Evans, and Gahagan, 1983) that police officers may create behaviours in the persons they are interacting with which are then falsely taken by the police to be indicative of something about those persons. However, at that time, while there had been published considerable psychological research to support this notion, almost none of it had directly involved police personnel. Given that then many police officers (i) considered themselves to be a special group immune from many typical human frailties, and (ii) believed that by experience alone their members would become skilled, it was hard in the 1980s to convince the majority of them that the established results of good psychological research which had not directly involved such personnel also would apply to them. In some countries (e.g. The Netherlands, England and Wales) this convincing became easier to achieve in the 1990s, and in the 21st century is now less problematic. However, in many countries it is still the case that the police are still failing to realise how human, and therefore how frail, they really are.

Five years after our book was published Frans Willem Winkel and Aldert Vrij commenced a series of crucial studies on this notion. In their first study Winkel, Koppelaar and Vrij (1988) noted that the term 'Personal space refers to the area surrounding a person that he or she wants to maintain, inside which others may not penetrate without arousing uncomfortable feelings in the person in question' (p. 308). This psychological topic of personal space had been extensively researched regarding the general population (including students) but had rarely been studied in the police setting. Winkel *et al.* noted that one of the few relevant previous studies concerned with this notion had been conducted in Canada by Rozelle and Baxter (1975) who had asked police officers what information they believed they used in forming an initial impression of a citizen with whom they were interacting. The information provided by the officers was categorised as being either 'person-linked' or 'situation-linked', partly because psychologists know (and one would assume that other professional groups should also be aware) that people's behaviour is the joint result of the situation they are in and the kind of person they are. However, Rozelle and Baxter found that the police said that their impressions were very much person-linked and to do with body movements, the way questions were answered, nervousness, hostility, co-operativeness, appearance and intelligence.

These two researchers decided to test whether the behaviour of a police officer could create the very citizen behaviours reported by the police to crucially affect their impressions. In their study Baxter and Rozelle (1975) asked the interviewer, who appeared to be a police officer, to take up a position either 62cm. from the interviewee or 21cm. Previous psychological research had found that the former distance does not usually represent an invasion of personal space, but the latter does. Their study found that the latter distance resulted in interviewees averting their gaze more, moving their head more, making more small hand movements, and placing their arms or hands between themselves and the interviewer.

Winkel *et al.* (1988) pointed out that such 'behaviours could be called defensive reactions' (p. 310) and that these could be taken by those who more readily classify behaviours as person-linked (i.e. police officers) to be the choice of the interviewees rather than be typical responses to the situation the interviewees find themselves in. These Dutch authors pointed out that their observations some years earlier of police training had noted 'that police officers frequently narrow the distance between themselves and civilians as a means of retaining the initiative in interaction' (p. 310).

In some police forces a greater emphasis on using in training the recent results of research, such as that just described, above began in the early 1980s (e.g. in the London Metropolitan Police – see Bull and Horncastle, 1994, 1989, 1988a and b). However, even nowadays in many countries police personnel do not receive adequate, if any, training on such issues.

In a follow up to their 1975 study, Rozelle and Baxter (1978) showed people one of two video recordings of an interaction between a law enforcement officer and a citizen. In one of the two versions of the recording the citizen was instructed by the researchers to display the defensive reactions to bodily proximity found in their prior study described above (Baxter and Rozelle, 1975).

For the other version the citizen did not receive these instructions. The people who saw the former version, more so than those who saw the latter version, evaluated the citizen as making a suspicious impression, not telling the whole truth, as more dangerous, and more worried.  Thus, the natural human behavioural responses to having one's personal space invaded were taken as negative, person-linked factors.  Furthermore, some of these responses are the behaviours erroneously taken by many people, including police officers, as indicative of lying (Vrij, 2000).

Winkel *et al.* decided to see whether the results of the Canadian research by Rozelle and Baxter would be replicated in a country on a different continent (i.e. The Netherlands). Firstly, however, they wanted to determine if what they themselves had noted in police training would also be found in a straightforward, simple research study. In this study police officers and citizens were each independently asked to approach a person to listen to the story the person was starting to tell. (The person was not actually present but visible on a TV screen). The study found that police officers stood significantly closer than did the citizens (61cm versus 72cm).

In their second study Winkel *et al.* (1988) firstly asked a police officer to stop a student to talk to her/him.  For some students (chosen at random) the officer was instructed to stand no closer that the greater distance used in Baxter and Rozelle's (1975) study (i.e. 60cm) and for other students he was instructed to stand at the close distance used in the 1975 study (i.e. 20cm).  These interactions were video recorded and those in which the natural behaviour of the students most resembled that found in the 1975 study were used in the second, main part of the study.

In this main part police officers were shown two video recordings from part one of the study. (Note that the civilians' behaviour was not an act by the students, but was spontaneous).  These recordings were made from the side so that the interpersonal distance was clearly visible.  The officers saw one recording with an interpersonal distance of no less that 60cm and one recording with a distance of around 20cm.  For each recording the officers completed a questionnaire.  This part of the study found that the civilian spoken to at the closer distance was evaluated as significantly more dangerous, suspicious, emotionally unstable and anxious, and creating a stronger 'caught-in-the-act' impression.  Winkel *et al.* noted that such findings support the notion that exhibiting defensive behaviour is labelled as suspicious by police officers even when a situation-linked explanation (i.e. the officer standing too close to the citizen) is readily available.

Here at Portsmouth Akehurst and Vrij (1999) noted that interviewer behaviour affected the behaviour of adult interviewees, and that observers took the resulting interviewee behaviour to be indicative of deception. In their study the interviewer (a police officer) in half the interviews (about the possession of an item) made more hand movements. The (adult) interviewees were affected by this in that those interviewed by the more 'lively' interviewer themselves exhibited more 'non functional' movements. The observers (police officers) of video clips of the interviews took the increased movements of these interviewees to be behaviours indicative of deception. This led them to make errors concerning whether the adult interviewees were telling the truth or not. This recent study again demonstrates that variation in interviewer manner can elicit cues taken to be indicative of deception.

**Effects of ethnicity**

Winkel and Vrij (1990) noted that previous Dutch work had found white people to be treated differently by investigative personnel (for example, police officers) from non-white people. They pointed out that this had also been found in Germany, in the USA, and in Britain. To explain this differential treatment some authors had contended that non-white people may behave in a more negative way. However, Winkel and Vrij stated that 'none of these authors support their argument with empirical evidence' (p. 336). In fact, in their own prior study (1989 – published in Dutch) they had observed that non-white people behaved more co-operatively during police interviews than did white people. They suggested an alternative explanation of the differential treatment of non-white people by white professionals which focuses on the hypothesis that 'in cross-cultural interaction, participants ... inadvertently misunderstand each other's non-verbal behaviour' (p. 336).

Prior research in several countries had demonstrated that in social interactions between two people their gaze behaviour and amount of eye contact is important. Reviews of this previous research had noted that gaze behaviour influences judgements of credibility, dominance, competence, liking and so on, with individuals who more frequently look the other person in the eye being rated higher on such factors. However, almost all of this previous research had only involved white people. Those few previous studies involving black people had found that they evaluated frequent eye contact as being impolite and as a sign of arrogance and disdain. Other studies had examined how frequently whites and non-whites actually engage in eye contact. These studies had found that, at least in the USA, whites look at each other more frequently than do non-whites.

Winkel and Vrij summarise these two bodies of previous research (i.e. on the meaning ascribed to eye contact and on how frequently eye contact occurs) by suggesting that they 'reveal a clear potential for non-verbal communication errors to occur in cross-cultural interactions' (p. 338). For example, a white investigatory or legal professional questioning a non-white adult or child may find this person to avert his or her eyes more than expected. Although the non-white person 'may do this, say, to show respect' (p.338), the white professional could erroneously interpret this as a sign of rudeness or suspicion. On the other hand, for non-white professionals the more frequent eye contact of a white interviewee may lead to a negative evaluation. Winkel and Vrij also noted that people's experience with other ethnic groups could perhaps reduce these mis-understandings.

They designed a number of studies to investigate these ideas. In one study white and non-white adult members of the public agreed to be interviewed by a police officer about whether or not they had on them a small item. These interviews were video recorded. Observation of the video recordings found that the white interviewees maintained significantly more eye contact/gaze behaviour with the interviewer than did the non-white interviewees. They also (Vrij and Winkel, 1991) found that the non-white interviewees had a slower speech rate, smiled and laughed more, made more trunk movements, and exhibited more self-touching behaviour. Vrij and Winkel pointed out that many of these behavioural differences relating to interviewee ethnicity concern the very behaviours people think are signs of lying. They suggested (p. 182) that 'these culturally determined nonverbal behaviour patterns might easily operate as perceived indicators of deception in white police officers'.

In their 1990 study Winkel and Vrij had an actor play the role of a suspect being interviewed by the police. Two actors were used, one white one non-white, and each in one interview displayed the gaze behaviour found by the previous research to be typical of white people, and in the other interview of non-white people. Dutch police officers who observed video recordings of the interviews evaluated the interviewees who displayed non-white gaze behaviour as more tense, unco-operative and as making a more suspect impression. (We are not told what proportion of these police officers were non-white but Winkel and Vrij's paper suggests that they were all white).

This series of exciting studies by Winkel and Vrij makes it clear that interviewers may often create the very behaviours in interviewees that they then take to be indicative of something important, ignoring the possibility that they actually created the behaviours themselves!


**Helping people remember more**

How much people recall of a crime is also influenced by police behaviour. Like Winkel and Vrij, Ron Fisher has made it clear that police officers' behaviour can affect the very behaviour they focus on, in this instance interviewee recall. In a landmark 1995 article reviewing his (plus colleagues) work on helping police interviewees to remember more he mentioned not only Moston *et al's* (1992) outstanding study of police interviewing (which I described above) but also his own study (Fisher, Geiselman and Raymond, 1987) of real-life police interviews, these being with witnesses to robberies.

While the Robbery Division of the Metro-Date (Florida) Police Department is to be congratulated on its willingness to audio tape interviews for research purposes and to release these to the researchers, it is criticised (justly) in the resulting publication for conducting poor interviews. In particular the officers regularly interrupted the witnesses while they were giving relevant accounts, asked many short-answer questions, and employed inappropriate sequencing of questions. They seemed to employ very few techniques known from psychological research on memory to aid recall. Thus, like their British counterparts, they seemed at that time to have received little or no appropriate interview training.

In his 1995 paper, Fisher reviews several principles of memory retrieval and of dyadic communication known from laboratory based research to be likely to increase the amount of correct information reported. These principles form the basis of the 'cognitive interview' (CI) which he began to develop with Ed Geiselman in the mid 1980's. When I first had the pleasure of hearing from Ron and Ed, at a conference, about the effectiveness of the CI techniques in enhancing witness recall I was a little suspicious. They were claiming, and had published studies in peer reviewed journals, that it aided adult witness recall by around 40 per cent. I was so impressed by the size of this increase and then so ignorant of standard police interviewing techniques (i.e. those prior to the 1990s), that I naively thought that at least part of this very large increase must be due to a confound in their studies. Surely nothing so sensible as the cognitive techniques of:

- Recreating the original context;
- Emphasising the need to report everything;
- Using varied retrieval paths; and,
- Using witness compatible questioning.

plus good social communication skills, would boost so much what 'professionals' could achieve?

I was interested in whether I could assist children and (as stated above) collaborated with Amina Memon, Günter Köhnken and then Becky Milne on this issue. Other researchers also became interested in the CI and our recent meta-analysis of several dozen prior studies shows that it is, indeed, very effective even compared to a good comparison interview which only differs in that it does not contain the CI's cognitive components (Köhnken, Milne, Memon, and Bull, 1999).

Fisher's 1995 reviews work not only on the CI but also that on hypnosis which Fisher, rightly, does not recommend to police interviewers. He then goes on to write about an even more important issue. This is concerned with developing positive procedures to foster effective interviewing. He notes that the steps that can be taken to improve police interviewing '... fall into the two traditional areas of organizational improvement: better training and more efficient use of personnel' (p.756-7). He had been saying this for nearly a decade stating in 1987 that 'The psychology of memory is advanced enough to be able to contribute positively to effective police interviewing ...' and that '... a major change must be enacted at institutional level, namely, to introduce formal training in the science of interviewing ...' (Fisher *et al.*, 1987, p.185).

In his conclusion Fisher, correctly, makes the rather pessimistic observation that 'Thus far, psychological research has been met with only a lukewarm reception by the legal-police community ...' (p. 758). I remember him asking me over ten years ago whether British police officers were receptive to psychology. I replied saying that our 1983 book seemed to have sold fairly well and that there was an ever increasing number of officers who had degrees in psychology (the co-editor of the present book being a notable example). I remember telling Ron that a combination of these 'police officer psychologists' and properly disseminated good quality, ecologically relevant research by psychologists such as himself would one day have a very positive effect.

At least in Britain this effect is now with us. Since 1992 all officers have become aware of the psychological principles related to an information gathering approach to interviewing. In fact, in 1992 all 127,000 police officers were issued with a booklet about this which was written by well informed police officers who were willing to take 'outside' advice (for more on this see Milne and Bull, 1999). In addition, in 1992 (to be updated and expanded in 2001) the British Government produced a *Memorandum of Good Practice* for the interviewing of (alleged) child witnesses/victims which was based on known psychological principles (Bull, 1992; 1995; 1996). Furthermore, when Ron Fisher biennially presents CI workshops in my department these are always full, mostly with police officers.

Unfortunately, the impact of published works like the ones I have chosen for this chapter is not universal. Nowadays, Britain does not lead the world in many things, but it does seem to regarding attempting to improve police interviewing. In my opinion readers from other countries have a duty to try to help persuade their country's police interviewing to improve.

I trust that, like me, you have found the five published works nominated in this chapter (i.e. Baldwin's, Winkel and Vrij's, Moston, Stephenson and Williamson's, Pearse and Gudjonsson's and Fisher's) to be of fundamental importance. They have certainly influenced the collaborative research that I have been and am involved in. Without their contributions, my programme of work would have been of lesser quality. Not that I planned three decades of such research!

# References

Akehurst, L. and Vrij, A. (1999). Creating suspects in police interviews. *Journal of Applied Social Psychology, 29*, 192-210.

Baldwin, J. (1993). Police interview techniques: Establishing truth or proof? *British Journal of Criminology, 33*, 325-351.

Baxter, J. and Rozelle, R. (1975). Nonverbal expression as a function of crowding during a simulated police-citizen encounter. *Journal of Personality and Social Psychology, 32*, 40-50.

Bull, R. (1992). Obtaining evidence expertly: The reliability of interviews with child witnesses. *Expert Evidence, 1*, 5-12.

Bull, R. (1995). Interviewing children in legal contexts. In R. Bull and D. Carson (eds), *Handbook of Psychology in Legal Contexts*. Chichester: Wiley.

Bull, R. (1996). Good practice for video recorded interviews with child witnesses for use in criminal proceedings. In G. Davies, S. Lloyd-Bostock, M. McMurran, and C. Wilson (eds), *Psychology, Law and Criminal Justice*. Berlin: de Gruyter.

Bull, R., Bustin, R., Evans, P. and Gahagan, D. (1983). *Psychology for Police Officers*. Chichester: Wiley.

Bull, R. and Cherryman, J. (1996). *Helping to Identify Skills Gaps in Specialist Investigative Interviewing : Enhancement of Professional Skills*. London : Home Office Police Department.

242   *Criminal Justice Research*

Bull, R. and Horncastle, P. (1988a). Evaluations of the effectiveness of police training involving psychology. In J. Reese and J. Horn (eds), *Police Psychology: Operational Assistance*. Washington DC: United States Department of Justice.

Bull, R. and Horncastle, P. (1988b). Evaluating training: The London Metropolitan Police's recruit training in human awareness/policing skills. In P. Southgate (ed), *New Directions in Police Training*. London: Her Majesty's Stationery Office.

Bull, R. and Horncastle, P. (1989). An evaluation of human awareness training. In R. Morgan and D. Smith (eds), *Coming to Terms with Policing*. London: Tavistock.

Bull, R and Horncastle, P. (1994). Evaluation of police recruit training involving psychology. *Psychology, Crime and Law*, 1, 157-163.

Cherryman, J., Bull, R. and Vrij, A. (1998a). *British Police Officers' Evaluations of Investigative Interviews with Suspects*. Poster presentation at the 24th International Congress of Applied Psychology, San Fransisco.

Cherryman, J., Bull, R. and Vrij, A. (1998b). *Investigative Interviewing: British Police Officers' Evaluations of Real Life Interviews with Suspects*. Paper presented at the Annual Conference of the European Association of Psychology and Law, Krakow.

Clifford, B. and Bull, R. (1978). *The Psychology of Person Identification*. London: Routledge.

Fisher, R. (1995). Interviewing victims and witnesses of crime. *Psychology, Public Policy and Law*, *1*, 732-764.

Fisher, R. and Geiselman, R.E. (1992). *Memory Enhancing Techniques for Investigative Interviewing: the Cognitive Interview*. Springfield, Illinois: Thomas.

Fisher, R., Geiselman, R.E. and Raymond, D. (1987). Critical analysis of police interview techniques. *Journal of Police Science and Administration*, *15*, 177-185.

Gudjonsson, G. (1992). *The Psychology of Interrogations, Confessions and Testimony*. Chichester: Wiley.

Gudjonsson, G. (1999). Police interviewing and disputed confessions. In A. Memon and R. Bull (eds), *Handbook of the Psychology of Interviewing*. Chichester: Wiley.

Köhnken, G., Milne, R., Memon, A. and Bull, R. (1999). The cognitive interview: A meta-analysis. *Psychology, Crime and Law*, 5, 3-27.

Irving, B. (1980). *Police Interrogation, A Case Study of Current Practice. Research Study Number 2, Royal Commission on Criminal Procedure*. London: HMSO.

Irving, B. and McKenzie, I. (1989). *Police Interrogation: The Effects of the Police and Criminal Evidence Act*. London: Police Foundation.

Memon, A., Vrij, A. and Bull, R. (1998). *Psychology and Law: Truthfulness, Accuracy and Credibility*. Maidenhead: McGraw-Hill.

Milne, R. and Bull, R. (1999). *Investigative Interviewing: Psychology and Practice*. Chichester:Wiley.

Mortimer, A. (1994a). *Cognitive Processes Underlying Police Investigative Interviewing Behaviour*. Unpublished Ph.D. thesis. University of Portsmouth.

Mortimer, B. (1994b). Asking the right questions. *Policing*, *10*, 111-124.

Mortimer, A. and Shepherd, E. (1999). Frames of mind: Schemata guiding cognition and conduct in the interviewing of suspected offenders. In A. Memon and R. Bull (eds), *Handbook of the Psychology of Interviewing*. Chichester: Wiley.

Moston, S., Stephenson, G., and Williamson, T. (1992). The incidence, antecedents and consequences of the use of right of silence during police questioning. *British Journal of Criminology*, *32*, 23-40.

Pearse, J. and Gudjonsson, G. (1999). Measuring influential police interviewing tactics: A factor analytic approach. *Legal and Criminological Psychology*, *4*, 221-238.

Pearse, J, and Gudjonsson, G. (1996). Police interviewing techniques of two south London police stations. *Psychology, Crime and Law, 3,* 63-74.

Plimmer, J. (1997). Confession rate. *Police Review,* February 7th, 16-18.

Rozelle, R. and Baxter, J. (1975). Impression formation and danger recognition in experienced police officers. *Journal of Social Psychology, 96,* 53-63.

Rozzelle, R. and Baxter, J. (1978). The interpretation of nonverbal behavior in a role-defined interaction sequence: The police-citizen encounter. *Environmental Psychology and Nonverbal Behavior, 2,* 167-181.

Stephenson, G. and Moston, S. (1994). Police interrogation. *Psychology, Crime and Law, 1,* 151-157.

Soukara, S., Bull, R., and Vrij, A. (in press). Police detectives' aims regarding their interviews with suspects: Any change at the turn of the Millennium? *International Journal of Police Science and Management.*

Vrij, A. and Winkel, F.W. (1991). Cultural patterns in Dutch and Surinam nonverbal behavior: An analysis of simulated police/citizen encounters. *Journal of Nonverbal Behavior, 15,* 169-184.

Winkel, F.W., Koppelaar, L., and Vrij, A. (1988). Creating suspects in police-citizen encounters: Two studies on personal space and being suspect. *Social Behaviour, 3,* 307-318.

Winkel, F.W. and Vrij, A. (1990). Interaction and impression formation in a cross-cultural dyad. *Social Behaviour, 5,* 335-350.

Wolchover, D. and Heaton-Armstrong, A. (1996). *Wolchover and Heaton-Armstrong on Confession Evidence.* London: Sweet and Maxwell.

Zander, M. (1990). *The Police and Criminal Evidence Act.* London: Sweet and Maxwell.

# Index